CULTURE AND POLITICAL-MILITARY BEHAVIOR: THE HINDUS IN PRE-MODERN INDIA

Culture and Political-Military Behavior : The Hindus in Pre-Modern India

JOEL LARUS

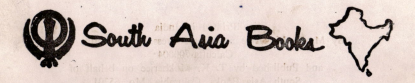

SOUTH ASIA BOOKS
Columbia, Mo. 65201, U.S.A.
in arrangement with

MINERVA ASSOCIATES (PUBLICATIONS) PVT. LTD.
7-B, Lake Place : Calcutta-700029 : INDIA

© Joel Larus, 1979

ISBN : 0-8364-0038-0

First Published : 1979

Printed in India
By M. K. Mukerjee at Temple Press, 2, Nayaratna Lane,
Calcutta-700004
and Published by T. K. Mukherjee on behalf of
South Asia Books, Columbia, Mo. 65201
U. S. A.

ACKNOWLEDGMENT

THE WRITING of this book was made possible with the aid of a fellowship from the Center for International Studies, New York University, and a research grant from the Institute of War and Peace Studies, Columbia University. I am most grateful to Professor Thomas M. Frank, Director of the Center, and to Professor William T. R. Fox, Director of the Institute, for the support and encouragement they gave me. A supplementary grant from the Arts and Science Council, New York University, allowed me to complete the manuscript.

A number of colleagues and friends very kindly read the manuscript at different stages of its development and offered comments and suggestions that improved it. I would like in particular to express my appreciation to Professor Ainslie T. Embree of Columbia University, Professor Walter Goldstein of the State University of New York at Albany, Professor Norman Palmer of the University of Pennsylvania, and Professor I. William Zartman of New York University. Each was most generous with his time and expertise. All errors of fact in the text, of course, as well as the interpretation of the facts, are of my own making.

I would like to acknowledge my particular debt to Mrs George Furniss of Reston, Virginia for her essential contribution in editing the manuscript and for offering many valuable suggestions on substance and language.

TABLE OF CONTENTS

CHAPTER I

INTRODUCTION

THE EXTENSION OF THE NATION STATE SYSTEM
AND THE CONSEQUENCES

THE ACADEMIC study of international relations is a relatively recent development of the field of political science. Stimulated by the advent of World War I, the British and American political science communities were especially active in introducing courses that attempted to examine in a structured fashion the interaction of nation states within the international political system. These offerings—variously named World Politics, International Politics, The Great Powers in World Affairs, and sometimes simply, The World Community—were a response by an imaginative group of academics to Great Britain and America's global responsibilities in the shrinking world of the twentieth century.

One significant feature of the early study of international relations here and abroad was its Western ethnocentrism. Because courses were the outgrowth of more traditional offerings of political science departments, such as foreign policy, international law, and European diplomatic history, the all-but-exclusive attention given to Western states and their foreign relations is understandable. Almost unfailingly, students examined the Western nation state experience and learned how Western countries (i.e. Great Britain, France, Germany, Russia and the United States) employed national power and applied diplomacy and international organization in their individual quests to help secure their vital interests and global positions. When countries of the non-Western world were discussed, the several states of Asia, Africa and the Middle East were treated as the objects of Western colonialism, that is, areas attractive for Western exploitation and colonization. It was a rare textbook or learned article of the inter-war period that dealt with non-Western countries as bonafide actors within the international political system. They were not examined as states with their own individualistic, pre-colonial styles for conducting foreign relations and managing national defense matters.

Given the strong Western parochialism present in the early growth period of international relations study, it is understandable that most courses carried the implicit message that the Western state system was the totality of the human political experience. Or, at the very best, it provided all of the record worthy of scholars' serious study and consideration. Several generations of undergraduates and probably graduates as well must have concluded that the entire non-Western world had nothing to contribute either about the ways political power could be employed in foreign relations or the most efficient manner that military power had been applied to put down aggression from abroad. Since international relations training was so narrowly conceived, its students had little reason to ask questions or to investigate the pre-colonial, non-western styles of political-military behavior.

This pervasive neglect of man's historic attempts to manage the international political system was less a consequence of Western racism, bigotry, or xenophobia than a general unfamiliarity with the pre-colonial non-Western world. Those who taught the first international relations courses in the United States and were responsible for much of the early research were primraily concerned with America's role in world affairs. Equally as significant, they were European-oriented. Few were able to read primary documentation of countries whose languages were not European-rooted and an even smaller number had in-depth knowledge about the cultural ethos of the peoples of the non-Western world. Furthermore, much of the then existing scholarship concerning the non-Western world was done by historians rather than political scientists and their emphasis was on the collection and interpretation of data.

In more recent years and especially since the end of World War II, the teachers of international relations have shown a steadily growing interest in the political-military behavior of the non-Western world. Their new concern for the nations of Asia, Africa and the Middle East is, of course, a direct outgrowth of the passing of the age of European colonialism. As a growing number of colonial territories acquired freedom after 1945, and ended foreign domination, it no longer was possible to ignore their increasingly important role in world affairs. Accordingly, there has been a considerable broadening of international relations course materials. It is not unusual to find an introductory text or more advanced studies including analyses of foreign policies, diplomatic practices, and military affairs of the non-Western world.

While attention to non-Western actors in today's international system is an important innovation, the study of international relations continues, in one sense, to be Western-oriented and parochial. Specifically, the contemporary international relations scholar tends to treat the political-military behavior of the non-Western world in a provincial and insular fashion. That is, they describe and evaluate the foreign policies and military programs of the non-Western world according to classical Western rules and principles. At the center of their analyses is the sovereign nation state, nationalism, and the phenomenon of power. In other words, Western political scientists are inclined to apply Western norms of politics, law, diplomacy, and military strategy onto the local scene and to evaluate the foreign relations of today's non-Western world accordingly. Almost no consideration is given to indigenous, pre-colonial styles of political-military behavior. But non-Western governments do not invariably conduct their foreign relations or formulate their military policies according to the Western model. As recent events in southeast Asia have demonstrated, patterns of inter-state relations developed long ago by Asians have not disappeared completely while century old fears and prejudices are not without contemporary significance.

The West has been remarkably successful in transporting its sovereign nation state system abroad and encouraging its duplication among non-Western governments. Concepts such as sovereignty, nationalism, military conscription, and a number of leading principles of international law originated in Europe or the United States and were introduced abroad during the eighteenth, nineteenth or twentieth centuries. As Western domination of overseas lands proceeded and more and more countries were conquered, local officials, either willingly or unwillingly, chose to duplicate Western institutions and practices relative to both their external affairs and national defense programs. What originally was the political-military form and behavior of Western nations exclusively in time became the dominant mode for all Asia, Africa and the Middle East.

I believe that the study of the contemporary non-Western

world is not complete without consideration being given to their pre-colonial styles of political-military behavior. Their traditional ideas about the world beyond their borders, their pre-colonial modes of thought concerning conflict resolution, and their classical responses to hostile threats from abroad are key issues that should no longer be discounted by international relations scholars and, indeed, this information may have utility for the contemporary policy maker. Accordingly, this study examines selected aspects of the political-military style of one great non-Western society, the Hindus of India, before it fell victim to foreign powers. Using a case study approach, this study attempts to develop two separate themes :

First, I hope to show that there is a direct and identifiable causal connection between the political-military behavior of a pre-modern, non-Western state and its cultural values and beliefs. The typical non-Western society, I believe, developed its foreign policies and conducted inter-state relations according to precepts and rules that were rooted in its cultural ethos and occurred with such regularity that they constitute a pattern.

To some degree, Western international relations scholars accept this idea. For example, most contemporary teachers know that Confucian China's system of inter-state conduct had few features that vaguely resembled the Western nation-state model. They are not aware, however, that China's traditional way of dealing with its neighbors is directly related to the ethnocentric world of the Chinese people, particularly various aspects of Confucian culture. Without some understanding of how premodern Chinese officials viewed Nature and man's place in it, much of the Middle Kingdom's political-military history becomes a blend of the amusing and the unfathomable. On the other hand, after leading tenets of Confucian thought and practices are described, the country's traditional relations with adjacent lands becomes far less obscure.

The patterns of political-military behavior of Hindu India are as confusing to Westerners as those of Confucian China. In the period of Indian history to be examined, Hindu kings and their staffs employed power in ways that to us seem devoid of enlightened statecraft or accomplished military performance. Once it is demonstrated that traditional Hindu patterns of political-military conduct are functions of Hindu cultural values and directly related to Hindu rules of social-economic organization, however, a quite different set of conclusions emerges. This study of Hindu India is an attempt to establish such a nexus. It sees pre-modern Hindu political-military conduct as the logical outgrowth of Hindu religious beliefs, philosophy of life, and conceptions of human relationships. It theorizes that this style was a natural consequence of the Hindu's social-economic ordering of society, everyday myths and local superstitions, the intellectual works of Hindu litterati, the creativity of artisans and technicians, and the physical environment in which the Hindus lived and functioned.

Secondly, I shall try to demonstrate how significantly the pre-colonial political-military patterns of behavior of the non-Western world differed from those favored in the contemporary period. Modern independent states facing a common aggressive neighbor, for example, tend to form an alliance to put down the threat to their future well-being. As the material that follows will show, the several Hindu kingdoms of pre-sixteenth century India did not follow this means of dealing with power threats. The Hindus furthermore did not become a strong sea-faring people although international relations texts frequently maintain that a long, attractive, well-situated littoral leads to the development of a dynamic naval tradition and the emergence of a powerful merchant marine.

To the extent that today's international relations students become familiar with an earlier, non-Western mode of conducting foreign and military relations, they will become more cosmopolitan and develop a growing capacity to empathize with the traditional preferences of non-Western peoples.

A final word about these themes : They are those that concern a political scientist rather than an historian. As a student of international politics and national defence affairs, my curiosity led me to issues and problems that historians generally discount. By training, historians seek out the answers to questions and concentrate on issues different from those that interest political scientists. In the case at hand, many historians have written extensively about the West's trade with early India and how Eastern luxury products were coveted in medieval Europe. In contrast, I am interested in learning why the Hindu people traditionally abjured all forms of naval power and neglected to capitalize on the geographic-economic attributes of the subcontinent by producing a class of overseas merchants who might have advanced India's power. Historians have also produced many accounts of the military history of early India, and they have geographically described the many Hindu-Muslim battles fought in the pre-modern era. My concern, on the other hand, is to identify the cultural pressures within Hindu society that repeatedly denied Hindu kings and troops success on the battlefield. Why did Hindu military leaders use outmoded and patently inefficient field tactics when clashing with armies from abroad ?

This study, therefore, follows the historical trail, but marches to the beat of a different drummer. And it is a study desirous of placing foreign relations and military affairs in a less parochial, non-exclusively Western context.

CHRONOLOGY OF STUDY

The chronological perimeters of the work are specific, albeit somewhat arbitrary. At one extreme is the Aryans' initial appearance in India about two millenia before the beginning of the Christian era. It was this pre-historic invasion of the subcontinent that led to the emergence of what today is known as Hinduism and the country's dominance by the Hindu people. The terminal point of the study is the Battle of Talikota in 1565 A.D., when Muslim forces decisively defeated the last politically significant Hindu kingdom of south India. Following this debacle, no Hindu ruler of any section of the Indian subcontinent possessed sufficient power to challenge the Muslim control of the country from the Himalayan mountains in the north to Cape Comorin in the South. The few scattered centers of Hindu power that did exist after Talikota were militarily ineffectual, politically crippled, and economically incapable of slowing the Muslims' consolidation of government as well as the imposition of Muslim culture in large areas of the land. It is, therefore, historically correct to maintain that after 1565 the Hindu people were forced to coexist in an India in which alien ideas about political-military behavior replaced their own traditional practices and military forms.

In the thirty centuries between the Aryans' settlement in

the north and the Battle of Talikota, Hindu ideas and theories about government, military affairs and the conduct of inter-state relations were developed and refined. These policies and programs were not without frequent challenge and interruptions both from abroad and from iconoclastic domestic groups, but a generally orderly and peaceful evolution of Hindu political institutions and military practices nevertheless took place. By concentrating on these centuries, the characteristic Hindu style of relating to other states of the pre-modern world and their traditional techniques of fighting wars can be isolated.

ORGANIZATION OF STUDY

The first two chapters of this study will present a survey of early Indian history and the principal tenets of Hinduism. This information, not oftentimes found within the everyday knowledge of international relations students, seems necessary for a good appreciation of the main body of the work. The first chapter, A Survey of Indian History, is an overview of the main political-military events and leading trends that comprise the Hindus' pre-modern experience. The succeeding chapter, Religion and Caste in India, explains in a general fashion the dominant characteristics and precepts about these areas and, particularly, their effect on the formulation and execution of Hindu public policies.

Following the background materials, the book's three main sections are presented. Chapters IV and V deal with the maritime behavior of the Indian people and the Arabs. This analysis is centered about the cultural specifics leading to the Hindus' aversion to overseas voyages and on why non-Hindu sailors and merchants of other areas of the world were so well prepared to take advantage of the Hindus' rejection of naval power.

The second main section concentrates on several leading features of the Hindus' military behavior in land fighting. Chapter VI sets the stage by explaining the role war and militarism played in classical Hindu literature. Chapter VII is devoted to an inquiry into why the Hindus were so attached to elephant warfare and also why cultural disabilities blocked them from becoming skillful cavalry fighters. Chapter VIII turns to the Hindu soldier and discusses why he performed so poorly when fighting Muslim invaders. The final chapter of this section takes up the lack of a strong tradition of military alliances among Hindu kings, and the cultural pressures that prevented rulers from coming together in joint military efforts are developed.

In the third section attention shifts to southeast Asia and its earliest colonial development. Chapter X explains why Hindus were able to bring such a wide section of this part of the world under their cultural control without resorting to the use of military power or a system of proconsuls.

The concluding chapter returns to the two central themes earlier cited—the close causal relationship between culture and political-military behavior among pre-modern, non-Western peoples and the importance of this relationship to contemporary scholars.

CHAPTER II

A SURVEY OF INDIAN HISTORY

THE HINDUS AND HISTORIOGRAPHY

BEFORE PRESENTING selected material dealing with the political-military experiences of the Hindu people, it is necessary to examine one of their strongly held philosophical beliefs, a value not to be found in other leading past civilizations of the Western world or Asia.

Pre-modern Hindu intellectuals were not in the least historically motivated. They were totally disinterested in producing a detailed historical record of the main events of the society's political achievements or the leading battles in their military record. Hindu kings, unlike rulers in other countries, in general, did not appoint an official chronicler whose duty it was to preserve for posterity a record of the accomplishments (and failures) of his master. As a result, the Hindu people, despite their venerability, failed to produce a notable historian whose accounts of pre-modern historical events might be used as a corpus of established facts to help contemporary scholars decipher their past.[1]

The Hindus' traditional indifference to historiography is entirely consistent with their cultural values and the prevailing philosophical beliefs of their society. They never developed what might be considered an historical sense because such attitudes were foreign to each Hindu's view of himself and his place within the cosmos. The world, they believed, was an illusion or *maya*. Life was a trial. Resignation or indifference to its multifold problems was a virtue. Events were said to occur in repetitive cycles, each a fleeting happening and so unworthy of recording in detail.

Brahmins, the principal contributors to classical Hindu literary productions and the only group within Hindu society sufficiently educated to have sponsored historical scholarship, concentrated all too frequently on their prayers while invaders' legions ripped the country apart. They were most involved with examining Man's proper role on earth, they were seeking ways to hasten his spiritual liberation rather than to improve the political-military environment. What today would be called the elite of the classical Hindu world, they concentrated their individual efforts on learning the secrets of the universe and seeking communion with the Infinite rather than struggling with more mundane problems such as the integration of the subcontinent, an improvement in the performance of Hindu armies, or broadening relations with the outside world. Brahmins assigned a low priority to what today we call foreign policy issues and national defense matters. A contemporary scholar who has examined the *maya* concept summarized his findings : "Indians are not interested in recording their history if only because they had no real interest in improving it."[2]

Another contributing cause of the absence of Hindu written histories is the lack of ancestor worship as a feature of their religious practices. In those societies cultivating a deep respect for one's forbears, life becomes something of a continuum. The living assume special responsibilities for the dead of their line even as they look to future generations. Societies favoring such traditions, such as the Chinese,[3] highly value the idea of passing on to their unborn descendants the lessons of their lives and the political-military record of their government. They consequently encouraged men to devote their full talents to such endeavors. In Hinduism these attitudes do not exist.

The failure of ancient and medieval Hindu society to produce an historian with the talent and insight of a Thucydides, Ssu-ma Ch'ien or Ibn Khaldun presents a serious obstacle to scholars attempting to deal objectively with Indian history before the contemporary period. Rather than read and evaluate a Hindu account of a political controversy between two rival Hindu rulers or the details of a military engagement, one is compelled to rely exclusively on non-Hindu texts. Much of this scholarship is at best biased when dealing with traditional Hindu political-military behavior, and in other instances texts totally ignore the subjects.

It is the Muslim conquerors of India who have provided us with the most detailed picture of Hindu civilization after the tenth century A.D. While the West is certainly indebted to them for their efforts, no one can claim that they were even remotely objective. Muslim historians regularly exaggerated and glorified the abilities and exploits of their troops to the point where some of their reports must be dismissed as fantasy and others seriously doubted. They found little praiseworthy in Hindu society since all Hindus were infidels and idol-worshippers. For the same reasons, they silently passed over what might otherwise have been considered exemplary Hindu conduct. In short, one must be exceedingly circumspect in using such source material.

NORTHERN INDIA : THE ANCIENT PERIOD
(C. 2000-1500 B.C. TO 647 A.D.)

Why the Aryans decided to leave their original homeland and migrate eastward remains one of the many unanswered questions about their earliest history. Their roots are generally believed to have been in the Ural mountains in southeastern Europe, probably the region known today as the Russian-Ukrainian steppes. They were unquestionably a pastoral people, fairskinned, vigorous and organized into tribes. Once having begun their search for a new home, the Aryans, or Noble Ones as they chose to call themselves, are thought to have spent several centuries wandering about the Middle East, particularly the region bordering the Black and Caspian Seas. Thereafter, they filtered through modern Iran, gradually reaching Bactria, where they are presumed to have settled for a fairly long period of time. Dissatisfied with local conditions, again for unknown reasons, the Aryan tribes resumed their nomadic existence. The general direction of their march was east-southeast, toward the Indian frontier. Finally, between 2000-1500 B.C., the first wave of Aryans made their way through the passes of the Himalayas and began settling the area of the Sindh River, territory that roughly corresponds to Western Pakistan. Successive groups of Aryans followed, each bringing with them their families, herds of livestock, and detachments of horse chariots. This procession continued over some time, but ultimately the main body of the Aryan people entered the subcontinent of India. When the last group of Aryan stragglers reached the Punjab is not known.

During the next four to five hundred years, the Aryans explored Sind and the Punjab, slowly expanding their control of the area until they secured the heartland of northern India. The

Dravidians, their dark-skinned, flat-nosed antagonists, were earlier inhabitants of India, thought to be the successors to an earlier Indus Valley civilization that flourished around 2500 B.C. In any event, the Aryan fighting forces managed to prevail over the aboriginal inhabitants who were either killed in battle or reduced to slavery. Inexorably the northern portion of India, that is, the land from the Himalayas to the Vindhya mountains, came under the undisputed control of the Aryans. They designated the area as Aryavarta or Aryan territory, a term which strongly suggests the elimination of all other competing centers of power.

Undoubtedly, the Aryans were a people of striking enterprise and considerable determination and spirit. They cleared the forest lands and drained the marshes. Cultivating barley, their favorite cereal, and tending animals became the principal occupation of most male members of the population. Tribal society was eventually discarded in favor of more sophisticated political arrangements as the new order was extended in all directions. A number of small kingdoms emerged, each headed by a ruler who frequently resorted to contests of force to demonstrate his power and martial capabilities. The two epics attributed to this early period of Hindu development, the *Mahabharata* and the *Ramayana,* depict considerable local fighting. A love of fighting thus became a fixed Aryan attitude. Rival leaders and their armies battled one another to control an ever larger area of the land. The emergence of prolonged and bitter internecine fighting among the Aryans, as will be seen in subsequent sections of this study, forecast a leading characteristic of later Hindu society.

The religious history of the Aryans presents an engaging although indistinct picture of a pantheistic people acquiring increasingly sophisticated ideas about theology and Man's worldly values. Their original gods were the personification of natural phenomena, chiefly sun, fire, rain, and dawn. It was during this pre-historic period that Brahmins first started to become India's hereditary, privileged class and to acquire a monopoly on learning and education in India. They alone conducted the many complicated ceremonies and sacrifices performed to local deities. The apex of the Aryans' social hierarchy, Brahmins also began to exercise a strong influence in political affairs, particularly when kings were made subservient to the instruction of Brahmins. The primary source of much of this information are the holy Vedas and this period is thus referred to as the Vedic age. The emerging religion, often identified as Brahmanism, is the root source of contemporary Hinduism.[4]

Rudiments of the caste system also appear for the first time during this period. The fair-skinned Aryans declined to deal with the dark-skinned Dravidian people as equals, probably fearing a loss of Aryan identity if assimilation were permitted to proceed too spiritedly. Somewhat later Aryan society became divided into four broad groups, each identified with a particular occupation.

The maturing of Aryan society proceeded without foreign influence and pressures over many centuries. Its isolation ended in 330 B.C. when Alexander the Great Macedon, the first of a long line of foreign kings to disrupt Aryan-Hindu society, invaded northwest India. Leading an impressive army of men and war-trained animals, Alexander entered the Punjab where he easily demonstrated his superior military power and tactical genius. The local defending forces fell back and were compelled to abandon territory which they earlier had controlled. Exactly how far Alexander's invasion force might have penetrated India is impossible to determine. Alexander was forced to discontinue his invasion when his troops threatened to revolt if they were made to march farther eastward into unknown territory they considered perilous. He withdrew his men from the subcontinent, but not before making provisions to retain control over some of the northwest areas he had conquered.

This initial confrontation between an Asian Society and troops from the Western world set in motion a train of events of the utmost importance in Indian history. Almost immediately after Alexander and his armies left the subcontinent for more familiar territory, the first important dynasty of ancient India emerged. The several kings of the Mauryan empire ruled parts of India for one hundred and thirty-six years (321-185 B.C.). Chandragupta Maurya, the first ruler of the dynasty, ended Greek territorial ambitions in India by defeating Seleucus. He is believed to have been greatly aided in the formulation of his policies by a little-known advisor named Kautilya. It is Kautilya who is given credit for compiling in whole or in part the *Arthasastra,* the earliest Indian treatise on political-military affairs and one of the most perceptive analyses on power and government ever written in any country in the pre-modern period.[5]

Chandragupta was followed by three kings of the same line. The most distinguished and innovative ruler of the Mauryan dynasty was Chandragupta's grandson, Ashoka Maurya. On the throne from 269-232 B.C., Ashoka was responsible for inaugurating an impressive number of political-religious policies remarkably advanced for the period, and he was strikingly benevolent to his subjects. Early in his reign Ashoka was attracted to the Buddhist faith, especially its guiding principle of humanitarianism and non-violence. He publicly announced that aggressive warfare would be discontinued and that he would eschew military force as an instrument of his state's policy. Nor did Ashoka's revolutionary programs stop there. Hoping to teach his subjects to live together in charity and common dedication, he promulgated a code of moral conduct (*dharma*) to be observed by all those living in his kingdom. These Edicts emphasized the ethics of Buddhism.[6] As a consequence of Ashoka's commitment, Buddhism became a world-wide religious movement.

Following Ashoka's death, the Mauryan dynasty was subjected to a number of fratricidal struggles, each more bitter than the previous, and it was ultimately overthrown in 183 B.C. by a military coup. The Mauryan dynasty had lasted less than a century and a half.

At the height of Mauryan power, all but an insignificant area of premodern India came under the control of this house. Mauryan ruled from the Himalayan mountains south to the Indian Ocean and from the Sind eastwards to the Bay of Bengal. However, and most importantly, the Mauryan failed to develop central governing institutions or to stimulate a feeling of community among those living in the subcontinent. They did help produce the origins of a common culture for all India, one which was based on the caste system and religion. They were considerably less effective, however, than the early Chinese whose talents for developing conditions of political stability and a highly centralized government were of an extraordinary order. The Mauryans were very capable warriors and able to put down local tribes that threatened to block their expansion and control. After they conquered large areas of northern India, they introduced no legislative and/or administrative system that would permanently serve as a forerunner of an all-Indian governing authority. Nor did the Mauryans stimulate a strong, enduring feeling of what today would be called inchoate nationalism. In brief, the Mauryans were not inspired bureaucrats; they lacked the genius to produce a governing system that would have united the people of India into a firm, strong and enduring polity.

Even while the Mauryan kings were conquering additional territory, local officials became increasingly independent until they alone were determining policies in the villages and championing centripetal political institutions. During the centuries following the Mauryan overthrow, the rural residents of India—the mass of its inhabitants—continued to view their villages as the hub of society. As long as their day-to-day lives were relatively untouched, the rural population of early India disassociated themselves from the political vicissitudes of the royal court and the military exploits of the kings and the caste that fought under his supervision. In consequence, many generations of farmers and artisans learned to ignore foreign invasions and threats to the safety and well-being of India. The disinterest of India's earliest settlers is legendary. Megasthenes who served as ambassador to Chandragupta's court (c. 300 B. C.) wrote :

> ... the tillers of the soil [of India], even when battle is raging in their neighbourhood, are undisturbed by any sense of danger, for the combatants on either side in waging the conflict make carnage of each other, but allow those engaged in husbandry to remain quite unmolested.[7]

For approximately five hundred years after the disintegration of the Mauryan empire, northern India was the scene of chaos. No one paramount local king was able to assert his military strength and prevail over other competing centers of power. Therefore, a multiplicity of petty rulers fought and quarrelled incessantly; internecine warfare was endemic throughout the period. Today's ally was tomorrow's victim; no kingdom was secure from an unprovoked attack of a neighbouring king for any appreciable length of time. This feature of Indian political-military life was well established long before the beginning of the Christian era.

Several successful invasions of northwest India by armies from beyond the Himalayan mountains contributed to political centripetalism. Beginning around 190 B.C. and continuing until the early part of the fourth century A.D., bands of aggressive warriors, led by ambitious kings, launched one disruptive attack after another against the residents of the Punjab and beyond. First it was the Bastrian Greeks (c. 250 B.C.). Their collapse was soon followed by the invasion of the Parthians or Pahlavas, who in the mid-second century B.C. began to occupy the lower Indus Valley. In about 60 B.C. the Sakas or Scythians arrived for the first time. Somewhat later the Kushans, a division of the Yuch-chi tribes, succeeded in establishing themselves in India. Their empire lasted little more than a century, and by the early part of the third century A.D. the Kushans' power had all but disappeared. The absence of a dynamic imperial dynasty following the Mauryan demise meant that various invaders from beyond India's borders settled there permanently, weakening the integrity of Hindu society.

The second great Indian dynasty was the Gupta, which emerged about 320 A.D., and dominated the northern area of the subcontinent for the next two hundred years. Chandra Gupta, the first king of this line, was so adroit that he gained control of much of the northern area. His several successors continued to expand their territorial holdings so that at its height the Gupta empire encompassed the entire upper portion of the subcontinent, and their policies and programs significantly influenced events occurring in a considerable area of the south. The Gupta centuries are generally thought to be the period of India's greatest cultural achievement. Art, education, science and philosophy flourished. The traditional Aryan beliefs and customs were reinterpreted and refined in the light of existing conditions, pressures, and experiences. Once it was challenged by a revitalized Hinduism, Buddhism began to decline. It was from this Brahmanical revival that modern Hinduism finally evolved.

Seeking to duplicate the all-India empire of the Mauryans, the Gupta kings strove to create a central authority powerful enough to govern and sustain their extensive kingdom. But like their predecessors, they failed to formulate institutions of central government and made few, if any, inroads in the firmly established village system of local autonomy. As a result, the Gupta power slowly diminished while their empire disintegrated.

During the middle of the fifth century A.D., Central Asian nomads again began invading Gupta strongholds in the subcontinent. This time it was the Hunas (White Huns) who moved south to test the northwestern frontiers of the Gupta kingdom. Gupta armies attempted to stem the Hunas' raids and to secure their frontiers, but were unable to defeat the invaders. By the mid-fifth century, the Hunas were in a position to invade India proper, once again using the Punjab as their point of entry. Unable to withstand the challenge, the Gupta kingdom disintegrated and fell in 535 A.D.

The Huna era of Indian history is very obscure. Specific events become clear only when Harsha, the first notable king to rule Indian soil after the Huna invasion, ascended to the throne in 606 A.D. Crowned when he was only sixteen years old, Harsha ruled for forty-one years until his death in 647 A.D. A devout Buddhist, he sponsored policies which protected Buddhism, thus arousing the enmity of the Brahmins in his court. Soon after his death, the empire began to deteriorate into a number of mutually hostile, independent kingdoms.

For the next three hundred years, upper India was the scene of extensive local fighting as king after king sought to establish his primacy. None was successful. Law and well-regulated communities were rare, and there was a great deal of co-mingling and assimilation of the people in the region. The institutions of Brahmanism recovered considerable strength during this time and played an increasingly vital role in the lives of most of the people.

Upper India was all but free from the disruptive effects of a major invasion force from the mid-sixth century A.D. until the very end of the tenth century. These years might have been used to foster political integration of the country and to develop an appropriate military strategy to protect the northwest frontier from further incursions. Leaders with sufficient foresight, ability, and backing to initiate such programs were lacking, however, and the centripetal features of Indian society solidified.

NORTHERN INDIA : THE MEDIEVAL PERIOD
(986 A.D. TO 1526 A.D.)

After the collapse of Huna hegemony, northern India once again fell apart both politically and militarily. Although conditions were strikingly similar to earlier chaotic periods of Indian history, one major shift had taken place within the Hindu community of the north. In the eighth-ninth centuries A.D. a new wave of invaders appeared, the Rajputs. They began their ascendency to power by first disrupting the peace of the countryside and thereafter by challenging the reigning kings more directly. They were a people of diverse descent and were not Hindus either religiously or culturally. Only after they had settled permanently in north India, exposed to Hindu ways and beliefs for some time, were the Rajputs assimilated into the mainstream of the larger Hindu community. They became, in effect, a latter-day caste, namely *kshatriyas,* and assumed the rights and privileges of this elite group of Hindu society.

When in the late tenth century northern India was again invaded, it was Rajput armies which were called upon to bear the brunt of the attack and to provide for the defense of Hinduism. The new aggressors were Muslim Turks.[8] In 986 A.D. they began overrunning the defense perimeters of the several Rajput kingdoms and continued hostilities until they had defeated the individual Rajput armies that moved to check their advance. As has been suggested, invading through the Hindu Kush passes was a feat accomplished with little or no difficulty by a determined, reasonably proficient army. As India's history makes clear, if troops from Central Asia, Persia or Afghanistan were resolute and moderately aggressive, the northwest could be penetrated successfully without inconvenience, hardship or loss of manpower. Once appearing on the scene, the Muslims were monotonously successful in seizing booty, prisoners or whatever else they desired.

This invasion confronted the Hindu people, the Rajputs, and the older segments of the community with a situation quite unlike any earlier threat to their independence. Since the invasion of the Bactrian Greeks in the post-Mauryan period, each succeeding invader had been culturally inferior to the people living on the Punjab and the Gangetic plain.[9] Large numbers of the early invading troops, it will be recalled, settled down permanently in India, and at this point their way of life changed fundamentally. Without exception, the invaders were less civilized than the local residents. The religious beliefs of the invaders were far less sophisticated than those practiced by the Hindus, the Buddhists or the Jains, and in general, the prevailing legal codes, social customs, and living standards of the people of India were superior. Accordingly, India's pre-tenth century invaders were regularly drawn into the local society and slowly assimilated. Integration of foreign invaders is not unique to the Indian subcontinent : many tribes or groups possessing a superior military capability, but whose general way of life was culturally inferior to their enemies' have succumbed in similar fashion. The late Ralph Linton describes what took place in India :

> ... In the slow, continuous struggle for survival which followed every new conquest and occupation, the older population always came off best. The invader could survive only by mingling their blood with that of the conquered and accepting much of the Indian way of life. Their descendants became an integral part of India, finding places in the elaborate yet flexible structure of Indian society and religion.[10]

When the Muslim Turks began to penetrate India, however, the Hindus no longer held their traditional advantage of cultural superiority. The Islamic religion and Persian culture the Turks had adopted some centuries earlier was, if not more sophisticated, at least as progressive as the Hindus'. Further, Islam was a highly structured religion offering an appealing message to those who were oppressed or disadvantaged, such as low caste Hindus. Islam did not countenance distinctions based on heredity; it was organized into a tightly knit community of believers without class distinctions. Islam preached a doctrine of *jihad* or holy war against infidels wherever they lived. Given such a mature and elaborate philosophy of life, the Muslims who invaded India in the tenth century were unwilling to be assimilated into the Hindu world no matter what privileged positions the Brahmin priesthood were willing to award them. In no way were they the cultural inferiors of the Hindus. Indeed, many Hindus, particularly those from the lower castes, freely converted to Mohammedanism because it offered promise of a fuller and more equitable life than the inflexible social order so fundamental to Hinduism. By the late eleventh century, therefore, northern India had become the principal Asian battleground of two antagonistic religious faiths with their mutually hostile means of attaining eternal salvation, two discordant ways of life, and two clashing societal arrangements. It was a conflict in which neither religious community could ever hope to assimilate the other.

Originally the semi-barbaric Turks concentrated on raiding key northern centers. They wanted to seize as much of India's legendary treasures as they could locate and transport back to their homes; they also wanted to smash as many Hindu shrines and temples as they could. Acquiring permanent control of Hindu territory was not among the original goals of the Muslim Turks, but this objective became increasingly attractive as their first sundry attacks met with such ineffectual resistance from the local Hindus that they began to enjoy the wealth of the country and the privileges of conquest and occupation.

Subuktigin, the first notable ruler of the Ghaznawid dynasty, was responsible for demonstrating to an invading Muslim army how rich a prize the northern area of India was. Raised in extremely modest circumstances, he managed, through talent and the force of his personality, to establish a kingdom which included Afghanistan, Khorasan, and parts of Central Asia. Ruling from his capital at Ghazni in Afghanistan, Subuktigin was strategically located to wreck havoc in the Punjab and surrounding areas.

When Subuktigin died, his son Mahmud of Ghazni succeeded to the throne (997 A.D.), and resolved to continue his father's forward policies of raiding Hindu territory. Mahmud is alleged to have resolved to invade India and plunder Hindu wealth every year he could manage to launch and direct a campaign. He succeeded magnificently and probably far beyond his original expectations. Between 1000 and 1027, he led sixteen or seventeen separate invasions into various areas of northern India, then as always, a welter of mutually hostile kingdoms. In a subsequent chapter, some of the details of these raids will be offered.[11] All the raids were unbelievably destructive to Hindu lives and property.

The Ghaznawids' supremacy quickly faded following Mahmud's death. One of his generals, Qutb-ud-din, ended his allegiance to Ghazni and established an independent Sultanate of
Delhi which, in turn, became the foundation for Muslim conquest of the subcontinent. Freed from the continuous threat of
invasions from abroad, the Hindu people of northern India returned to their former ways, including their decentralized political-military policies.

For the next century Rajput kings, as well as other Hindus
whose religious affiliations were far older, proceeded as though
the Ghaznawids' invasions had never taken place. Internecine
fighting resumed. No Hindu king or general seemed to have
considered improving the general military security of the northwest in order to prevent a future invasion. Although considerably poorer in both a religious and a material sense as a
result of the intense, prolonged Muslim raids, the Hindus of the
north all but ignored events occurring in Central Asia. Beginning about 1030 A.D., and continuing throughout the remainder
of the eleventh and most of the twelfth centuries, the never-
ending struggle to determine which Hindu ruler would dominate
the area persisted. Indian leaders acted as though the disintegration of the Ghaznawid empire permanently removed the danger of further threats to India. In the late twelfth century, the
short-sighted policies of the Hindus brought their toll. A new
Muslim invasion got under-way; this time the troops originated
from the kingdom of Ghuri. Their leader was Muhammad of
Ghor, a Turk of the Khilji tribe, and he was as rapacious as
his predecessors. The Hindus were as unprepared as when
Mahmud's troops struck.

The key battle between the invading forces and the defending Hindus took place at Tarain in 1192. The Rajput armies
were soundly trounced, a defeat so conclusive that there was
no stopping the Muslim advance into India. The defenses of
the area were eliminated all the way back to Delhi.

Having seized the key city of Tarain, the invaders proceeded to consolidate their power throughout Upper India, but
not without decades of political machinations, royal murders and
battles for succession. In 1206, the so-called Delhi Sultanate
was formed, the event generally regarded as establishing Muslims
as the politically dominant group in India for the coming seven

centuries. While there was some opposition in the early period, the Hindus became increasingly a humbled, conquered people, whose right to determine their own political fortunes and to exercise their religion freely grew more and more restricted as time passed. Caught in an area of the subcontinent inimical to their traditional way of life, northern Hindus learned to accommodate themselves to their new situation. As a result, the vital centers of Hindu political and military life shifted to south India, as will be discussed in the following section.

By the late thirteenth century a third Muslim invasion of north India further disrupted the mainstream of Hindu society. This time the invaders were the Moghuls, the Indianized version of Mongols,[12] the able successors of the great Ghengis Khan whose exploits in Asia and eastern Europe are well documented. In 1398, Timor (Tamerlane in English), who ascended to the Samarkand throne twenty years earlier, moved against the subcontinent of India. His reputation as one of the most cruel, rapacious and inexorable conquerors known throughout history was well deserved. Marching his armies to the gates of Delhi, Timur defeated its Muslim defenders and sacked the city and its environs with a cruelty and vengeance unique even for this part of the world. While Timur did not annex any section of India to his empire, he was responsible for creating a power vacuum there, and his heirs skillfully exploited this situation. Babur, a direct descendent, founded the Moghul Empire, and it continued for almost two hundred years under six Moghul kings who ruled an ever expanding part of the subcontinent.

The corruption and inefficiency of the Moghul empire in the closing years of its history produced a return to earlier trends in Indian history. New waves of Asian invaders moved against the subcontinent. The Moghuls were unable to re-direct the centrifugal pressures of the local political scene; many local rulers declared their independence from Delhi and struck out on their own. After the West Europeans began their invasions of India, the situation became increasingly fluid. Led by troops from Portugal, Britain, and France, the European forces steadily expanded their sovereignty within the country. Now it was the Muslims of India who became a conquered people. But these events had little effect on the Hindus, particularly those living in the north.

SOUTHERN INDIA : (C. 2000 B.C. TO 1565 A.D.)

The history of political and military events of southern India[13] is even more fragmentary and illusive than that in the north.   Despite the gaps in our knowledge of the way southern Hindu kings ruled their respective polities, certain facts emerge : (1) Hinduism became the prevailing religion and the dominant cultural force in the southern section of the subcontinent later than the north.   (2) The blending of orthodox Hinduism and the prevailing religions of the southern Dravidians was less successful than in the north.   (3) It was northern Brahmins, seeking to escape from situations they believed compromised their religious purity, who are thought to have been leaders in propagating Hindu beliefs and values among the Dravidians.

When the Vedic Aryan tribes first began to invade northwest India and to upset the existing aboriginal society, the dark-skinned Dravidian people were their opponents.   So little is known of the Dravidians—their lifestyles, political institutions and religious ceremonies—that it is possible to offer only the most general observations concerning their pre-history traits and peculiarities.

There are reasons to believe the Dravidians originally migrated to India from the West, early enough for some authorities to conclude that the region is one of the oldest inhabited areas of the world.   When the Aryans arrived, the contrast between their fair complexions and the swarthy Dravidians was conspicuous, and so were the dramatic differences in their physical stature.   The Dravidians practiced a type of animism in these prehistoric centuries and closely identified with the major forces found in their surroundings.   Their Tamil language had little in common with the Sanscrit favored by the Aryans.   There are indications that they built crude boats and sailed local waters, possibly even participating in some limited maritime commercial activity during their pre-Aryan history.

At a physical (military ?) disadvantage, the Dravidians were unable to prevail over the more aggressive and proficient Aryan challengers, and their political-military system ultimately fell apart under the Aryan pressure.   Some Dravidian tribes may have allied themselves to one of the Aryan armies in order to reinforce their ranks during the prolonged internecine fighting among the Vedic Aryan tribes. Other Dravidians, perhaps less willing to surrender their traditions and independence, declined to join forces with the newcomers. They probably migrated southward. For a time, these Dravidians are believed to have tried to settle in or near the Deccan plateau. For reasons that are unclear, they were apparently unable to establish themselves there and continued their migration southward. At last they reached peninsular India, where the geography of the subcontinent prohibited further travel. It was here in the lower section of the country that the Dravidian people began making what was to become their permanent home in India.

If the Dravidians thought in quitting the north that they would be free of Aryan pressures and domination they were quite wrong. Probably as early as 1000 B.C., Aryan ideas, including Aryan religious beliefs, were being carried, most likely by Brahmins, to peninsular India. Certainly during the Ashoka period (the late third century B.C.) the northern religions were, for a brief period, spreading into the area.

Somewhere around 600-800 A.D., however, northern Brahmins moved to incorporate the Dravidians into the Brahmanical fold because of their unsettled conditions in the Punjab and Gangetic plains. Once armies from Central Asia began periodic invasions of this region, and after foreigners (*mleccha*) had settled in their midsts, the Brahmins moved south to establish an area where their ceremonies and folkways could be practiced without challenge or adulteration. It will be recalled that according to orthodox Hindu values those who wished to remain pure and unsullied had to live in isolation from foreigners. This freedom was no longer possible in the north after the Greeks, Persians and Huns had settled the area, and as a result many Brahmins left. A contending theory maintains that the Brahmins moved because they were unwilling to accept the presence of a culturally antagonistic community (i.e. the Dravidians) so close to their centers or to allow non-Brahmanical institutions to coexist with those they favored. Whatever be the reason, there was a migration of northern Aryans to the southern portion of the subcontinent. There the Aryans assumed a dominant position in local affairs by eventually grafting Hinduism onto the existing Dravidian ethos. Their efforts to incorporate Dravidians into the mainstream of Brahmanical society, while attaining a good measure of success, never totally eliminated all traces of classical Dravidian values and beliefs.

The early southern people were most selective in their values. The caste system, so vital a feature of northern Aryan-Hindu life, was not accepted by the southerners with any enthusiasm. Their indigenous societal organization permitted mobility and favored change, two characteristics antithetical to a caste order. Moreover, the *kshatriya* caste was never able to entrench itself in the south's caste hierarchy. Once the Brahmins established their elite position in Tamil-nad and commenced to exercise an ever-growing influence, the Dravidians were compelled by circumstances to accept some caste forms and practices, but there seems to have been a good deal of hesitation and resistance to reorganizing Dravidian society along narrow and restrictive lines. To this day caste rules and regulations have been less rigorously followed in the southern regions of India than north of the Tungabhadra River.

From as early as the second century B.C. and continuing without interruption until the fourteenth century A.D., three Tamil speaking groups dominated political-military events in the south. The inter-state relations of these kingdoms were as mercurial and aggressive as those that typified north Indian history during the comparable centuries. The Tamils engaged in frequent battles to determine which of the three was the paramount power, and there is no evidence of a serious attempt to compromise their political differences for the sake of a central organisation.

The Pandyas, the first tribe about which any hard information is available, appeared in strength by the fourth century B.C. By 300 B.C. they had sufficient military resources and ability to launch a campaign against Ceylon and conquer the island. From observations of early Greek writers, it is known that the Pandyas were prominent in the commercial-export activity then taking place with the Mediterranean world. Eventually, the Pandya power ebbed and their kingdom became increasingly vulnerable. Their first challengers were the Cheras (or Keralas) people, followed by the more important Cholas.

By the beginning of the Christian era, the political-military fortunes of the Cholas were on the ascendency. The Chola-Pandya wars lasted several centuries, the fortunes of war shifting back and forth. Beginning in the latter part of the ninth century A.D., however, the Cholas demonstrated the greater strength and determination. Once they had decisively reduced Pandya power, the Cholas were able to extend and consolidate their operations in peninsular India. For the next three centuries—from about the ninth to twelfth centuries A.D.—the Cholas were the foremost power. At its peak, their empire included most of the southern region, Ceylon, the Nicobar Islands, and some territory as far away as Bengal in the north.

In the closing years of the thirteenth century, a revived Pandya dynasty began to take advantage of the Cholas' sagging fortunes. Marco Polo, returning from China in 1293, visited parts of the Pandya kingdom and was much impressed with local conditions. He noted that :

> When you depart from Seilan (Ceylon—ed.) and go westward about sixty miles, you come to the extensive province of Maabar, on the mainland. It is called India the Greater, and indeed the noblest and richest country in the whole world.[14]

By the fourteenth century the growing power of the Muslim kingdoms of the north was a steady menace to the Hindus of the south. Previous Islamic invaders had secured themselves in Upper India, leaving their descendants to rule the area and the Hindu population which continued to live there. In the Deccan, five Muhammadan kings fought among themselves for local primacy and when not so occupied, challenged their southern Hindu neighbors. At first the Deccan Muslims only probed the northernmost defenses of the Hindu kingdoms located across the Tungabhadra River, but their ultimate objective was clear. As northern Hindus had done throughout the previous two thousand years of their history, the Hindu kings of the south declined to form a united front against the encroaching Muslims. Interminable bickering and internecine warfare continued unabated, the Muslim threat notwithstanding.

In the course of a Muslim raid deep into the south, two local Hindu princes were captured and quickly sent back to Delhi as prisoners. For reasons that still remain vague, both princes agreed to abandon their faith and accept Muhammadanism.[15] The Sultan, upon being informed of the conversion and convinced of their newfound dedication to Islam, allowed them to return to their homelands with the understanding that they would work to advance his cause and fortunes. Once freed, however, both princes decided to subvert the Sultan's plans. One of them, Harihara, soon managed to become ruler of a small kingdom and once upon the throne, he thoroughly denounced Islam and offered public testimony of his devotion to Hinduism. It was Harihara who later founded the Vijayanagar Empire, in about 1336, south India's last major Hindu kingdom before the entire area fell to the Muslims.

Harihara and his several heirs were capable leaders and equally talented military commanders. Their empire prospered and expanded steadily. Throughout the remainder of the four-teenth century and continuing until the first half of the sixteenth century, a considerable political and military relationship deve-loped between the Muslims of the Deccan and the Hindus of Vijayanagar. Treaties were concluded; alliances were formed; trade was opened. These events, however, took place against a background of accelerating Muslim-Hindu tensions and quarrels.

By the mid-1550's the Deccan Muslims were determined to crush, once and for all, the last bastion of Hindu power in India. Triggering the decision to act were the openly hostile policies of Rama Raya, chief minister of the Vijayanagars. In 1565, the several Muslim kings formed an alliance and agreed to move jointly against their Hindu neighbors. In the same year they crossed the Tungabhadra River and marched on Talikota, a key point of access to the entire south. The defending Hindus ral-lied their armies. On January 23, 1565, the troops of the two sides clashed in one of the most significant battles in Hindu-Muslim history. The Vijayanagar Hindus were trounced and forced to capitulate. Having eliminated their main opposition, the Muslims were in a position to take control of the entire southern region of India free of further Hindu challenges. Throughout India, the Hindus were a conquered people, doomed to live at the sufferance of their Muslim overlords until the poli-cies of the British, French and Portuguese colonialists allowed them to regain the power they had lost.

REFERENCES

1. In this regard, see R. C. Majumdar, *Historiography in Modern India* (New York : Asia Publishing House, 1970); James Tod, *Annals and Antiquities of Rajasthan* (London : Oxford University Press, 1920), pp. 2-3; and S. J. Samartha, *The Hindu View of History* (Bangalore : Christian Institute for the Study of Religion and Society, (1959). For somewhat different conclusions also see Romesh Chunder Dutt, *A History of Civilization in Ancient India* (Rev. ed.; London : Kegan Paul, Trench, Truber, 1893), pp. 1-4; and A. K. Warder, *An Introduction to Indian Historiography* (Bombay : Popular Prakashan, 1972).

2. In calling his reader's attention to this feature of Hindu scholarship, John McCrindle in 1896 wrote that "The Indians themselves did not write history. They produced, no doubt, a literature both voluminous and varied, and containing works which rank as masterpieces in various departments of Philosophy, Poetry, and Science, but within its vast range history is conspicuous by its absence. Their learned men were Brahmins whose modes and habits of thought almost necessarily incapacitated them for the task of historical composition. Absorbed in devout meditation on the Divine Nature or in profound speculation on the insoluble mystery of existence, they regarded with indifference or contempt the concerns of this transitory world which they accounted as unreal, as a scene of illusion, or to use their own expression, as *Maya*. Hence, they allowed events, even those of the greatest public moment, to pass unrecorded, and so to perish from memory . . ." Quoted in J. C. van Leur, *Indonesian Trade and Society* (The Hague : W. Van Hoeve, 1955), p. 326, note 96.

3. Speaking of the Chinese historical tradition, Reischaur and Fairbank state, "Much of earlier Chinese literature . . . was actually historical writings of one type or another. In the time of Wu Ti (141-87 B.C.—ed.), however, there appeared a history much greater in scope and far more advanced in scholarship than anything that had preceded it. This was the *Shih chi*, or *Historical Records*, of Ssu-ma Ch'ien.
"Ssu-ma Ch'ien (died about 85 B.C.) . . . claimed to be simply completing the historical work which his father, Ssu-ma T'an, had commenced, but this may have been partly a pious excuse for what was in reality a most presumptuous undertaking—the continuation and amplification of what was supposed to be Confucius' greatest accomplishment, that is, the arrangement of the record of the past in proper form. Ssu-ma Ch'ien was obviously a man of great daring as well as prodigious learning. . .
"Ssu-ma Ch'ien not only set the pattern for most later Chinese historical works but also determined their style and scholarly aproach. He limited himself to a concise and straightforward

statement of the facts as he knew them, avoiding the dramatic but largely imaginary embellishments of historical incident
that characterized some of the earlier Chinese histories as well
as those of the ancient Occident. His technique was to quote
with a minimum of alterations those sources which he felt to
be the most reliable. On dubious points that he did not feel
he could himself resolve, such as the variant traditions regarding high antiquity, he simply copied the different accounts side
by side. His book, therefore, like those of later Chinese
historians, is for the most part a complicated patchwork of
passages and paraphrases from earlier books and documents.
Ssu-ma Ch'ien thus set a standard for historical scholarship
in China that was probably not equalled in the West until relatively modern times. His succinct prose style also set a literary
standard that strongly influenced later generations of historians."
For a fuller description of Ssu-ma Ch'ien's contribution to Chinese historiography, see Edwin O. Reischauer and John K.
Fairbank, *East Asia—The Great Tradition* (Boston : Houghton
Mifflin Company, 1958), pp. 112 ff.

4. The evolution of Hinduism from its early roots is not of fundamental importance to this study, nor is it possible to make precise
delineations between Brahmanism and its successor modern Hinduism, without extended analysis. (For a worthwhile discussion on this point, see Heinrich Zimmer, *Philosophie of India,*
ed. Joseph Campbell (Cleveland : World Publishing Company,
1951, pp. 77 ff.) Scholars who are not especially concerned with
such sophisticated material frequently refer only to Hinduism
throughout their writings. The later style will be employed in
this study.

5. Concerning the *Arthasastra,* a recently published analysis claims it
to be "the most comprehensive treatise on the subject (of political theory and administrative organization) and was rightly regarded as the standard work on politics throughout the Hindu
period and probably even long after it." R. C. Majumdar,
Ancient India (6th Rev. ed.: Delhi : Motilal Banarsidass, 1971),
p. 140.

6. For a translation of the *Edicts of Ashoka* along with a brilliant
history of the Mauryan empire, see Romila Thapar, *Ashoka and
the Decline of the Mauryas* (London : Oxford University Press,
1961).

7. *Ancient India as Described by Megasthenes and Arrian,* J. W.
McCrindle, Trans. (London : Trübner, 1877) p. 33.

8. To be historically correct, the initial Muslim invasion of India was
a maritime enterprise executed by Arab armies in 711-712 A.D.
Landing in the Sind, they secured an area along the coastal regions and some adjoining territory. They did not, however, continue their conquest deeper into the Sind or more remote parts
of the subcontinent. Internal dissention within the Arab camp as

well as the difficult terrain they encountered are the two reasons most frequently given to explain why the first Muslim invasion of India was not more impressive in scope. While settling permanently in this region, the Arabs did not play a major role in the forthcoming Muslim-Hindu conflict for control of India. This contest began in the tenth century A.D. as the main body of this work indicates, and was undertaken by Turkish, Persian and Afghan tribes that had converted to Islam as a result of the proselytizing efforts of Muslim leaders.

9. Professor Percival Spear calls special attention to two types of invasions India has experienced in the premodern period. The first he designates as a "folk movement," that is, a culturally inferior invader conquering the local residents and thereafter being easily assimilated so that only the physical effects remain. The second type of invasion Spear labels "military conquests." These produce few physical effects because "there is nothing so transitory as pure military action." See *India, Pakistan and the West* (3rd ed., London : Oxford University Press, 1967), pp. 94-95.

10. Ralph Linton, *The Tree Of Culture* (New York : Alfred A. Knopf, 1956), p. 468.

11. See infra, notes, Chapter IX.

12. The word Moghuls, if used correctly, should refer only to the troops of Ghengis Khan. However, it has been broadened to apply to all foreign Muhammadans from Central Asia who invaded and settled India.

13. Southern India, as used in this study, refers to that area of the subcontinent below the Tungabhadra River and extending, of course, to Cape Comorin. Frequently this region is also referred to as Tamil-nad or the land of the Tamil people. A third designation of the area is peninsular India.

14. Hugh Murray, trans. *The Travels of Marco Polo* (New York : Harper and Brothers, 1845), pp. 257-8.

15. See infra, Chapter VII.

CHAPTER III

RELIGION AND CASTE IN INDIA

HINDUISM

PERHAPS MORE than with any other people, the religious-philosophical beliefs and practices of the Hindus have influenced what political-military policies their leaders favored and also how government officials sought to implement these decisions. The genesis and evolution of Hinduism is a long and complicated story, one marked by the vitality of competing ideologies, numerous re-interpretations concerning the meaning of life and the way to attain salvation, one that was burdened by the need to assimilate local antagonistic cults and pagan gods. A detailed recital of the growth and maturation of Hinduism can be found elsewhere. But in order to gain an appreciation of the traditional political-military responses of the Hindu people, some familiarity with their religious philosophy and the general aspects of their day to day caste behavior is required. What is offered here is an overview that emphasizes these features of Hinduism which help explain the Hindus' conduct in war and peace.

Hinduism did not always exist in its current form; not even the principal gods in the Hindu pantheon have been constant throughout the ages. As a religion, Hinduism has been exceedingly flexible, susceptible to outside (i.e. non-Hindu) influences, and free of dogmatism.[1] In these respects classical Hinduism differs markedly from Judaism, Christianity, Islam and Confucianism.

The earliest version of what is regarded today as Hinduism is generally called Brahmanism because of the dominant role played by the Brahmin priests within the Vedic-Aryan community. Early Brahmins were the most influential group in both religious and non-religious affairs, even exceeding the king in authority and prominence. The modern version of Hinduism evolved in the early centuries of the Christian era and is sometimes known as Pauranic Hinduism. If these two observances are treated as parts of a common religious experience and the earlier tradition, Brahmanism was the forerunner of later events —the approach followed in this study—then Hinduism is a religion at least five thousand years old.

Hinduism emerged from the experiences and insights of the earliest Vedic community, but whether during residence in their original homeland or while migrating to India proper cannot be determined. In any event, it was these pre-historic Brahmins who developed the central philosophical theories, ceremonial practices, and literary texts that generations of subsequent Hindus have followed and revered. Early Hinduism (Brahmanism) did not originate according to what Westerners generally regard as the normal genesis of a religious faith. It lacks a founding philosopher or messiah : Hinduism never has been identified with a man of extraordinary capabilities or profound mysticism whose earthly experiences are the central point of departure for its religious growth. It is not even possible to state with any degree of accuracy when Hinduism first attracted followers outside of the Brahmin group in significant numbers.

By the time the Vedic Aryans began to expand their political control over the Punjab and later the Gangetic plain, many of the leading tenets of Hinduism had been defined. A careful reading of the Vedas, the oldest Sanskrit text available, as well as the two leading epics of early Aryan society, the *Mahabharata* and the *Ramayana,* supports this conclusion. Central to the Hindu faith was the idea that individual salvation and the group's happiness were obtainable only by frequent sacrifice to honoured deities and meticulous attention to elaborate rituals of observance. In the liturgy these rites were to be conducted only by the Brahmin elite; non-Brahmins were precluded from any but an observer role. An emphasis on polytheism is identifiable in early Hinduism (Brahmanism). The Vedic Aryan community revered a multiplicity of gods found in nature. They came to regard the sun, wind, rain and storms as divinities who, if correctly appealed to by the proper priestly group, would come to the aid of the supplicant. But Hinduism also contains concepts which stress a monotheistic approach to God. Sections of Vedic literature express the idea of one dominant, all-pervading supreme being or spirit in the world who would assist those who sought and merited his divine help if the proper rites were conducted by Brahmins.

Given a privileged role in Aryan society, the power and authority of the small group of Brahmins steadily grew. By the sixth century B.C., not only had they assumed spiritual leadership among all followers of the faith, performing difficult rites when the need arose, but they had become its leaders in non-spiritual affairs. They were the group to whom all other Aryans—including the tribal kings—deferred and honored. Their knowledge of religious matters and their assigned duties at religious observances entitled them to such privileges. As time passed, Brahmins became the central figure in every ceremony designed to attract the attention of the gods : births, marriages, deaths, and other community events.

According to scholars specializing in the earliest period of India's religious history, the Brahmanical movement had become exceedingly rigid by the sixth century B.C. The rituals that had been developed satisfied the ecclesiastical drives and political ambitions of the Brahmin elite within Aryan society, but they blocked direct, personal participation by other members of the community and offered them something less than a full measure of spiritual satisfaction. The Brahmins continued to dominate the Aryan's religious life, but more and more, they concentrated on its elaborate ritualism at the expense of the philosophical doctrines and spiritual tenets of the Vedas. This situation, similar in some regards to later Western religious experiences, could not go on indefinitely : major changes had to be introduced if Hinduism were not to be eclipsed. The appearance and propagation of Buddhism and Jainism in the sixth century B.C. offered an alternate way to salvation to those disaffected Aryans who could no longer countenance Brahmin elitism. The rapid growth of these two heterodoxical movements in India eventually led to a counter-response within the Aryan community. Brahmin leaders initiated policies designed to re-establish their key role within Aryan society. Beginning during the Gupta period of the fourth century A.D. and lasting for several centuries, many of the leading religious and social tenets of Brahmanism were examined and debated. Some were reinterpreted or eliminated; others were synthetized with schemes of salvation preached by fringe groups; almost all were in some manner updated so that what ultimately emerged—what today is called

Hinduism—was more attractive and religiously significant to the mass of the people of India.

Another factor led to the decline of early Hinduism. As Aryans settled the countryside and Brahmins consolidated their position throughout the upper part of the subcontinent, more and more of their number began to marry women from the many indigenous tribes with whom they came in contact. Marriage of Brahmins was not forbidden, but each liason diluted the blood lines of these families. The non-Brahmin elements within the society expressed growing doubts about the virtue, orthodoxy, and dedication of the Brahmin caste as inter-marriage became increasingly common.

Adding to the general erosion of Brahmin power and status was their policy of conferring high caste status on invading tribes that settled in their midst. At this early period of Aryan development, the Brahmin leadership was exceedingly tolerant of the foreigners from Central Asia, provided they accepted their values and their leadership. Many of the invaders were little more than militarily proficient barbarians, men whose level of religious consciousness was either primitive or non-existent. Seeking to protect their elite role within Aryan society, the Brahmins decided to absorb the alien priesthood into their group rather than coexist with a dissident element in their midst. The neo-Brahmins were accordingly permitted to exercise many of the privileges otherwise restricted to those born of legitimate Brahmin families who had been duly instructed in the mysteries of the faith. Although proof is lacking, it is likely that over the centuries this situation disturbed many Aryans of lower caste status. Faced with accepting as bona fide Brahmins intruders whose right to lead in Vedic rituals was not governed according to classical rules, some turned to Buddhism and Jainism as alternate religious outlets. Of course, these developments did not take place within a few years or decades but over a number of centuries. Throughout this period, the leaders of Buddhism and Jainism are known to have aggressively sought out the discontents within the Aryan community, converting them and steadily decreasing the power and prominence of the traditional Brahmanical leadership.

The Hindu Concepts of Karma and Dharma

When the principal beliefs and practices of the Hindu people are isolated, a stark contrast emerges between their doctrine and practices and what Westerners generally expect a theology to represent. Hinduism differs from other foremost religious movements of the world in a number of ways. It has no obligatory religious ideology. It never produced a common bible or, indeed, a generally applied text dictating how to attain salvation. It has no integrated, highly structured philosophical system of ideas. It did not establish a supreme authority to promulgate new doctrine or direct the day to day life of the faithful. Hinduism did not include a subordinate clergy, priests expected to operate within a recognizable ecclesiastical format. Throughout the period under discussion, Brahmins maintained their ecclesiastical prominence, although in varying degrees; they were the authoritative teachers of the sacred Vedas. As such, they were the only group allowed to administer the various sacraments of Hindu life. Their conduct or misconduct, however, was never subject to the discipline or criticism of a superior authority or a council of religious elders. Congregational worship, that is a common service occurring on a regular, pre-arranged schedule, is unknown to Hinduism.[2] Finally, no one born outside of the Brahmin caste, no matter how dedicated he becomes to Hinduism and its advancement, can ever attain a position of religious leadership within the mainstream of this faith.

On the other hand, traditional Hinduism is notably tolerant of other religious movements, able to absorb dissonant philosophies of life and to assimilate people of other cultures. Within the Hindu community there have been a wide assortment of differing and frequently conflicting interpretations of philosophical beliefs and ceremonial practices. For example, some Hindus are committed to a highly abstract monism; others of equally good standing are resolute polytheists and highly value superstition and esoteric occult ceremonies. A middle group individually selects aspects of Hinduism they find personally or intellectually attractive, disdaining all else. The eclectic quality of Hinduism has been well portrayed by Professor W. Norman Brown :

> ... As a religion Hinduism ... is a conglomerate, a

chaotic chance association, at best a loose confederation. Theologically Hinduism is not a single religion but many religions, tolerating one another within the shifting social framework of caste. To see them as a unified and coherent whole would be as difficult as to find unity and coherence in the total landscape of the subcontinent.[3]

Professor Donald Smith has provided another summary of the unique features of Hinduism and it is also worth citing in part :

Hinduism . . . never held a General Council or Convention; never defined the relations of the laity and clergy; never regulated the canonization of saints or their worship; never established a single center of religious life, like Rome or Canterbury; never prescribed a course of training for its priests.[4]

Within the "chaotic chance association" of Hinduism three primary philosophical ideas have been persistently honored and emphasized by all Hindus. The doctrines of *karma* and *dharma* are fundamental concepts in every observant Hindu's life. Each in its own way affects nearly every aspect of a Hindu's approach to life from birth until death. Each has profoundly influenced the cultural values of the Hindu people throughout their history. Conversely, together they explain some of the limitations and conservatism found in the traditional Hindu pattern of political-military behavior.

The doctrine of *karma* provides Hindus with a philosophy concerning the evolutionary transmigration of the soul and a rationalization for the caste system. It explains what forces determine a man's future incarnations or, resorting to Hindu terminology, the wheel of births. According to Hindu belief, life is an episode in the career of the soul. The soul is eternal, indestructible. It is scheduled to be born again unless it is ultimately rewarded with a final release or deliverance. Hindus are taught that one's soul is destined to live a countless number of lives here on earth, but that its evolution is not the result of fortuitous circumstances. Rather, its metempsychosis is narrowly determined by a cause and effect relationship based on the premise that the soul's development in one's previous incarnation has prescribed one's current position. For example, a Hindu who leads a life regulated by ethical, generous behavior, piously following religious and societal rules, believes he will be rewarded

with a position in a higher social caste in a forthcoming life.
Hindus believe that personal rewards and punishments are dis-
pensed from one birth to the next re-birth.   On the other hand,
the Hindu who disregards the various codes of righteous conduct, failing to observe the required ceremonies with proper
attention and respect, is doomed according to the doctrine of
karma to experience his coming life in a reduced position, such
as an outcaste or a pariah.   He may even be reborn in a different form and returned to earth as an animal if his conduct was
sufficiently unobservant.

To a pious Hindu, therefore, *karma* is as inspirational and
consequential as the heaven-hell doctrine in Christianity.   It postulates that one's lives are interconnected : a person will be
punished or rewarded in each subsequent incarnation because
of earlier sins or virtues in Hindu theology.   No significance is
given to the Western idea that every man will be punished or
rewarded in the hereafter for his sins or purity while on earth.
The *karma* doctrine offers a different message, namely that the
observant Hindu in his next reincarnation will be punished or
rewarded because earlier he failed to act in a pious fashion or,
alternatively, he performed some duty in a laudable, correct
manner.

Karma consequently has provided Hindus throughout the
ages with a complete explanation of why they are members of
a particular high or low caste group.   It answers questions about
one's lofty or humble socio-economic status, family's circumstances, and of all other features of one's life.   The doctrine
encourages those in pleasing, fruitful circumstances to continue
their past pious lives to insure even more attractive coming lives
and their soul's ultimate release from the wheel of birth.   Such
people believe that the endless cycle of birth, death and re-birth
is nearer completion than for others within the Hindu community of a less elevated standing.   To those whose present life
is spent in miserable circumstances, *karma* teaches acceptance
of humiliations as punishment for misconduct in a former life.
Karma also teaches that a person's lot in a future incarnation
will improve if he strives now to be a more observant and commendable Hindu.

Given the indestructible quality of one's soul and the endless cycles it must experience before deliverance, the spiritual

goal all pious Hindus seek is the soul's metempsychoses. When a soul is no longer subjected to the wheel of birth, Hindus say that it has attained Nirvana, i.e. the soul has been re-absorbed in Brahman from which it emanated. In Hindu theology, Nirvana is the ultimate goal, one as illusive as heavenly salvation in Christianity.

Very closely connected to *karma* is *dharma. Dharma* is difficult to define precisely because in classical Hindu literature it has been broadly interpreted. The word itself is often translated as "the code of right conduct" or "absolute righteousness". While correct, these phrases fail to suggest the full ambiance of the word. More exactly, *dharma* connotes the idea of Hindu morality; it deals with the divinely ordained way a Hindu is expected to behave in his daily routine and in his inter-personal relationships. *Dharma* encompasses duty, virtue, law and justice. It pertains to the socially correct standard of personal behavior vis-à-vis every other person, caste and vocation. It is akin to a fundamental moral law that incorporates the concept of obligations and the discharge of moral duties to oneself and others. Thus, *dharma* determines and regulates the functions of a Hindu's daily life and influences his larger life goals.

What greatly complicates an understanding of *dharma* is the fact that it is neither static nor specifically identifiable. In the Hindu ethos, every person is expected to act in harmony (i.e. his *dharma*) with his current station in life and also according to the responsibilities and limitations indicated by that role. *Dharma,* consequently, fluctuates in each stage of a man's life. If a man is born a tradesman or a peasant farmer, the doctrine of *dharma* requires him to conduct himself according to the *dharma* of a trader or agriculturist. Furthermore, the *dharma* of a young trader or farmer are not those of a senior trader or farmer. It is inappropriate for either a farmer or a trader to aspire to or emulate the *dharma* of a soldier or that of a Brahmin. Such *dharma* codes are not appropriate to his caste, his occupational role within society, and his duties and obligations. Rather, Hindus are instructed to concentrate their full efforts on compliance with the *dharma* relevant to their given position. One's *dharma* is also determined by such variables as age, geographical location, education, wealth, intellectual capabilities, and even the era in which a Hindu lives.

CASTE

Next to the religious-philosophical ideas of Hinduism, the four tiered caste system is the most persistent, prominent feature of pre-modern Hindu civilization. It is the basis for both the religious and social structure of the Hindu people. Caste is without question one of the key determinants of traditional Hindu political and military behavior and institutions, and it has been called the steel structure of the Hindu community.

The idea of arranging Aryan society along socially closed caste lines first appeared in northern India, according to some scholars, soon after the invasion of the Vedic Aryans. Some authorities believe contact with the darker-skinned, less sophisticated Dravidians prompted the Aryans to arrange themselves in a hierarchical division to protect themselves from miscegenation. This thesis is supported by the fact that the Sanskrit word for caste, *varna*, means color. Other scholars disagree and believe the Dravidians themselves developed something approximating a caste society in the several centuries before the Vedic Aryans appeared. Regardless of which theory is accepted, no one in any way familiar with the ancient and medieval history of the Hindu people can question the enormous impact that caste has had in shaping values and in organizing Hindu society into a highly stratified, economically dominated entity.

In its purest period, Vedic Aryan society was divided into four main social-occupational groups or *varnas,* or what we designate today as castes. The first three represented the "twice born". They received their first birth at the time of their physical birth. Upon attaining adolescence, each male Hindu member of one of the upper three castes was required to undergo a special religious ceremony that initiated him into his second life, that of the spirit. Therefore these people were known as "twice born." After the ceremony, every twice born Hindu was authorized to wear the sacred threads around his neck as evidence of his privileged role within the community. The three original twice born castes were (1) Brahmins or priests, (2) *Kshatriyas* or warriors and aristocracy, and (3) *Vaishays* or those who engaged in agricultural or pastoral work. (With the passage of time, the *Vaishayas* included the merchant-traders of the community).

The fourth caste group were the *Sudras* and comprised the peasant farmer, the hunters and the fishermen. They were designated "once born" because they were not permitted to be initiated into a spiritual life.

Divorced from the traditional caste groupings were the so-called outcastes, people who were scorned, isolated and forced to undergo a long list of social and economic disabilities because of their lowly origins. The outcastes were not permitted to participate fully in Hindu life and had to exist on its fringes in the best way they could.

The caste system has never been static and unbending. Sometime after the collapse of the Mauryan empire the fourfold caste system underwent a change to become more responsive to an increasingly complex society. As a result, a far more complicated and elaborate system of sub-castes or *jati* (literally, birth) evolved. This arrangement retained many of the basic features of the original caste system, but compartmentalized Hindus along much tighter, hereditary vertical lines. In India, the *jati* traditionally has been the primary social unit, the group within which marriages are arranged and dining normally takes place. In analyzing the relationship between caste and *jati*, Romila Thapar concludes that "the sub-caste came to have more relevance for the day-to-day working of Hindu society than the main caste, but the *varna* arrangement remained the over-all theoretical framework."[5]

As the caste system evolved in India, Hindu leaders formulated innumerable rules which prescribed inter-personal, inter-caste behavior. Four of these taboos warrant special consideration because they illustrate how highly stratified Hindu society became. A violation, even though unintentional and of a minor nature, was sometimes sufficient cause to banish the wrong-doer permanently from Hindu society.

First, endogamy was rigidly observed. The caste into which a person was born determined the group from which a suitable marriage partner could be selected. To marry outside one's designated *jati* was an act of defiance that resulted in the iconoclast's permanent banishment from his home, family, and friends.

Secondly, caste prescribed occupation. In a general fashion, each sub-caste specialized in one particular form of work. A son was expected to follow his father's work role; the son of a sweeper became a sweeper; a tinsmith became a tinsmith, and so on. Hindu society made no provisions for individual social and occupational mobility, that is for a young man to discontinue the sequential family-caste arrangement and turn to a different trade or profession. On the other hand, it was possible for an entire caste to upgrade (or lower) itself over an extended period of time, generally through a joint dedication to such a goal.

A third caste prohibition dealt with eating, drinking and other aspects of everyday social intercourse. A free co-mingling of diverse caste members either in private homes or public restaurants has never been sanctioned by observant Hindus. Men and women were expected to restrict their social life to people from the same group. Furthermore, each caste (but especially, the upper castes) regulated what foods were acceptable, how and by whom they should be prepared, and of course, what had to be avoided and under what circumstances.

The fourth regulation related to the collegial effects of the caste system. The members of a group in many respects resembled a large family unit. In times of adversity when one of its members suffered some misfortune, the caste was expected to provide some assistance. Conversely, the caste leadership possessed the authority to drive from the caste anyone who violated its code of behavior. Few punishments had such dire consequences as expulsion from one's traditional group. The offender was isolated from all members of his immediate family and friends. He was even barred from entering his home. No longer was he permitted to work his trade since he was denied acceptance by his former co-workers. All such a stigmatized, ostracized Hindu could do was to spend his remaining years in lonely disgrace or undergo whatever punishment was stipulated for regaining caste purity.

These rigid sets of social and religious taboos, as will be seen in the chapters that follow, influenced a number of fundamental political-military attitudes and practices of the Hindu people.

BUDDHISM AND JAINISM

India is oftentimes exclusively identified with Hinduism, both as to its socio-cultural expressions and its varied religious rites. This point of view neglects the other two religious movements so vital a part of India's religious history. Six centuries before the Christian era, Buddhism and Jainism emerged in the north and began to compete for the spiritual and ethical allegiance of the people. The contest between these two heterodoxical schools of ethics and Hinduism was not decided conclusively until the seventh century A.D., or about one thousand years later. The eclipse of Buddhism and Jainism in India, however, did not result in the disappearance of their teachings and philosophical beliefs. Each had a profound and permanent influence on Hinduism. Because Buddhism and Jainism espoused ideas and principles that were incorporated by the Hindus into their faith and lifestyle, it is important to mention both in this study.

Early Buddhism was firmly rooted in the Brahmanical traditions and cultural manifestations. According to popular legend, Gautama Buddha, or the Enlightened One, was from the *kshatriya* caste. As he matured he found much in his early life that repelled him, and he also concluded that a good deal of the training he had received was untrue. Brahmanism, he decided, had become too formalized; its priesthood were without piety, and their rites, while highly stylized and elaborate, lacked religious significance. It was an inappropriate means to attain deliverance from the re-birth cycle. Sometime between 533 and 528 B.C., in a now famous Deer Park near Benares, Gautama, it is claimed, received enlightenment, and thereafter began his life's ministry.

He taught his disciples that life is epitomized by extensive, prolonged, personal suffering which arises because of human desires and attachments. The salvation of Buddhism became rooted in The Four Noble Truths or the Middle Way. The Buddha observed that "all things . . . are on fire with passion, hatred, infatuation, misery, grief and despair." Such sorrowful and lamentable circumstances, he continued, can be observed at birth, death, during illness and, finally, throughout old age. The Second Truth provided an explanation for this unbecoming state of the human condition : continuous desire and craving. Man thirsts for things and experiences; he seeks an existence he does not have and he dreams about events he longs to experience. Much time is spent seeking sensual satisfaction, worldly possessions, and personal power which will add to his temporal indulgences. As a result of such insatiable cravings, Buddha preached, Man goes through endless births and re-births. What he seeks to attain and realize in one life are manifestations of his earlier existence. Furthermore, his conduct helps determine future acts and decisions in lives yet to be experienced. The one way to win release from the painful pessimism of the *karma* wheel is for each man to abandon his desires and to renounce any need for earthly possession. This is The Third Noble Truth.

Having postulated a cycle of birth and re-birth replete with suffering and sorrow, The Buddha offered his followers a way to attain salvation. The Fourth Noble Truth, which differs significantly with Brahmanism and its theories of salvation, required the pious to adhere throughout their lives to (1) the right views, (2) the right aspirations, (3) the right speech, (4) the right conduct, (5) the right livelihood, (6) the right effort, (7) the right mindfulness, and (8) the right meditation. A life rooted in these Truths would achieve Nirvana. Royalty or those without caste had the same opportunity to realize salvation provided they faithfully followed The Middle Way.

Other features of early Buddhism were of great importance to its expansion. The idiom of Buddhism was Prakit, the language of the common people of the subcontinent, rather than Sanskrit, favored by the elitist members of the Brahmanical-Hindu community. Also, monastic Buddhist orders were established where monks and nuns dedicated themselves to the propagation of their faith. These orders required their members to go out each day beyond the community to preach, beg for alms, and associate with the outside world directly and intimately. The contrast between the simple behavior of the Buddhists and the demanding codes of the Brahmins was an important reason that so many people turned to Buddhism in India. Directly connected with the obligation to preach locally was Buddhism's missionary orientation. Priests and lay disciples of the Buddha were regularly dispatched to various regions of Asia to propagate their faith and in so doing carried many Indian cultural values and, indeed, parts of Indian civilization to vast areas of that part of the world. Finally, Buddhism rejected the caste system, thus freeing this community from the stultifying arrangement favored by the Brahmins.

The first period of growth and expansion of Buddhism took place during the reign of Ashoka Maurya. Whether Ashoka converted to Buddhism, making it the official religion of his empire, or merely championed its credo for his own self-serving reasons, is an issue hotly debated among scholars. The consequences of his actions, however, are not in dispute. Sometime after 260 B.C., Ashoka is known to have encouraged his subjects to adopt what appears to be The Middle Way or something remarkably similar to The Buddha's moral and ethical teachings. Ashoka dispatched missionaries to Ceylon and points farther to the East. Moved by The Buddha's instructions concerning non-violence, Ashoka formally introduced a series of royal edicts that discontinued the use of military force as a means of territorial conquest. This was the first time in history that a reigning monarch had adopted such policies.

For the reasons noted, the appeal of Buddhism was profound among the people of India. The Buddhist congregation expanded, although not without interruptions, until at least the very early centuries of the Christian era and possibly beyond. Then a change took place. The vitality and singleness of purpose of the Buddhists began to ebb during the revitalization of Hinduism so that by the third and fourth centuries A.D. Buddhism in India was declining in importance, and by the sixth century, it had all but died throughout the subcontinent.

What were some of the main reasons for the disappearance of Buddhism in India while it was continuing to be strong in China, Japan, Nepal, Burma, Tibet, and Indonesia? One factor was the exceedingly ascetic nature of early Buddhism. It called for a large measure of self-denial and dedication by those professing orthodoxy. Brahmanism-Hinduism, in contrast, made no stringent demands on its followers, and the Aryan and non-Aryan people of India chose the less exacting and severe faith. Secondly, following the death of Gautama, the leadership of the Buddhist Church could not agree on a single doctrine and a great many schisms developed. According to legend, the first disagreement over the form and substance of Buddhism emerged the day after Gautama's death. Each splinter group that appeared thereafter stressed some change it deemed salutory, or pressed for some particular interpretation of the faith. One question in dispute was whether Gautama was a man or a divi-

nity.   Others involved such issues as whether his teachings were
to be interpreted in an esoteric fashion, and the proper role for
the monasteries and the monks.   Ten years after The Buddha's
death (c. 470 B.C.) it has been estimated there were six major
quarreling factions within the Buddhist congregation and a dozen
lesser groups.

A third explanation for the decline of Buddhism was the
determination of the Brahmins not to be overwhelmed by their
religious opponents and their willingness to make philosophical
accommodations in order to try to win back their former disciples.   Brahmin scholars, particularly those living in the south,
organized in what today would be called a revival movement.
They introduced a series of reforms, up-dated concepts that had
for centuries lessened their attraction to the masses, and generally infused the movement with a new vitality. Many aspects of
The Buddha's moral and philosophical message were incorporated into Hinduism so that the two religions were considerably
less hostile to one another.   As a result of these rejuvenating
efforts, the Brahmins not only redressed the appeal of their faith,
but also re-established their central role in Hindu society.

Jainism, while containing a number of features quite similar to Buddhism, was traditionally more conservative and far
less influential within India.   The central figure to Jains is
Mahavira, also believed to have lived in the sixth century B.C.
Like Gautama, he originally belonged to the *kshatriya* caste.
Only after years of wandering about the countryside and sub-
jecting himself to a series of severe personal tests, did his enlightenment come.   As a result of his experiences and revela-
tions, Mahavira taught his followers that the ultimate happiness
of each man does not rest with a supreme being(s), but de-
pends on his right living and proper conduct.   If a Jain properly
purifies his body by austere living and prolonged meditation, and
follows five great vows, Mahavira preached, he can be released
from the cycle of re-birth.   The five tenets of Jainism are : (1)
truthfulness, (2) abstention from stealing, (3) non-attachment,
(4) continence, and (5) *ahimsa* or non-violence.   During his
ministry, he deplored the obscure ritualism of the Brahmins as
well as various expressions of occultism then prominent in
Brahmanism-Hinduism. Here the Jains and the Buddhists shared
the same point of view, and both rejected the caste system.

A unique feature of Jainism is its idea that everything in the world, living creatures and inanimate objects, has an eternal soul seeking to be freed from the *karma* wheel. Another central Jain tenet is the importance of a life extolling *ahimsa* or non-violence. Taking of any life whatsoever, under whatever circumstances is a forbidden practice; observant Jains work zealously to avoid this sin. Those most deeply committed to *ahimsa* wear face masks so as not to inhale and thus destroy organisms living in the air.

A further consequence of the *ahimsa* doctrine pertains to the occupational pursuits Jains have traditionally been willing to perform. Early in their history, it was decided that agricultural work of any type was unacceptable because plowing the fields meant the inadvertent death of the creatures living in the soil. To avoid all possibility of such desecration, Jains over the centuries became leading figures in India's banking and business community. The buying and selling of commodities or similar speculative commercial enterprises allowed Jains to maintain themselves without violating their religious faith.

REFERENCES

1. The traditional willingness of the Hindus to accept diversity and heterodoxy has been well stated by W. Norman Brown, who has written "... As a religion Hinduism has set side by side in peaceful co-existence every shade of belief ranging from the most primitive set of animism to a highly sophisticated philosophical monism, and with this has gone a corresponding range of worship or practice extending from the simplest sort of effort to propriate fertility or vegetation or disease spirits to the most concentrated meditation designed to produce knowledge of abstract personal reality. Theologically Hinduism is not a single religion but many religions, tolerating one another within the shifting social framework of caste ..." W. Norman Brown, "Mythology in India", *Mythologies of the Ancient World,* ed. Noah Kramer (New York : Doubleday Anchor, 1961) and quoted in Seymour Fersh, "India : Tradition in Transition", *Goals of Democracy Annual* 1973 (New York : Macmillan Company, 1962), p. 207.

2. For comment concerning the contemporary relevance of these characteristics of Hinduism, see Donald Eugene Smith, *India as a
Secular State* (Princeton : Princeton University Press, 1963),
p. 27.

3. Quoted in Seymour Fersh, *India : Tradition in Transition* (New
York : Macmillan Company, 1962), p. 207.

4. Donald Eugene Smith, *India as a Secular State* (Princeton : Princeton University Press, 1963), p. 27.

5. Romila Thapar, *A History Of India* (Baltimore : Penguin Books,
1966), p. 40.

CHAPTER IV

HINDUS AS TRANSMARINE SAILORS AND OVERSEAS MERCHANTS

INTRODUCTION

AFTER EXAMINING a map of Southeast Asia, Westerners only casually informed about the pre-modern development of India and the culture of its people might conclude that Hindus played a notable role in Asia's transmarine history, and that Hindu crews traditionally have been conspicuous on ships sailing to Western and Eastern ports. Both conclusions are factually incorrect.

In European history, a country (or a much smaller political entity such as a city state) provided with ready access to an ocean or sea and endowed with a talented and energetic population normally became a marine power. The maritime achievements of the Greeks, Romans, and other early Mediterranean peoples, as well as the several Nordic kingdoms far to the north, illustrate how an enterprising population controlling a coastal area resulted in the emergence of a sea-oriented state. Similarly, the policies of the British, French, Portuguese and Spanish governments of the sixteenth and seventeenth centuries stimulated a high level of marine activity and, as every schoolboy knows, each country was amply rewarded.

India, in contrast, has no comparable nautical history. Early Hindu kings built no navies either for military adventure or for the enhancement of their political power. They did not encourage merchants to construct cargo ships to export local products. The oceans surrounding India, as a recent study points out, "played no part in the building of Indian culture and civilization . . .and the Indians had no organic relations with the ocean."[1]

Why were transmarine policies of the early Hindus in such marked contrast with the marine programs of their Western contemporaries? The Hindus' disinterest in sailing the high seas was not the result of India's unfavourable geography or its physical deficiencies. Ancient India possessed impressive topographical features and material resources that if judged by

Western experiences, could have made the subcontinent a dynamic sea power.

India forfeited an ongoing maritime development because its male population had no dedicated interest in sea travel. For at least 2,500 years the young men of the Hindu community lived close to two of the world's greatest commercial highways, but almost totally rejected the opportunity to become mariners or overseas merchants, and Hindu kings, despite the fact that they were committed to programs of military aggrandizement, neglected the development of naval power.

The Hindus' rejection of transmarine enterprises has long been recognized by those who have written about the Indian people, but why they did so has not been considered in any detail. Professor A. L. Basham, for example, noted in one of his early essays that "the high-caste Hindu became the world's most thorough-going landlubber."[2] Other authors who have contrasted India's impressive maritime potential and its almost non-existent naval record have been more candid and far more critical. In 1918, General Sir O'Moore Creagh, a former Commander in Chief of Indian Army, who had lived more than forty years of his life in India wrote that "No Indian race has ever shown any capacity as sea-warriors, although, as merchant seamen some few of them are of undisputed value." As a sea-oriented people, he concluded, "Indians are, and ever have been, inferior to every other Asiatic people."[3]

This chapter offers a series of cultural pressures which helped shape the anti-marine attitudes and practices of the Hindu people.

INDIA'S PRO-MARINE ATTRIBUTES
Marine Geography and Topography

No pre-modern kingdom that lacked attractive coastal features such as deep harbors, sheltered bays, and an absence of reefs could hope to establish itself as a significant maritime power. India's marine geography and general topography therefore warrant primary consideration.

The Indian subcontinent, the largest land mass jutting out from the Asian mainland, resembles a slightly askew bow of a ship, bounded by the Arabian Sea on its starboard and the Bay of Bengal on the portside. Its two coastlines are among the longest in the world. Until recent times, India's western littoral was well over 2,000 miles long. Beginning in what is today known as the Sind, this coast fell in a southwestern direction, through the Malabar district and ultimately reached its southernmost extremity at Cape Comorin. Ships sailing from one of the several harbors on India's western shore such as Bombay, Calicut, Diu or Trivandrum, had ready access to the Persian Gulf and the Red Sea, each an avenue of entry into the Mediterranean and Arabian kingdoms and their commercial communities. India's classical eastern shoreline was approximately as long and no less well situated. It began in the vicinity of the mouth of the Ganges River, followed a southwestern line, past the Palk Straight and the island of Ceylon, and it also terminated at Cape Comorin. Ships departing from Calcutta, Madras or one of the ports on the Coromandel coast were within sailing distance of Burma, Malaysia and the island kingdoms of the South Pacific. From these locations they could continue their voyages and ultimately reach the ports of the Chinese empire.

India's two coasts were not only geographically impressive but also had topographical attributes that should have stimulated a steady expansion of Hindu sea power. The ports cited contained natural harbor facilities to accommodate a number of ships at the same time. The subcontinent itself was surrounded by an impressive number of navigable channels and deep roadsteads, good inlets, and several sheltered islands that could be used as secondary ports of debarkation. In addition, India's river network should have advanced the people's transmarine sailing skills. Many cut directly across the subcontinent before emptying into the sea, a feature used in other countries to good advantage by exporters and mariners. Even the prevailing winds and the dominant ocean currents favored marine traffic.

NATURAL RESOURCES AND BOAT CONSTRUCTION

Until recent times wood was the primary material for all nautical construction, commercial vessels as well as men-of-war. Secondary materials, such as metal nails, iron fittings, cloth sails, leather kegs and cordage were essential to make a ship seaworthy. It was wood, however, that formed the vessel's outer framework, its inner ribs and its deck planking. Consequently, any early community aspiring to become a sea power either required extensive forests located within its own territory, or a large supply of imported logs to supplement whatever meager supplies it possessed. Without wood, no kingdom could undertake a major ship building program.

Not all types of wood known to the ancient world possessed the requisite characteristics essential to building sailing ships. The logs most sought after were those possessing great strength, elasticity, and considerable resistance to saline corrosion. It was necessary to grow them in abundance, to harvest them without extraordinary difficulty, and finally, to cure and prepare the logs with a minimum of technical sophistication. Of the various types of wood known to have been used in early ship construction, in either the West or the East, teakwood was the most highly prized. Few woods are as well endowed for use in sailing ships. Teak trees can be felled and cut into planks or beams without much difficulty; since the wood is not notably hard it can be worked with relative ease. Of greater significance are the qualities of teak-wood after submergence in the water. Properly cured, teak neither shrinks, splits, cracks, nor varies its shape even when exposed to salt water over long periods of time. Also, metal fittings can be affixed to teak without destroying its structural integrity.[4]

In the ancient world teak trees grew profusely in two principal locations. One of these areas was south India, the so-called peninsular region of the subcontinent. The other area was the Burma-Siam-Indonesia triangle. For centuries the hot, rain-soaked hills of India's Malabar coast have been known for teak. Even to this day, Malabar teak forests flourish. The people living in the Malabar area had started harvesting and exporting teakwood almost from the beginning of organized trade between Asia and the Mediterranean world. Archeologists believe the teak used in the construction of the Moon Temple of the Sumerian city of Ur on the Euphrates River (c. 3000 b.c.) originated in Malabar and was sent north by overland route to its final destination, probably via the Arabian peninsula and the Persian Gulf. Considerably later, Theophrastus, the Greek philosopher who lived between 370 and 285 b.c., mentioned in his writings that he had seen ship-wrights in Arabia build vessels from a type of wood that could only be teak.

In the island of Tylos off the Arabian coast they say

there is a kind of wood of which they build their ships, and that in sea-water this is almost proof against decay; for it lasts more than 200 years if it is kept under water, while, if it is kept out of water, it decays sooner, though not for some years.[5]

Since teak is not native to any locale within the Arab world, Theophrastus had to be describing logs or planking imported either from southern India or the more remote forests.

Authors of later periods were more specific in their assessments of the importance of teakwood in ship construction. In one of his books, Al-Masudi, a ninth century A.D. historian, mentioned how frequently the ships sailing the Indian Ocean were made of imported Indian teak.[6]   Another Arab, Ibn-Jubayr, visited the prominent shipbuilding center of Aydhāb on the west coast of the Red Sea in the early part of the twelfth century, and called attention to teak's common use and desirable qualities.[7]

These chronologically scattered references illustrate two points : First, southern India, in the ancient period, was a leading source of the teakwood imported by the West.   Second, the people of the Malabar coast must have been familiar with the nautical importance of teak planking and its use in ship construction by artisans in other lands.   Had they been so inclined, Indians were advantageously located to develop their own centers of ship construction rather than to export teak, thus advancing the marine development of India's neighbors, but in no way furthering the subcontinent's nautical progress.

India had other material advantages for competing in nautical enterprises before the Christian era.   Iron, for example, is believed to have first appeared in India about 1000 B.C.   Over the next five or six centuries its use spread widely.   Although costly to produce, iron nails, rods, fastenings and similar items employed in ship construction were available in India. Copper, another metal used frequently by early shipwrights, is believed to have pre-dated the appearance of iron.   The art of weaving cloth was yet another skill the Indians acquired very early in their history.   India is also known to have produced sturdy cordage made from the outer fibers of coconuts, which could have been used both for making sails and for binding sails to masts.

INDIA'S MARINE DEFICIENCIES
The Hindus and the Sea

The last factor essential to the development of sea power is personnel. If a pre-modern king were to establish naval strength or a fleet of commercial carriers, he had to have a continuous stream of men and boys willing to turn to the sea as a way of life and a means of earning a livelihood. A life at sea had to appeal to a significant segment of the population; it had to be a socially acceptable way of life. Crewmen had to be willing to undergo long, rigorous periods of apprenticeship to become proficient deckhands. Pilots, navigators and other officers needed special training. The crew had to be prepared to live an uncertain life at sea because they found great personal satisfaction aboard a sailing vessel. They had to accept the loneliness and daily deprivations while sailing from port to port that their land-based cousins did not experience. As is true today, early sailors had to be willing to leave their families and the comforts of their homes to live in cramped, inhospitable quarters for extended periods. Of necessity, they had to survive on a very restricted diet and one that was invariably monotonous. When given shore leave, these men often had to mix with unfriendly or even hostile people and try to adapt a strange customs and manners.

Whatever the inner factors that motivated pre-modern men to become sailors and sail the hostile seas,—and the issues of motivation of any sailing community is too complex to more than suggest a series of generalization—their bravery and accomplishments are well documented. Among the Mediterranean peoples, the marine exploits of the Egyptians, Carthaginians, Athenians, Corinthians, and Romans have been fully recorded. Each kingdom regularly turned out crews that sailed the high seas and brought great credit (and profit) to their respective countries. Some centuries later the northern Europeans produced the Vikings, seamen equally as brave and highly motivated. Both the northern and southern seamen accepted the hardships and dangers of seafaring because of the excitement and adventure that they experienced.

Within the pre-modern Hindu community, however, a strong pro-marine tradition failed to emerge. For most of the men of the Hindu community, going to sea as transmarine sailors was neither a socially acceptable nor even an honorable thing to do. Some time in the Vedic Age, the idea developed that deep sea travel was a religious sin and a social disaster. The early Aryans gradually accepted the idea that all forms of transmarine activity must be avoided if at all possible. The men of this society were indoctrinated with ideas and values stressing the importance of remaining on land and, more specifically, of residing within the subcontinent itself. Later, the Hindus, legatees of the Aryan cultural tradition, continued to shun transoceanic sailing and marine adventures. They were content to live in the area they were born, following the same occupations as their fathers with no urge to roam the world. The Arabian Ocean, the Indian Ocean, and the Bay of Bengal were part of the general landscape, but Hindu men rarely looked on these waterways either as a way of escaping from India or as a means of seeking new information about the world in which they lived.

One reason that the men in ancient India were content to stay at home was their felicitous environment. Early Hindus were able to live reasonably well in all areas of the subcontinent with a nominal amount of effort. Hunger does not seem to have been a significant problem. Undeveloped land was in abundant supply, and could be readily cultivated. There was also land for grazing cattle. For those disinclined toward any work, nature provided a variety of wild-growing fruits and nuts for sustenance. The economic productiveness of the subcontinent, however, offers only a partial explanation for the Hindus' abstinence from deep sea travels.

A more compelling explanation for the Hindus' rejection of the mariner's life is found in cultural values and taboos that stifled whatever sea-going tendencies existed at one time on the subcontinent. Beginning in the northwest during the earliest years of the Aryan invasion, the belief took hold that the orthodox should avoid sailing the high seas even for relatively short periods of time. The community was taught to isolate themselves from others who did not share their religious convictions or their way of life, that is, from foreigners. These ideas ultimately became firmly fixed within the Hindu ethos. Those who disregarded the tradition—who sailed abroad and took up residence in a non-Hindu country—were marked for exceedingly harsh and humiliating sanctions when and if they returned to India.

A number of inter-related factors had a direct bearing on the origin and growth of the Hindu religion and social values. By identifying these cultural forces, it is possible to understand why the Hindus shunned the ocean and failed to foster a vigorous and dynamic marine tradition similar to those of other premodern people located adjacent to the main sea lanes of the world.

ANTI-MARINE THEMES IN HINDU LITERATURE

Before they invaded the subcontinent, prehistoric Aryans were a land-based people with no direct sailing experience. In the course of their prolonged migration from their original habitat to the northwest section of India, they are thought to have survived by engaging in occupations connected with the land, such as hunting, tending herds, or gathering whatever edibles were available. There is no reason to believe that before settling in India proper the first influx of Aryans had ever seen a large body of water or engaged in marine travel. There is a possibility that the earliest Aryans who lived in eastern Europe were familiar with the ocean, but such contact had long since been erased from the memory of those who first arrived and settled in India. If in the period before reaching India the Aryans were compelled to cross local rivers and streams, they probably managed to circumvent or ford them without difficulty. They most likely had no reason to experiment with building a ship, and consequently, never discovered that sailing could stimulate, excite, and demonstrate courage and virility.

As the invasion progressed, more and more Aryans settled in northern India, forcing the indigenous Dravidians to migrate south. Ultimately Aryans dominated the entire countryside of upper India. The land was suitable for agricultural development, and the Aryans were able without difficulty to maintain their earlier pastoral folkways and land-oriented values. Because the sea was beyond their immediate horizon, the disinterest in all types of marine activities earlier established by the Aryans endured. The Punjab, the location of the first Aryan settlement in India, is literally hundreds of miles from the Arabian Sea. Furthermore, there was no reason for the people to undertake such a long and arduous journey to India's eastern or western shores. Land was plentiful. As the Aryan community multiplied and more land was needed for settlements and agricultural pursuits, they moved eastward toward the Jumna and Ganges Rivers. By developing the subcontinent along its widest axis, Aryans further postponed coming into prolonged contact with India's maritime frontiers. Most revealingly, the *Rig Veda* never once mentions fish as a basic component of the Aryans' diet. It is not impossible, of course, that some adventuresome and particularly aggressive men explored the broader countryside and actually reached the seashore.[8] If they did report back on the vastness of the waters or its possibilities for travel, it does not appear to have been in such enthusiastic terms that other Aryan men followed their lead. While much of their earliest history is lost, it seems likely that of those Aryans who settled in India between c. 2000 B.C., and 400 B.C., few made their homes near the coast or had any but the most superficial contact with the waters surrounding the subcontinent.[9]

During the centuries immediately preceding the Christian era, many of the dominant cultural values today associated with the Hindus were well established, or at least emerging in a recognizable form. Interest in sailing vessels, fishing, transmarine travel, or fascination with the sea do not emerge as strong features of the Aryan people.

An examination of the sacred *Vedas,* the collection of ritual texts, hymns and *mantras* embodying the central truths of the Aryans' philosophy of life, supports the conclusion that these men were not sea-oriented and had no concept of how the development of a marine capability could advance their political-military goals. This body of Sanskrit literature is associated with the period immediately following the Aryan settlement of India and consists of more than one hundred individual verses (*slokas*). The *Rig Veda,* for example, reveal how the Aryan people occupied their time, what pleasures were valued, and how their leaders and priests interpreted the natural world about them. A careful examination of the *Vedas* fails to indicate a strong, emerging maritime tradition. While there is no prohibition against sailing in the *Rig Veda,* and there are several references bearing on shipping and shipbuilding, the *Vedas* are all but silent about the material advantages of inter-state commerce or the possible enjoyment realized by a man sailing on the high seas. One passage of the *Rig Veda* speaks disparingly of merchants "under the influence of greed, sending out ships to foreign countries." Other references are brief, almost incidental, allusions to the sea. One *sloka* reads : "When Varuna and I went on a boat and took her out to sea, I lived in the boat floating on the water and was happy in it, rocking gracefully (on the waves)."[10] A third passage that seems to support the prevalence of sea voyages is certainly the most interesting in form, but not much more precise than other references. It concerns the misfortunes that befall Bhujya, a resourceful warrior ship wrecked and later rescued by his patron-god. The narrator who recounts the incident in the *Rig Veda* describes how Bhujya is placed aboard a boat that comes to his aid and then praises the escape in the following manner :

> Ye wrought that hero exploit *in the ocean*
> which giveth no support, no hold, nor station
> What time ye carried Bhujya to his dwelling
> Borne in a ship with hundred oars. . .[11]

These *slokas*[12] suggest widespread navigation of the Indian Ocean and extensive trading voyages by the Aryan people in ancient India. According to the opinions of some experts who have studied the original Sanskrit and have attempted to translate the words in a culturally correct manner, the word "sea" is poorly chosen and improper. The activity described in the *Vedas,* they maintain, is either sailing on an inland river or lake, or alternatively, sailing close to the shoreline of India. They decline to accept a literal interpretation of the words in question. Thus, the late Professor Romesh Chunder Dutt, commented in connection with the Bhujya *sloka* that "there are distinct references to voyages by sea, though of course the words used may mean rivers only, and not the sea."[13]

Next to the *Vedas,* the most important body of literary material from the Aryan period are the *smritis.* The *Vedas* are alleged to be of divine authorship, but the *smritis* are believed to have been written by men who lived within the Aryan community and knew its peculiarities first-hand. While it is most difficult to be chronologically precise, it is widely assumed that the *smritis* describe Aryan society beginning about 500 B.C. By the time the *smritis* first appeared, Aryan society had experienced a number of major changes. Tribal life had slowly collapsed. People had begun to settle in cities and villages scattered about the entire northern section of the subcontinent. Warrior-kings had acquired greater power than formerly, and they began to dominate the political-military policies in the areas where Aryans established themselves. Aryan society had become considerably more complex and difficult to govern as more and more of the community discontinued their earlier habits and began assuming roles as permanent settlers of the subcontinent. The caste system by this time had taken on a much sharper definition, but many of its rules were still vague, conflicting and probably unevenly applied. In terms of interpersonal relations, the emerging caste system must have produced innumerable situations in which there was considerable tension and dispute. Aryan leaders accordingly sought to formulate a societal code that was functional and appropriate to their new situation. For the first time in Aryan history, statements began to appear explaining the rationale for the caste system, codifying a number of its leading practices, and also specifying what penalties and punishments could be expected if violations occurred. The *smriti* treatises reflect this stage of Aryan civilization.

Of the several authors of *smriti* whose treatises are available today, and whose writings are believed to have been especially influential on Aryan thinking, Baudhayana is considered among the first to have been active. His *Dharmasastra* [14] is generally thought to have been compiled between five and six centuries before the Christian era. Among the specific topics Baudhyana addressed was what individual acts are sinful and destructive to Aryan life and caste arrangements. In this context Baudhayana declared—without elaboration—that "making voyages by sea" constitutes a very serious offense against pious Aryan life and will automatically bring about the loss of the traveller's caste status. [15] This admonition is believed to have been the reason orthodox Brahmins were so reluctant to make sea voyages to other continents.

Another section of the *Dharmasastra* lists the sanctions to be applied against those who violated the non-sailing rule and the expiation for this sin. His statement dictating sanctions for overseas travellers is among the earliest that can be located in the literature. The severity and meannesss of Baudhayana's

punishment, along with the details he provided for its imple-
mentation, suggests that Aryans of the period had started to be
attracted to maritime activities and that the society's leaders
formulated a harsh and cruel expiation rite so as to put an end
to such ideas. Any Aryan found guilty of violating the edict
against overseas travel, the *Dharmasastra* proclaimed, would be
punished not only by loss of caste but advised that :

> For those who have committed [the offence of sailing
> abroad . . . ed.] the following penance is prescribed : They
> shall eat every fourth meal-time a little food, bathe at the
> time of the three libations . . . passing the day standing and
> the night sitting. After a lapse of three years they throw
> off their guilt.[16]

Baudhayana's work is among the earliest *smriti* produced,
but it was not as influential within Aryan-Hindu society as the
Manusmriti[17] (The Laws of Manu). It has been refined and
elaborated upon by dozens of successive *smriti* commentators
since it first appeared, somewhere near the beginning of the
Christian era. It has been singularly influential over the centuries in helping to shape societal beliefs. The central themes
of the *Manusmriti* are similar to those advanced by Baudhayana.
Both are concerned with establishing what conduct is acceptable
and what actions and attitudes are forbidden within the Aryan
community. The rules and regulations that Manu noted, however, are stipulated in far greater detail than those Baudhayana
offered.

One area of great specificity involves transmarine travel. In
an elaborate fashion Manu told how the most orthodox members
of the Aryan community were to regard those who sailed the
high seas and how marines were to be penalized.

He listed those people with whom Brahmins were not to associate. He prescribed that those guilty of conduct destructive to the
purity and well-being of the individual must be ostracized from
Brahmanic society. He thereafter named those who were so regarded. Incendiaries (i.e., men who burned corpses at funerals), prisoners, men who ate food given by sons of an adulteress, a seller
of Soma (i.e., a man who sold the merits gained by sacrifice), a
suborner to perjury, and lastly, a man "who undertakes voyages
by sea"[18] were among the offenders. Any twice-born orthodox
Hindu guilty of such actions was a "locust" and despised. For

his transgression he was to be denied participation in caste activities. He could not participate in funeral rites, was denied religious instruction and could not join in the everyday social life of the community. Finally, Manu advised those who faithfully observed the laws and who had not engaged in such prohibitions that they :

> ... should shun at sacrifice ... these locust of twice-born men, whose conduct is reprehensible and who are unworthy to sit in the company at a repast.[19]

In another section of the *Manusmriti,* further evidence appears of the Aryan community's prejudices against high sea sailing and residence abroad. Here Manu discussed the geographical areas of the world where observant Hindus are allowed to reside without violating their religious credo and cultural standards. The permissible territory he designated as Aryavarta or the country under the control of the Aryans where Brahmanism was in force. It consisted of the territory between the Himavat mountains (today identified within the Himalayan range) and the Vindhya mountains (the range that marks the division between north and south India). The east-west terminals of Aryavarta, according to Manu's description, are the two great bodies of water flanking the subcontinent. Residence in any location outside this area, he decreed was unacceptable behavior for an observant twice-born Aryan and so prescribed. Manu maintained that beyond Aryavarta lived only people who were religiously and socially impure. They were *mléccha,* barbarians and most despised foreigners. No Aryan who valued his religious principles and wished to remain a member of good standing in the community was allowed to reside in territory under *mléccha's* control.[20]

The two cited passages of the *Manusmriti,* when taken together, all but destroyed whatever inclination any of the early, more adventuresome upper caste Brahmins might have had to explore the world. Lesser caste men, almost certainly influenced by the conduct idealized for Brahmins,[21] probably acted similarly. For generations, Manu's laws discouraged the Aryans from sailing on the high seas and residing abroad in merchants.

The ban against travelling outside of Aryavarta was not completely successful. Small groups of Hindus did migrate to foreign countries. Others sailed the seas and some even resided in foreign lands for months or years before returning to India. The

status and reputation of these adventurers suffered because of
their travels, but their numbers were relatively small and their
actions did not significantly influence Hindu travel standards. The
vast majority of men within the Aryan-Hindu community both
before and after the Christian era abided by the injunction against
sea travel and living abroad. They remained geographically
rooted, many living adjacent to the ocean but without venturing
beyond local waters.[22]

Many of the *smriti* writers who followed Manu did little more
than repeat verbatim Manu's admonitions to remain in India and
to avoid inter-oceanic travel. Those few later authors who did
advance new ideas, far from liberalizing the ban against sea travel, invented novel ways to further humiliate those found guilty
of such offences. The new and more crippling sanctions demonstrate the determination of the Aryan leaders to force their people
to remain in their own country. They also indicate that the
passage of time and the gradual opening of the subcontinent to
foreigners from several lands had not served to open the way
to marine travel and residence abroad.

Naradasmriti[23] (The Laws of Narada), a typical later *smriti*,
is believed to have been written during the fifth or sixth century
A.D. As a compendium of rules and regulations, *Naradasmriti* was
never a major treatise, but its text forcefully projects the unabated
prejudice against sea travel within the Hindu community in the
medieval period.

By the time Narada's work appeared, Hindu judicial processes in some ways resembled Western legal institutions and trial
procedures. In one section of his book Narada provided Hindu
courts of law with a list of Hindus who were to be considered
as incompetent and not credible witnesses, whose testimony, even
if taken under oath, was not admissible. Whatever they said or
did outside of the courtroom also was to be considered of dubious
value by the more pious members of the community. Among
these individuals that Narada disenfranchised were men who made
long voyages and merchants who traveled to trans-marine countries, along with actors, eunuchs, the irreligious, the sick and the
deformed.[24]

Some seven hundred years later, despite India's longtime
prominence in trading affairs, Hindu publicists had not appreciably softened their attitude toward mariners and transoceanic

travellers. By the thirteenth century A.D., India's export trade
to both the Mediterranean world and southeast Asia had been
flourishing for centuries. Shipping local products abroad had
brought the Indian people enormous wealth. The subcontinent
had been visited by a steady stream of foreign merchants, sailors,
curious visitors and religious missionaries. In spite of such ex-
posure to the world beyond India and to non-Hindu sailing activity, leading Hindu authors continued to renounce deep-sea sailors, travellers and foreign merchants. A prominent law digest
of the thirteenth century A.D., the *Catutvargacintamani* of Hemadri, for example, was as unbending in its denunciation of these men
as Baudhayana and Manu had been some two thousand years
earlier. In his treatise Hemadri warned that a person guilty of
such transgression must purify himself before he could resume his
customary role within the daily life of his caste. Hemadri added
one new prescription. According to his interpretation, a party
guilty of violating the maritime ban could never expiate for his
behavior. After performing the necessary acts of purification and
contrition, the offender was no longer to be considered impure by the community, but under no conditions could he regain his status among his caste peers. He was permanently
banned from participation in his family's day-to-day activities
as well as from all caste meetings and celebrations. Hemadri,
unlike his predecessors, doomed the voyager to the life of a
permanent outcaste, forcing him to live apart until he died.[25]

The *sastras* comprise a third body of literature of early
India reflecting the classical attitudes toward the sea. *Sastras*
deal with government and economic matters, and the most distinguished is Kautilya's *Arthasastra*.[26] This work, associated
with the formation of the Mauryan empire of the 4th century
B.C., is frequently compared to Machiavelli's *The Prince* because it discounts the importance of ethics and morality in the
political process. Without question, no other pre-modern Indian text discusses how rulers should determine political, economic, and military policies as thoroughly or with as much insight, and none was as influential.

The *Arthasastra* reinforces the early Indians' prejudice
against deep sea travel. Kautilya devoted extensive passages to
an analysis of sailing, navigational routes, import-export taxes,
and the proper organization of Mauryan custom facilities. Kau-

tilya was obviously aware of the advantages of a thriving export trade. He understood that taxing all types of commerce would enhance the royal treasury, and hence, the king's reputation and power. On the other hand, Kautilya strongly advised against transmarine shipping. Kautilya stated that if a merchant could choose between shipping cargo by a land or a marine route, the former was preferable. The land route, he wrote, presented fewer dangers than sailing on the seas, as it was easier to provide security to a land caravan than to protect ships from maritime disasters. He recognized that certain situations might require an exporter to use water facilities to deliver the cargo to the purchaser. When conditions necessitated a water route, Kautilya favored the coastal route. Given a choice between a water route that generally followed the shore line of the subcontinent, he wrote, and one that required the vessel to sail in "mid ocean," the former was to be selected. "The route along and close to the shore is better, as it touches at many trading port towns," Kautilya wrote.[27]

In another passage of the *Arthasastra*, Kautilya discusses the anti-marine prejudices of both the people of early India and their officials. This section, entitled "The Superintendent of Shipping,"[28] consists of a lengthy description of the various duties and responsibilities of the maritime official. He was to be given authority to examine all the records pertaining to the country's maritime enterprises, both of ships and cargoes coming into Mauryan ports and of those leaving for foreign destinations. The official had the right to audit the records of ships travelling "not only on [the] *oceans* and the mouth of rivers, but also on lakes, natural or artificial, and rivers in the vicinity of sthāniya and other fortified cities."[29]

The key word in the passage is "ocean," which in the original Sanskrit is *samudrasamyána*. If the translation of Kautilya's text is to be accepted literally, the Superintendent of Shipping had authority to supervise ships engaging in transmarine voyages. Unless qualified in some way, such an interpretation would conflict with Kautilya's earlier admonition against deep sea travel. There is, however, no discrepancy between the two cited passages. According to the footnote provided by the translator of the *Arthasastra*, the Sanskrit word *samudrasamyāna* refers to "sailing or boating close to the shore."[30] Thus

Kautilya assigned to the Superintendent of Shipping the responsibility of reviewing the records of ships traversing what today would be called the marginal or territorial sea. The omission of all reference to inter-continental shipping conforms with the other literary works reviewed.

HINDU MARINE MYTHS : LODESTONES AND NAILS

In very early Western history, the people who lived adjacent to the coast and the men who sailed on the high seas made up many lurid, frightening stories about the ocean and the monsters who lived beneath its waves. They told of the dangers that awaited crews who ventured too far out from shore or became lost. The accounts of the voyages of Homer and Ulysses, as well as the less episodic literature of the West, contain innumerable tales about devilish sea monsters, exotic and destructive mermaids, mountain-high geysers, boiling hot whirlpools and the like. Such marine myths which were common among all coastal people, are understandable. In those days, any large body of water that stretched far beyond the horizon was an unknown, forbidding frontier. It was to be both feared and respected.

As Western sailing people gained a greater appreciation of the world beyond their homes and became more proficient sailors, they developed clearer understanding of the sea and its nature. Western marine myths gradually disappeared. Stories entered the general fictional literature, where they were enjoyed as a pleasant and amusing remembrance of the past. The Lorelei myth is a typical example of how a belief early Western sailors had in an alluring enchantress of the sea was ultimately relegated to fiction and opera. Among pre-modern Western sailing communities there were any number of such stories.

The Aryans had their own marine myths, and some were similar to those identified with Western sailing. The Aryans, however, originated at least one fanciful tale about the sea that thereafter influenced their marine conduct. They acted as though the myth they created was factual. Long after they had greater knowledge of the sea and better understood its nature, they did not relegate the myth as an amusing anachronism of their early past but continued to be captive to its effects.

At an indeterminate period in Indian history the belief took hold that scattered about the ocean floor were extensive fields of gigantic lodestones. They were said to contain sharp peaks, jagged edges, and most important, were extremely magnetic. Aryans believed that if a sailing vessel was constructed with iron nails or metal fittings and sailed too close to the lodestones, the submerged magnetic fields would draw the ship onto the rocks where it would be destroyed. Consequently, the Indian sailors of the ancient period concluded that only vessels constructed of materials impervious to the magnetic pull of the lodestones, that is, ships using wooden pegs and braided rope rather than nails and rivets, could sail the seas without disaster.

The precise origin of the lodestone myth cannot be determined, although there is no question about its longevity or the effects of its wide circulation. According to one contemporary treatise on ship construction and the sailing practices of early Eastern people, Indian mariners as early as the fifth century B.C. were deliberately avoiding the use of metal in their sailing vessels.[31] Ptolemy's *Geography,* a work generally attributed to the first half of the second century A.D., gives an example of the effect of the myth :

> There are said to be also ten other islands forming a continuous group called Maniolai, from which ships fastened with iron nails are said to be unable to move away, (perhaps on account of the magnetic iron in the islands) and hence they are built with wooden bolts.[32]

Many later Western accounts of India recite the same dread consequences.[33] An eleventh century A.D. Hindu treatise must have had considerable influence on maritime construction within the entire Indian subcontinent. The *Yuktikalpataru* (The Wishing Tree of Useful Arts) is a compilation of diverse handicraft techniques accredited to Bhoja Narapati.[34] The late Professor Mookerji described it as the "one Sanskrit work, which is something like a treatise on the art of shipbuilding in ancient India." Included in the contents are instructions for the proper design and construction of sailing vessels and the materials from which they were to be built. The work, he concludes, "sums up in a condensed form all the available information and knowledge about that truly ancient industry of India."[35] Particularly revealing are Bhoja's comments about proper materials because they probably represent the prevailing views of eleventh century India on nautical construction. As summarized by Mookerji, Bhoja warned :

> ... care should be taken that no iron is used in holding or joining together the planks of bottoms intended to be seagoing vessels, for the iron will inevitably expose them to the influence of magnetic rocks in the sea, or bring them within a magnetic field and so lead them to risks. Hence the planks of bottoms are to be fitted together or mortised by means of substances other than iron.[36]

As a result, Indian ships were traditionally lashed or strapped together with yards and yards of heavy cordage, and planks and beams were joined together in like manner. Early mariners and ship owners were thus spared concern about the magnetic pull of the lodestones.

Today this type of ship construction, known as "stitching the planks together," continues to be used in some areas of the East.[37] In fact, vessels stitched together and avoiding the use of metal can be highly functional, notably in coastal waters, such as along the western coast of India where treacherous, unseen reefs threaten passing vessels.[38] If an accident occurs, the damaged section of the undersurface is more easily repaired than if nails and heavy metal spikes had been used. These vessels are, however, far less capable of making extended voyages across the high seas than those with metal fittings.

In any event, "stitching the planks together" became the prevailing mode of ship construction throughout India until about the end of the fifteenth century A.D. By that time, Arabs and other seafaring peoples had become remarkably proficient in building functional, Western style ships, and their technological capabilities were so advanced that it is doubtful whether Indian shipwrights could have bridged the gap even had they been so inclined. They had no interest in changing their traditional ways and utilizing their Western neighbors' more utilitarian methods. The following two citations were recorded approximately thirteen hundred years apart. They nicely illustrate the persistency of Indian shipwrights in avoiding metal constructions. In the first century(?) A.D., Hippalus told of his travels in southern India, and describes the local ships as "very large vessels made of single logs bound together."[39] A more elaborate but basically identical description of Indian shipping is found in Friar John of Monte Corvino's journal, written in the thirteenth century. Because he came from the Mediterranean where nautical affairs played a vital part in the lives of many men, he paid special attention to Indian marine practices. He wrote home about the poor quality of the local ships and the ineptitude of the mariners he observed. Never before having seen stitched planking used in marine construction, he wrote :

> Their ships in these parts are mighty frail and uncouth, with no iron in them, and no caulking. They are sewn like clothes with twine. And so if the twine breaks anywhere there is a breach indeed ! Once every year therefore there is a mending of this, more or less, if they propose to go to sea. And they have a frail and flimsy rudder like the top of a table, of a cubit in width, in the middle of the stern; and when they have to tack, it is done with a vast deal of trouble; and if it is blowing in any way hard, they cannot tack at all. They have but one sail and one mast, and the sails are either of matting or of some miserable cloth. The ropes are of husks.
>
> Moreover, their mariners are few and far from good.[40]

India's marine development was undoubtedly retarded by the primitive anti-sea myths that led to the persistent use of stitched planking instead of metal-fastened vessels. Over many centuries, India's mariners and shipwrights continued to act as if the anti-sea myths were factual and accordingly placed ships of the subcontinent in a decidedly disadvantageous position. In contrast, the Arabs and Mediterranean shipyards were building increasingly sea-worthy vessels and allowing their crews to venture farther and farther out to sea.

CASTE RULES AND MARINE LIFE

Traditionally Hindus from the upper castes have been deeply concerned with cleanliness and the need to be free from all forms of contamination. In the Hindu value system, contamination can result either from physical contact with those considered unclean, or from failure to observe one of the sundry regulations that Hinduism prescribes for personal hygiene.

In order to appreciate how an observant Hindu's personal

determination to remain unsullied inhibited marine development, it is necessary to understand the extent and complexity of their rules and regulations. For example, intricate instructions on eating, drinking and bathing practices are given to each of the principal castes. The complexity and nuances of what was permitted and what was not authorized is exceeded only by the concern for minutiae. A Brahmin may eat rice or grain cooked with water only if it has been prepared by another Brahmin, but is permitted to eat vegetables cooked in clarified butter even when handled and cooked by a member of a lower caste. In contrast, Hindus of the lower castes are not barred from accepting any type of cooked food prepared by higher caste members or from taking water they offer.[41]

Rules of the Hindu religion are especially rigid regarding the use of water—whether how to draw it from a well, hand it to another person, drink it or use it in the preparation of food. Throughout their history orthodox Hindus have been deeply committed to obeying the regulations laid out for them. They are concerned with what caste has the right to draw water from what well and what castes are prohibited from so doing; who has touched a container or vessel of water and his caste membership; and who has the right to serve it. There are many stories of ultra orthodox Hindus, for example, who would use water only if it came from a single, very specific source. There is even a report of a Brahmin who carried a sufficient supply of his customary water in his baggage when travelling abroad so that his daily ablutions could continue and his food be prepared without fear of contamination.[42]

Caste rules narrowly prescribed the Hindu's dining companions. As a general rule, one could not eat with others of lesser caste status. A Brahmin dined only when others at the table were his caste equals. Otherwise he ate alone. Other castes were similarly restricted. Participation in a social situation involving a mix of people from contrasting socio-economic groups has been all but unknown throughout Indian history.

Bathing is another rite that is prescribed in great detail and calls for an extremely demanding regimen. Under the precepts of their religion, the Hindu, particularly a Brahmin, is required to bathe a minimum of three times a day. The conditions under which these ablutions are to take place—even such minutia as which hand is to be used in washing what part of the body—are specified in the required ritual. This feature of Hinduism is centuries old and was commented upon by a number of early visitors to the subcontinent. Alberuni, for example, reported in one of his writings :

> Every day he [the observant Brahmin—ed.] wash himself thrice : at the [time] of rising . . . at the [time] of setting, i.e. evening twilight, and between them in the middle of the day.[43]

A contemporary Indian author, describing the typical Hindu's enthusiasm for cleanliness believes they display "a maniacal anxiety for physical cleanliness" and that among Hindus "cleanliness (is) superior to godliness."[44]

Under these circumstances, it is no wonder that the Hindus avoided long voyages at sea and had no desire to live in foreign countries. Travelling on the high seas for any appreciable period of time meant the discontinuance of many, if not most, caste rituals. Crowded indiscriminately aboard a vessel that could offer its passengers few of the amenities of life on land,[45] and threatened with one of the most destructive societal sanctions (outcasting), the Hindus' long aversion to sea travelling becomes understandable. If by chance he was able to conduct himself at sea in a manner that preserved caste purity, he faced equally grave problems at the port of debarkation. An alien residing among foreigners, he could hardly hope to continue to observe the required forms and regulations of his earlier life.

The sailing vessels of India before the sixteenth-seventeenth centuries appear to have been small and exceedingly confining. Passengers and the crew must have been forced to accommodate themselves in hundreds of different ways to their immediate situation. Social mixing was of necessity indiscriminate and obviously no dietary prescriptions could be followed. Dining only in the presence of one's caste equals or bathing three times per day was equally impractical. To an orthodox Hindu, especially a devout Brahmin, the prospect of living on board for several weeks or months under such conditions represented an evil to be avoided if at all possible.[46] A short voyage (a few hours at best) might be tolerable for Hindus, but to sail on the high seas, or to live in a non-Hindu environment in a foreign land would violate one of the leading drives of a pious, upper caste Hindu, namely, the preservation of his personal purity.

REFERENCES

1. Amaury De Reincourt, *The Soul Of India* (New York : Harper and Brothers, 1960), p. 158. On this point, also see Alan Villiers, *The Indian Ocean* (London : Museum Press Limited, 1952), pp. 93ff. He concludes, "India *should* have dominated eastern trade and its rulers should have dominated eastern sea power. Yet little evidence they did so . . . ." (italics in original). However, for a quite different interpretation of India's prehistoric maritime traditions and experiences, see K. M. Panikkar, *India and the Indian Ocean* (London : George Allen & Unwin Ltd., 1945), pp. 17-27.

2. A. L. Basham, "Notes on Seafaring in Ancient India," *Arts and Letters*, XXIII, No. 2 (London : The Royal India and Pakistan Society, 1949), pp. 69-70. Also see William Vincent, *The Commerce and Navigation of the Ancients in the Indian Ocean* (London : T. Cadell and W. Davies, 1807), II, p. 404. He refers to Barthema's early sixteenth century chronicle to support his conclusion that "the Hindoos at Calicut/the principal southern port/left all navigation to the Mohamedans, so it should seem that the prohibition of their religion had been uniform from all ages . . .". pp. 404-5.

   It should be made quite specific that many Indian historians refuse to accept the idea that early Indians were not men of the sea. Professors Moreland and Chatterjee, for example, without making clear the origins of the sailors and captains, state : ". . . it is not possible, then, to say when seagoing ships began to be built on the western side of India . . . all that we really know is that Indians used the sea freely in the centuries between the foundation of Buddhism and the Christian era . . . there appears to be no clear evidence that in the earlier days they sailed the open sea." *A Short History of India*, 4th ed. rev., (New York : David McKay, 1967), pp. 71-74. Other Indian historians have reached the opposite conclusion. In discussing a twelfth century edict protecting foreign merchants, K. A. Nilakantha Sastri states that "we may draw the inference that the overseas trade of the country had passed more or less completely into the hands of foreigners and that the indigenous population had already lost their maritime instincts and developed a new dread of the seas that has been so general in modern India." "Foreign Trade Under the Kakatiyas," *Journal of Oriental Research*, VIII (Oct.-Dec. 1934), p. 320.

3. General Sir O'Moore Creagh, *Indian Studies*, 2nd ed. rev., (London : Hutchinson and Company, 1919), p. 234. For material disagreeing with such sentiments, see Stephen P. Cohen, "The Untouchable Soldier : Caste, Politics and the Indian Army," *Journal Of Asian Studies*, XXVIII, May 1969, p. 457.

4. On the attractiveness of teak in pre-modern nautical construction as well as India's prominent role as a teak exporter, see George Fadlo Hourani, *Arab Seafaring in the Indian Ocean In Ancient and Early Medieval Times* (Beirut : Khayata, 1963), pp. 90ff; and E. B. Havell, *The History of Aryan Rule in India* (London : George G. Harrap, nd.,) pp. 129ff. On the evolution of maritime construction in the East in general, see James Hornell, *Water Transport : Origins and Early Evolution* (Cambridge : Cambridge University Press, 1946).

5. Theophrastus, *Enquiry into Plants*, trans. Sir Arthur Hort (London : William Heinemann, 1916), 1, p. 445. Also quoted in George Fadlo Hourani, *Arab Seafaring* (Beirut : Khayata, 1963), p. 90.

6. See George Fadlo Hourani, *Arab Seafaring*, p. 90.

7. *ibid.* See also William Wright, ed., *The Travels of Ibn Jubayr*, 2nd ed., rev., (London : Luzac and Company, 1907), p. 71; and R. J. C. Broadhurst, trans. *Travels of Ibn Jubayr* (London : J. Cape, 1952), p. 65.

8. There currently exists considerable disagreement among scholars concerning maritime activities in the Rig-Vedic period. Taking the affirmative position, Professor H. C. Raychaudhuri has noted that "A great controversy has centered around the question as to whether marine navigation was practiced in Rig-Vedic times. According to one view, navigation was limited to the crossing of rivers in boats, but we have undoubted references to navigators sailing in ships with a hundred oars. In the story of the shipwreck of Bhujyu, mention is made of the *Samudra*, 'which giveth no support, or hold, or station.' Some think that *Samudra* means no more than the stream of the Indus in its lower course. Others regard the story as a matter of heresay knowledge gathered from travellers, but acquaintance with the sea is rendered probable by references to the 'treasures of the deep.' If the identification of the Vedic *mana* with the Babylonian *manah* is correct, we have indubitable testimony to a very early intercourse between Vedic India and distant lands beyond the sea." *An Advanced History of India*, 2nd ed. rev., (London : Macmillan, 1965), p. 35.

In the opinion of the author of this work, Professor Raychaudhuri's argument is less than convincing, and the better view is that Vedic India, that is Upper India shunned maritime travel.

9. Thus Panikkar reports, ". . . To the people of North India, with their Central Asian traditions, the sea meant very little. Their conception of politics is well expressed by Kalidasa, who describes the ideal king of the Raghu Dynasty as *Āsamudra Kshitiesanām*—rulers whose territory extended to the shores of the sea. The idea of ruling seas, far less of ruling lands across the sea, never entered the minds of the monarchs of the north . . . ." *Geographical Factors in Indian History* (Bombay : Bharatiya Vidya Bhavan, 1959), pp. 78-79.

10. Romesh Chunder Dutt, *A History of Civilization in Ancient India*, Rev. ed., (London : Kegan Paul, Trench, Trübner, 1893), I. p. 40.

11. Quoted in A. L. Basham, "Notes on Seafaring in Ancient India," *Arts and Letters*, XXIII, No. 2 (London : The Royal India and Pakistan Society, 1949), p. 60.

12. For the six specific references to sailing found in the *Rig Veda*, see Radha Kumud Mookerji, *Indian Shipping*, 2nd ed., (Bombay : Orient Longmans, 1957), pp. 37-38 and also see Romesh Chunder Dutt, *A History of Civilization in Ancient India*, I, p. 40.

13. *ibid.*

14. F. Max Müller, ed., *Sacred Books of the East*, Vol. XIV; *The Sacred Laws of the Aryas*, trans. Georg Bühler (Oxford : Clarendon Press, 1879), p. 217.

15. *ibid.* p. 217. In a footnote to this passage, Georg Bühler repeated the accepted translation of the verse, that "making voyages by sea" means "voyaging by means of ships to another continent." Also on Baudhyana, see A. L. Basham, "Notes on Seafaring in Ancient India," *Arts and Letters*, Vol. XXII, No. 2, p. 67. Considerable confusion has arisen about Baudhayana's position vis-à-vis sea-associated occupations in early India. In another section he lists a number of customs peculiar to the north of the subcontinent and reports that men there did not "go to sea." See *ibid.*, p. 146. Also consult Mookerji, *Indian Shipping*, pp. 41-42.

16. *ibid.*, p. 218.

17. F. Max Müller, ed., *Sacred Books of the East*, Vol. XXV; *The Laws of Manu*, trans. Georg Bühler (Oxford : Clarendon Press, 1886).

18. *ibid.*, p. 105.

19. *ibid.*, p. 107.

20. *ibid.*, p. 33. The injunction against residing outside of Aryavatra persisted throughout the period of Indian history under discussion. For example, Alberuni in the eleventh century A.D. commented on the determination of orthodox Hindus to reside only within specified areas of the subcontinent. "He (a pious Hindu—ed.) is obliged to dwell between the river Sindh in the north and the river Camanvati in the south. He is not allowed to cross either of these frontiers so as to enter the country of the Turks or of the Karnâta. Further, he must live between the ocean in the

east and west . . . If he passes beyond them he commits a sin."
Alberuni's India, ed. Edward C. Sachau (London : Trübner,
1888), II, pp. 134-5.

21. The close relationship between Hindus' anti-marine beliefs and Brahmins has been indicated in a recently published study of *Hindu
Culture and Personality.* Without offering any original supporting evidence P. Spratt states : "Some of the lawgivers prescribed sailing on the sea for a hundred yojanas (i.e. 7 or 9 miles
—ed.) as a penance for killing a Brahmin . . . Going to sea was
prescribed as a penance presumably because, though disagree-
able and dangerous, it was holy. The curious prohibition on
travel by sea may therefore be attributed in a roundabout way
to the mother fixation." p. 195.

22. The persistance of the Hindus' prejudice against foreigners becomes
strikingly evident from Alberuni's eleventh century A·D. com-
mentary. Speaking of the Hindus' general traits, he wrote that
"their fanaticism is directed against those who do not belong
to them—against all foreigners. They call them *mléccha,* i.e.
impure, and forbid having connection with them, be it by inter-
marriage or any other kind of relationship, or by sitting, eating,
and drinking with them, because thereby, they think, they would
be polluted." E. C. Sachau, ed. and trans., *Alberuni's India,*
(London : Trubner, 1888), I, pp. 19-20.

23. F. Max Müller, ed., *Sacred Books of the East,* Vol. XXXIII; *The
Minor Law-Books,* trans. Julius Jolly (Oxford : Clarendon Press,
1889).

24. *ibid.,* p. 87. The Hindus' prejudices against mariners' testimony in
law courts persisted for centuries. In the thirteenth century A.D.,
for example, Marco Polo noted that the courts of Malabar and
those who helped adjudicate cases being heard there "reject
the testimony or guarantee of . . . mariners, (because they are)
accounted a reckless and desperate race." Hugh Murray, ed.,
Travels of Marco Polo (New York : Harper and Brothers,
1845), p. 263.

25. A. L. Basham, Vol. XXIII, No. 2, p. 68.

26. Kautilya, *Arthasastra,* trans. R. Shamasastry (Mysore : Mysore
Printing and Publishing House, 1961), p. 329.

27. *ibid.,* p. 329.

28. *ibid.,* Chapter XXVIII, p. 139.

29. ibid., p. 139. Underscoring added.

30. *ibid.*

31. George Fadlo Hourani, *Arab Seafaring in the Indian Ocean in
Ancient and early Medieval Times* (Beirut : Khayata, 1963),
p. 94.

32. See J. W. McCrindle, ed. and trans., *Ancient India as Described by
Ptolemy* (London Trübner and Company, 1885), p. 239.

33. McCrindle added the following : "In an account of India, written
at the close of the 4th or beginning of the 5th century, at the

request either of Palladius or of Lausius, to whom Palladius ins-
cribed his *Historia Lausiaca,* mention is made of these rocks :
'At Muziris,' says Priaulx, in his notice of this account, 'our traveller stayed some time, and occupied himself in studying the soil
and climate of the place and the customs and manners of its inhabitants. He also made enquiries about Ceylon, and the best
mode of getting there, but did not care to undertake the voyage
when he heard of the dangers of the Sinhalese channel, of the
thousand isles, the Maniolai which impede its navigation, and the
lodestone rocks which bring disaster and wreck on all iron
bound ships.' And Masudi, who had traversed this sea, says that
ships sailing on it were not fastened with iron nails, its waters
so wasted them ... Aristotle speaks of a magnetic mountain on the
coast of India, and Pliny repeats the story......". ibid., pp. 242-3.

34. This work is not available in English translation. See Radha Kumud
     Mookerji, *Indian Shipping,* 2nd. ed., (Bombay : Orient Long-
     man's 1957), pp. 13-14.

35. *ibid.,* p. 13.

36. ibid., p. 14. Concerning the *Yuktikalpataru* and Bhoja Narapati
     generally, see A. L. Basham Vol. XXIII, No. 2, p. 65, and
     H. G. Rawlinson, *Intercourse Between India and the Western
     World,* Vol. I (Cambridge : University Press, 1926), p. 139.

37. In 1946, for example, James Horness wrote, "In India at the present
     day many of the large fishing canoes on the Malabar coast are
     built up of a few broad planks sewn together while on the Mad-
     ras coast the surf boats used for the lighterage of cargo in the
     open roadsteads ... are deep-sided craft *built without ribs,* the
     strakes sewn together with coir and the seams covered by caul-
     king bands of fibre, laced on." *Water Transport : Origin and
     Early Evolution* (Cambridge : University Press, 1946), p. 236.
     A. L. Basham, Vol. XXII, No. 2, p. 65.

38. Ibn Battuta, a scholar from Morocco who travelled in India during
     the mid-fourteenth century A·D., wrote that "the Indian Ocean
     is full of reefs and if a ship is nailed with iron nails it breaks
     up on striking the rocks, whereas if it is sewn together it is given
     a certain resilience and does not fall to pieces." Quoted in
     A. L. Basham, Vol. XXII, No. 2, p. 65,

39. Wilfred H. Schoff, trans., *The Periplus of the Erythraean Sea* (New
     York : Longmans, Green, 1912), pp. 46ff.

40. Colonel Sir Henry Yule, ed. and trans., *Cathay and the Way Thither*
     (London : The Hakluyt Society, 1863), I, p. 217. Another Chris-
     tian missionary passing through India on his way to the East
     about the same time as Friar John wrote, "In this country men
     make use of a kink of vessel which they call *jase* (Persian for a
     ship—ed.), which is fastened only with stitching of twine. On
     one of these vessels I embarked, I could find no iron at all
     therein." ibid., p. 57.

41. Frequently Westerners are unable to appreciate the awful determination of orthodox Hindus in complying with caste dining and drinking regulations, and exactly how far they will go to avoid violating these time-honoured practices. For example, there are reports of Brahmins who were victims of local famine facing certain death by malnutrition, but who firmly rejected food offered by relief workers because of the possibility that it had been contaminated by lower caste Hindus someplace along the way. Further, Amaury De Reincourt in his valuable study, *The Soul of India* (New York : Harper and Brothers, 1960), reports that British officials in the nineteenth century discovered Brahmins who were dying of starvation, and yet refused to work on some public relief project because of the likelihood of associating with members of other castes. See pp. 222ff. It has also been reported that the Brahmin delegation that attended the Round Table Conferences in London (early 1930's) brought with them large casks of Ganges water for their personal use and also arranged that a weekly shipment be sent to them. See L. S. S. O'Malley, *Indian Caste Customs* (Cambridge : University Press, 1932), p. 111.

42. The pre-modern Hindus' compulsive cleanliness continues to the present time. In 1967 C. Morris Carstairs wrote as follows : "At the end of an Indian meal, one goes to a place apart, and water is brought and poured over one's fingers, while one washes them. Next, it is proper to wash out one's mouth several times with water, rubbing the teeth with one's right forefinger, then one leans forward holding the cupped right hand palm upward against one's chin in order to drink a few swallows of water poured into one's hand—this gesture, and the quick tilt of the head which means 'Enough' become second nature when one lives and travels in company with Hindus. Finally, the fingers are washed once more. It is made clear, in this cleansing ritual, that whatever has been in contact with the lips or the inside of the mouth, is defiling. The Hindu's daily early morning bath further illustrates this concept.

"Every informant who was asked to describe the happenings of a day in his life began by mentioning his going to stool, and then bathing, as being two of the most significant events of the day. During these morning ablutions, he would pay especial attention to washing out his ears, eyes and nostrils, as well as his mouth. Any secretion from the inside of the body is defiling, but the most defiling, of all is human excrement. 'To do it properly', said Devi Lal, 'a man should cleanse himself with earth and then with water twelve times after going to stool, and three times after making water—but few are so particular nowadays......". C. Morris Carstairs, *The Twice Born* (Bloomington : Indiana University Press, 1967), pp. 80-82.

43. Edward C. Sachau, *Alberuni's India*, II, p. 133.

76

Concerning the people of Malabar, Marco Polo wrote, "Both men and women wash their whole bodies in water twice every day, morning and evening, and till then will neither eat nor drink. He who omits this observation is regarded as we do a heretic." *The Travels of Marco Polo,* ed. Hugh Murray Gilbert, (New York : Harper and Brothers, 1845), p. 262.

44. Nirad C. Chaudhuri, *The Continent of Circe* (New York : Oxford University Press, 1966), pp. 181-82.

45. P. Spratt in his psycho-analytic study of *Hindu Culture and Personality* argues that a characteristic of Hindus is aloofness, inaccessibility and a love of privacy. He then suggests that their tendency toward aloofness and keeping people at a distance might explain the Hindus' aversion to travel overseas. See p. 23.

46. Basham may be overexaggerating when he states that "Indians of all castes, including Brahmans, frequently travelled by sea during the Hindu period. The texts which forbade or discouraged ocean voyages cannot have been followed by more than a small section of the population." "Notes on Seafaring in Ancient India," *Arts and Letters,* Vol. XXII, No. 2 (London : Royal India and Pakistan Society, 1949), p. 68.

Chapter V

THE SAILORS AND TRADERS OF INDIA

The Dravidians

The dark-skinned Dravidians, as noted earlier, were displaced some time after the invading Aryans settled the north. Overwhelmed by more powerful Aryan forces, the Dravidians migrated south where they ultimately established a new home and where even today their descendants prosper. Their relocation probably got under way as early as 1500 B.C. and continued for several centuries.

In contrast to the Aryans, the Dravidian people were traditionally sea-oriented and their men became capable mariners and traders. Scholars having researched this feature of Dravidian society agree that from the beginning the Dravidians had none of the Aryan-Hindu aversion to deep sea voyages nor shared their societal prejudices against living abroad as resident traders. *The Oxford History of India,* for example, states without qualifications that "The Dravidians were not afraid to cross the sea."[1] The Dravidians established trading patterns similar to those developed in non-Indian lands : They controlled a number of commercially attractive export items and, free from the anti-marine fears of northern Aryans, they sailed abroad to locate markets for their products. The early sea trade of India was therefore a Dravidian development. Sea-oriented occupations became an accepted, socially approved way of life among the Dravidians. One inscription found in the western province of Mysore honors the marine traditions of the men of this area :

> Brave men, born to wander over many countries since the beginning of the Krita age penetrating regions of the six continents by land and water routes and dealing in various articles such as horses and elephants, precious stones, perfumes, and drugs, either wholesale or retail.[2]

By the Hellenistic and Roman periods, the luxury items of the East had become attractive commodities for the affluent of the Mediterranean world. The people who lived there became increasingly determined and aggressive in their search for spices, perfumes, exotic woods, cloths and resins. In ever greater numbers Western traders and sailors visited the ports of India to locate new supplies or to arrange for larger shipments. The natives of southern India, no later than the closing centuries before the Christian era, found themselves in a profitable sellers' market. The West's demands were insatiable : no matter how large a supply of these products were assembled for export from Indian ports, the traders from the West wanted more. From archeological discoveries it is known that Western gold and silver coins were abundant throughout most of southern India.

Given this situation, the Dravidians realized that they did not need to make dangerous voyages in order to take advantage of the Western markets. They learned it was equally profitable —and far more conducive to a long life—to allow Western traders and mariners to bear the many risks. And they did : Western ships, manned by Western sailors, began to dominate coastal trading, even as the number of Western visitors arranging for a shipment of luxury products from India steadily expanded. The Indians of the south began to assume what was to become their traditional role in West-East trade, namely, land-based middlemen.[3] They prospered at home by arranging cargo exports while the sailors of other lands manned the carriers. Thus the Dravidians did not assume as dynamic a maritime role in the Indian Ocean as did the Greeks in the Mediterranean or the Vikings in the Baltic area.

The south Indian sailors discontinued their nautical prowess for another reason : cultural pressure. The appearance of Brahmins and other upper caste Hindus in southern India helped to weaken the Dravidians' interest in trans-oceanic sailing. The Hinduization of south India is believed to have commenced as early as 1000 B.C. It was, however, a slow, irregular process, sustained by orthodox Hindus who championed their religion and its cultural values. A major turning point in the assimilative process began about a century and a half before the Christian era when a number of nomadic tribes of Central Asia were forced to leave their traditional pasture lands after they had been defeated by the more militarily proficient Huns. One of the displaced tribes was the Kushans. Seeking a new homeland, they eventually invaded northwestern India, and by 78 A.D. their influence was pronounced. Kushan rulers developed a strong affinity for the Buddhist religion as practiced there, as well as for Buddhist culture in general.

Most threatened by the Kushan advances were the Brahmins of the region who feared their status would be changed. The prospect of living in a section of Aryavarta in which Hindu values and the Hindu religion did not prevail was in direct conflict with Manu's earlier quoted admonition about avoiding areas in control of *mlècchas*.[4] Once the Kushans had begun to assume political control where formerly Aryan-Hindu kings had ruled, an increasing number of the more puritanical northern Brahmins began migrating to southern India, specifically to the areas still dominated by the Dravidian peoples. South India thus became a refuge for many northerners.

During the first century A.D., the process of blending the Hindu and Dravidian cultures intensified. The Brahmins had the advantage. They were not only a more vigorous and learned group, but the more highly motivated. Unless they were able to establish themselves as the elite of southern India, as they had been in the north before their migration, their caste status and religious orthodoxy was at an end. As is often true when dissimilar and basically antagonistic peoples interact, the more advanced prevailed. The Brahmins succeeded in bringing an increasing number of Dravidians into their religion, and the Hindu pantheon was broadened to include many indigenous Dravidian gods. A number of Hindu social practices were superimposed on Dravidian practices. For example, the caste system emerged in south India about this time, although it never became nearly as prominent a feature of southern life as it was of other sections of India.[5]

The dominating presence of the growing group of Brahmins probably did much to dampen the Dravidians' interest in transmarine activities. To ensure the success of Brahmin acculturization efforts, it was essential that the Dravidian men, like the Hindus, remain at home. Every Dravidian who exposed himself to a lengthy ocean voyage or lived abroad and returned home violated the Hindu ethos and was subject to strict sanctions that awaited the returning traveller. If such expeditions were allowed to go unchecked, there was less and less chance that Hinduism would become firmly rooted in south India. Consequently, the newly arrived Hindu elite moved in to curtail Dravidian travelling, although the precise techniques used to accomplish this goal are unknown. Hindus do not appear to have interfered with local or coastal Dravidian sailing.[6] The emphasis was on curtailing foreign voyages.[7]

One event known to have occurred about this time must have aided the Brahmins' campaign. The migration of the Brahmins to south India coincided with the monumental discovery of Hippalus, an enterprising Alexandrian ship captain who specialized in trading with Eastern countries.[8] He came to understand that there was a pattern in the winds in this part of the world. A ship leaving a Western port at the proper time, he concluded, could take advantage of the seasonal monsoon winds blowing across the Indian Ocean and reach its destination by sailing directly across the Arabian Sea.[9] No longer was it necessary for Western ships to hug the coastline as they proceeded to south Indian ports. With this information, Western ship captains reduced their travel time appreciably. Knowledge of the monsoon wind patterns was so revolutionary a discovery that Western sailors attempted for a time to keep the information from the sailors of south India. Although eventually the vessels from the Malabar coasts applied the monsoon discovery in reverse, the advantage stayed with Western mariners because they were constructing more seaworthy vessels and also because they were free of the Hindus' prejudices against deep sea sailing and residence abroad.[10]

By the second or third centuries A.D. the men of south India were no longer sailing the seas as they had before. Brahmin influences and pressures had modified their attitudes and practices. Local fishing continued in southern waters, but it was now an occupation reserved for the lower members of society.[11] Commercial sailing up and down India's coasts and inland rivers was still important, but this work too, was relegated to the lower castes. Those southerners who devoted themselves to India's export trade assumed middlemen roles, or what today might be called wholesalers or jobbers. Even though these men remained close to their home communities and did not sail abroad, they were castigated by the Hindu society. For example, Dio Chrysostom, the sophist and rhetorician of the first century

A.D., visited the west coast of the country and noted the considerable discrimination against local residents who engaged in commerce. He wrote that the castes engaging in trade were "in low repute, and all the others say harsh things of them."[12]

THE BUDDHISTS

Dravidians were not the only people of early India who did not disapprove of inter-oceanic travel and residence abroad. As early as the latter part of the sixth century B.C., the Buddhists began to form a religious community in India. Until their group was all but submerged by Hinduism, the Buddhists were extremely active at sea and were remarkably talented sailors. In marked contrast to the landbound attitudes of the Aryans, the Buddhists had no fear of contamination and they were spared the regimentation and isolation required by the caste system. Because they were dedicated to proselytizing The Four Noble Truths of The Buddha, Buddhists looked upon sea travel and prolonged residence in foreign countries as essential to the growth and future well-being of their faith. Between the sixth century B.C. and the eighth-ninth centuries A.D., Buddhists steadily migrated from India, apparently aboard ships manned by Buddhist sailors. Only after a resurgent Hinduism succeeded in turning back the challenge of Buddhism was there a noticeable drop in Buddhist marine activity. Once Hindus had established their leadership throughout the subcontinent, the Indian Buddhist community grew smaller, less dynamic, and their nautical enterprises decreased. The rise and fall of the marine history of the early Buddhists of India is, in effect, a chronicle of the growth and prosperity of their community in the Far East. It indicates no inherent disability to Indian nautical activity in the pre-modern era other than the cultural disabilities Hinduism imposed on its adherents and the country in general. Had it been Buddhism that prevailed as the dominant religion of India instead of Hinduism, the subcontinent's maritime history might well have been distinguished.

The roots of the early Buddhists' interest in the sea are identifiable. Before The Buddha died in the seventh century, he exorted his followers many times to be resolute in their proselytizing efforts. "Go forth, Oh, Bhikkus, on your wanderings," he preached, "for the good of Bahujana." Such exhortations,

6

along with the detailed sermons he preached on the need to attract new disciples to the faith, led to the missionary programs of the Buddhist movement. At the third Buddhist Council held in Pataliputra during the reign of Ashoka (c. 250 B.C.), for example, the clergy formally approved of a highly structured, centrally organized campaign of missionary efforts. The goal of the program was to bring the teachings of The Buddha to the people who lived in the lands surrounding India. Groups of evangelical Buddhist monks and nuns regularly departed from India for areas that appeared promising. Some went via land caravan routes, but many boarded ships and sailed to Ceylon, Burma, Malaya, the Indonesian islands and probably China.[13] Missionary Buddhists are also known to have been active as far west as Rome.

The history of the Buddhist nautical development is well documented in their Pali literature, (a derivative of Sanskrit). Unlike Aryan-Hindu treatises that are all but devoid of citations relating to the sea and sea travel, the Pali texts abound with such references. Scattered throughout these several works are astute, well-informed observations about the sea and its possible use as a highway for travel and commerce. Unmistakably, by the third or second century B.C., the Buddhist community of India was well on its way to developing a large group of efficient, dedicated mariners. Buddhist literature repeatedly mentions the usefulness of lighthouses they had constructed at the mouth of river ports to facilitate the docking of their intercontinental ships. Other passages explain how trained birds, probably crows, were carried aboard Buddhist ships to locate land not yet visible to the crew and passengers. It is known that Buddhists organized a pilot guild so that the members could share information about their sailing experiences, navigational techniques and the road-steads and routes to follow or avoid, and mariners returning to India reported on the docking facilities of host ports, if any. Buddhists' comments about the sea and sea travel are so extensive and detailed that it is clear they were people deeply involved in marine affairs, aggressively pursuing export-import trade, and determined to increase their mastery of deep sea sailing.

Several extractions from representative Buddhist stories illustrate the contrast between the landbound Aryan-Hindus and the traveling Buddhists. A verse in a leading Pali treatise, *The*

Question of King Milinda,[14] which is believed to have been written in Northern India around the beginning of the Christian era, indicates the geographical sweep of Buddhist maritime travels and how they pursued foreign commerce. The speaker is addressing his ruler and encouraging him to adopt policies that forswear war and militarism. Reaching the summation of his argument, he says :

> Just, O king, as a shipowner who has become wealthy by constantly levying freight in some seaport town, will be able to traverse the high seas, and go to Vanga, or Takkola, or China, or Sovira, or Surat, or Alexandrea, or the Koromandel coast, or Further India, or any other place where ships do congregate—just so, O king, it is he who . . . acquires, . . all . . . ecstacy of peace and bliss. . . .[15]

An even richer source of material about early Buddhist involvement in marine affairs appears in *The Jataka*[16] or *Birth Stories,* a collection of five hundred and fifty tales and riddles about Buddhist life and interests, many of them fanciful and allegorical. Viewed in its entirety, *The Jataka* could only been produced by a people who were fond of marine travel. The following illustrations suggest the extent of Buddhist voyages, the techniques used in navigation, and their overall identity with the sea.

The 196th Jataka story opens :

> ". . . Once upon a time, there was in the island of Ceylon a goblin town . . . people by she-goblins. . .
>
> "Now it happened once that five hundred ship-wrecked traders were cast ashore near the city of these she-goblins . . ."[17]

Both the 339th and 384th Jataka tales suggest how frequently Buddhist sailors used crows to locate the direction of the nearest land :

> ". . . some merchants came to the kingdom of Baveru, bringing on board ship with them a foreign crow . . . This bird perched on the top of the mast. . . ."[18]
>
> ". . . when he grew up he lived amidst a retinue of birds on an island in the middle of the sea. Certain merchants of Kasi got a travelled crow and started on a voyage by sea."[19]

A number of Jataka stories offer explicit details concerning the maritime ideas, customs, and superstitions of the Buddhists.

The 463rd tale is among the most colorful and complete. It
says in part :

> . . . the Bodhisatta [literally the enlightened being—ed.]
> was born into the family of a master mariner there. . . when
> he was no more than sixteen years old, he had gained a
> complete mastery over the art of seamanship. Afterwards
> when his father died he became the head of the mariners
> and plied the mariner's calling : wise he was, and full of
> intelligence; with him aboard, no ship came ever to harm.

In time it so happened that injured by the salt water both
his eyes lost their sight. After which, head of the mariners
though he was, he plied no more the mariner's trade; but resolved
to live in the king's service. . . It happened that some merchants
had got ready a ship, and were casting about for a skipper. . .
As they pressed him unceasingly, he at length consented. . . Then
he went aboard their vessel.

They sailed in their ship upon the high seas. For seven days
the ship sailed without mishap : then an unseasonable wind
arose. Four months the vessel tost (sic) about on a primeaval
ocean. . .

> . . . Now there were seven hundred souls aboard this
> ship, and they were in fear of death . . . The Great Being,
> (The Buddha—ed.) thought, "Except me, no other can save
> those; I will save them by an Act of Truth. . ."

> Four months the vessel had been voyaging in far dis-
> tant regions; and now as though endued (sic) with super-
> natural power it returned in one single day to the seaport
> town of Bharukaccha, and even upon the dry land it went,
> till it rested before the mariner's door, having sprung over
> a space of eleven hundred cubits. . ."[20]

It was during the Gupta period (c. 300-637 A.D.) that
Hinduism began to reassert itself throughout the Indian subcontinent and initiated a far-reaching program of reforms to
save their faith from usurpation by Buddhism. Some six centuries later, Hinduism had become the dominant faith in India.
By 1000 A.D., scattered centers of Buddhist power in India remained, but never again was Buddhism a dynamic force in the
land where it originated although its growth and influence in
many other areas of Asia were spectacular.

Buddhism's decline throughout the subcontinent corresponded to a drop in the marine activity. As had been true centuries earlier when the Brahmins forced the Dravidians to discontinue their sailing activities, Buddhist mariners found it expedient to relocate permanently in another country or to find a new occupation, one more compatible with the Hindu values of Indian society.

THE CHOLAS

Only once in the history of India did a Hindu king, after undertaking an intensive program of shipbuilding, use his fleet to conquer overseas territory. This unique naval undertaking took place after 1017 A.D., and was led by Rajendra Chola.

The Cholas[21] were a Tamil speaking people who lived along the Coromandel coast in south India. They probably had made their homes in this region since pre-historic times, but were for centuries under the dominance of other local kingdoms. Somehow the Cholas were able to assert their independence during the close of the ninth century A.D., and soon after they became aggressively militaristic. One southern state after another was defeated until the Cholas dominated a considerable part of southern India. In 985 A.D., Rajaraja the Great ascended to the Chola throne. Under his direction, Chola troops moved to extend the boundaries of their kingdom.

Simultaneously, Rajaraja decided to undertake a major program of ship construction, either to improve his position in the thriving trade with the Far East or to conquer an overseas empire to add to his holdings. The exact reasons for Rajaraja's embarking on a program of overseas colonialism are not known, but several theories can be advanced. The Chola people were followers of Siva, and consequently were less orthodox Hindus than their northern co-religionists. The Hindu taboos against maritime activities are known to have been less scrupulously observed in this part of the subcontinent than elsewhere. Traditionally, southerners engaged in local sailing and fishing in coastal waters. Given a pro-maritime tradition, Rajaraja might have realized that a sizable fleet of ships would help him realize his political goals. It is also feasible that he built his fleet in order to acquire new sources of revenue that would enable him to continue his extensive land campaigns.

In any event, some time after Rajaraja's accession to the throne the construction of the Chola navy began, and over the next thirty years its strength steadily increased. During the king's lifetime his ships and crews came to dominate the trade routes from the Indian subcontinent to the Malayan peninsula and beyond to the southern ports of China. Cholas eventually controlled an even larger area of territory in the South Pacific. When Rajaraja died in 1015 A.D., his son Rajendra succeeded to the throne. The new king took control of a sizable fleet, a proficient cadre of sailors, pilots and ship's captains, plus a far-flung overseas empire.

In the tenth-eleventh centuries, even as is true today, acquiring control of the Straits of Malacca was the key to access to the trading opportunities of the South China Sea. Whatever political authority controlled the shores of the Straits decided which ships would pass into the South China Sea without challenge and which would be turned back. It meant that the local maritime administrators were able to determine which ships were to be allowed to carry China's exports to the West.

While the Chola navy was growing into a powerful force in the South Pacific, the Straits were controlled by the Sailendra rulers and part of their Srivijaya empire. Their capital was located at Palembang in southeast Sumatra, and their power extended to most of the Malayan peninsula, Java, the lesser islands of the region, and for a while, Cambodia. Initially the relationship between the Cholas and the people of Srivijaya was friendly. There is evidence that Chola ships were welcomed in local ports and allowed to trade freely. As Rajendra's fleet increased its power and size and as the Hindus sought to establish a more dominant position in the region, tensions and hostility between the two kingdoms arose. Some contemporary scholars are of the opinion that the king of the Srivijaya empire, aware of the commercial and military threat presented by Cholan sea power, attempted to block all direct maritime intercourse between the Cholas and the Chinese. They believe the Srivijaya king issued orders prohibiting Chola ships from sailing through the Straits of Malacca and required local middlemen to arrange for the sale of Chinese exports and local shippers to carry all cargos to their destination. The Cholas refused to accept such interference, probably realizing that their continued growth and prosperity depended upon unimpeded access to the China Sea.[22] The war that finally broke out between the Cholas and the Srivijaya kingdom probably occurred some time between 1016 and 1033 A.D. Fighting was not confined to the sea, but for the first time in pre-modern Indian history, naval battles did take place. The Cholas were victorious and for the following fifty years they dominated the sea lanes between their home ports in India and those of the China coast. Delegations of Chola merchants are known to have travelled with regularity to China to arrange for the purchase of the luxury items that were in great demand in the West. The wealth and prosperity of the Cholas at that time was probably as great as in any Hindu kingdom of India. As so frequently happens in Indian history, however, the Cholas became deeply involved in a series of prolonged, costly internecine struggles among would-be contenders for the throne. A series of local wars with hostile neighboring kingdoms—the chronic subversive pattern of Indian political dynamics of the period—added to the gradual erosion of Chola strength and military prowess. Also, the Chola administrative machinery was probably insufficient to the tasks assigned it. As their power ebbed on the mainland, the Chola fleet became a less effective military force and the suzerainty they had established generations earlier over Srivijaya territory ended.

The ability of the Cholas to plan and follow through on the construction of a large fleet of ships, the staffing of these vessels, and the adaptability of their men in learning to fight at sea, approximately 1,200 miles of sea between the Coromandel coast and the territory originally controlled by the Srivijaya forces and fleet, was a remarkable accomplishment. Chola ships that sailed across such an expanse of open water, loaded down with men and armament must be recognised as a tour de force of impressive dimensions. What type of ships they used is not known nor is the armament they carried or the naval strategy they employed to defeat their rivals. Despite our lack of information about their development of ocean transports, the exploits of the Vijayanagar mariners in the South Pacific are so remarkable that they must be considered pre-modern India's leading nautical people. As Spate and Learmonth conclude, "Certainly no European power of the day could have dreamed of such oceanic adventures : only the Viking voyages are as impressive, while the Crusading fleets were in comparison mere coastal forays."[23]

THE ARABS AND THE SEA

The Arabs, as has been observed earlier, played a leading role in commercial naval enterprises, and their preeminence is an additional reason for the Hindus' becoming a land-locked people.

Before the emergence of Islam in the seventh century A.D., the Arabs were largely a nomadic desert people, organized into tribes and frequently fighting bitterly amongst themselves for choice camping sites and essential water resources. The early Arabs specialized in desert caravans—long parades of camels, heavily laden with luxury items from the East—that slowly moved across the sand dunes until arriving at some leading entrepôt of the eastern Mediterranean world. With the appearance of Mohammed and his ministry of Islamic brotherhood and call for Arab unity, the political-military attitudes of these people changed. They became great fighters and ardent missionaries. Peacefully or by the sword, the Arab Muslims moved out from their traditional homelands. In the century following Mohammed's death (632-732 A.D.), the Arab armies triumphed across a broad strip of north Africa, Spain and gained control of territory as far away as the Sind on the Indian subcontinent.

The Arabs' earliest antipathy toward the sea and nautical affairs reflected the superstitions of other land-based people whose familiarity with the ocean and its challenges was nominal. Mohammed, incorporating the desert heritage of most of his original disciples, is reported to have advised his followers that "he who twice embarks on the sea is truly an infidel."[24] Such thinking persisted within the Arab world for some time after Mohammed's death. For example, Amr ibn el'As, the general who commanded Islamic troops preparing to invade Egypt for the first time, failed to appreciate the importance of nautical power and the use of an Arab fleet to advance Arab military programs. Early in his career he was asked to sanction a ship building program to expedite the transport of soldiers to Egypt, thus allowing them to reach the battle ground better prepared to fight the Egyptians and defeat these enemies of Islam. The general is reported to have rejected the projected naval expedition in toto. For Arabs to build a fleet of sailing vessels and then sail across the Mediterranean to Egypt, he noted, was deliberately to forfeit the chance for eventual military victory. "Men at sea," he is alleged to have warned, "is (sic) an insect on a splinter, now engulfed, now scared to death."[25]

These views did not endure for long. As they expanded the world they controlled, the Arabs experienced a complete change of heart about the sea and all forms of marine activity. By 670 A.D., they had conquered both Syria and Persia and gained control of the Persian Gulf. Once established in this region, they came into contact with Greek and Byzantine sailors as well as Persian shipwrights and pilots. An exchange of cultural-religious values took place between the Arab Muslims and the conquered-converted people. Before long, the Arabs developed a healthy respect for sea power, both to further their commercial interests and to augment their military power.[26]

One principal reason that the Arabs became proficient at sea (and in a relatively short time) was their ability to adapt their traditional behavior to new experiences. They were adept at learning to appreciate the relevancy of unfamiliar occupations and unknown techniques dealing with the environment. Consequently, before the end of the seventh century A.D., Arabs were constructing seaworthy ships and gaining proficiency in handling their vessels, and their traders were shifting from land caravans to nautical transportation.

Arab navigational superiority which contributed to their eventual domination of the sea lanes to Asia was a skill they brought with them out of the deserts. Long before the appearance of Mohammed, they had learned to cross a wide unmarked desert by celestial landmarks. For generations young boys were taught by their fathers how to select the correct route for a caravan to reach its planned destination, and they, in turn, transmitted the information to their sons and grandsons. Such skills became commonplace within the Arab desert community. As Professor Parkinson has noted, the ability to carry out complicate land navigational exercises while astride a camel was readily adaptable to the marine exploits of Arab mariners in the post-Mohammed period. "The problem of crossing a desert is much the same as crossing the open sea, but that the caravan leader has a more stable platform from which to follow the stars,"[27] he observed.

By the beginning of the Christian era, what little indigenous interest in trans-oceanic sailing and foreign trading existed at one time in India had faltered and gradually disappeared. More from choice than necessity, India became a nation of men resolved to remain at home rather than to advance their fortunes by going abroad. Successive generations of Arab mariners capitalized on their advantages, and they became leaders in the nautical life of the region.

CONCLUSION

India's lack of interest in trans-oceanic sailing and overseas trading represents one of the oldest cultural values of the people of the subcontinent. The early land-oriented pastoral Aryan tribes were ignorant of the political, military and commercial importance of the sea. Slowly their distaste for deep sea sailing matured into an intense prejudice, particularly by the upper caste members of the Hindu community. Probably as early as the first century A.D., India's disinterest in maritime activities was firmly entrenched. It became a value that has markedly affected Indian history. Seamanship was not a skill that was highly regarded. Only lower caste men became sailors, and even they seldom strayed from local waters. The merchant castes concentrated their talents and energies on local enterprises, rather than seeking out trading arrangements in foreign lands. The many Hindu rulers ignored the development of naval power and chose instead to concentrate their martial energies on building up armies and fighting land campaigns. Although generation after generation of Hindus lived along India's long coastlines, they ignored its opportunities and challenges.[28] Sailing abroad was not compatible with Hindu orthodoxy, and so the people of India allowed other nations and their traders to sail the seas in search of power, profit and adventure while they remained at home. For their part, pious Hindus remained ashore and avoided what one Westerner has correctly labeled the terrible punishment of outcasting.[29]

REFERENCES

1. Vincent A. Smith, *The Oxford History of India,* ed. Percival Spear, 3rd ed., (Oxford : Clarendon Press, 1958), p. 43. Also see K. M. Panikkar, *India and the Indian Ocean : An Essay on the Influence of Sea Power in Indian History* (London : George Allen & Unwin Ltd., 1945),p. 29.

2. Quoted in K. M. Panikkar, *Geographical Factors in Indian History* (Bombay : Bharatiya Vidya Bhavan, 1959), p. 43.

    For an extended analysis of southern India's mercantile activity, see Burton Stein, "Coromandel Trade in Medieval India" in John Parker, ed., *Merchants & Scholars : Essays in the History of Exploration and Trade* (Minneapolis : University of Minnesota Press 1965), pp. 49-60.

3. This theory was first expressed in 1807 by William Vincent in his two volume study, *The Commerce and Navigation of the Ancients in the Indian Ocean* (London : Cadell and Davies, 1807), II. p. 404

4. The prohibition against *mlécchas* remained in force for centuries. According to the comments of Alberuni, a number of orthodox Hindus he encountered refused to engage in normal social intercourse with foreign travellers within India for fear of becoming polluted and losing their caste status. See Edward C. Sachau, ed. *Alberuni's India* (London : Trübner and Company, 1888), I, pp. 19-20.

5. H. G. Rawlinson, *India : A Short Cultural History,* ed. C. G. Seligman (New York : Appleton-Century, 1938), pp. 176-77.

6. On the other hand, there is some evidence that even local fishermen were not immune to the pressures of Brahmins to remain ashore. Hornell reports, for example, that in the area of Cape Comorin "the only important caste of fishermen is that of the Roman Catholic Parawas." Their ancestors, he continues, converted to Christianity almost immediately after the Portuguese arrived because it was the politically expedient thing to do. While political considerations may have influenced the Parawas, one cannot help wondering whether they rejected their Hindu values and religion when they realized that Christianity did not scorn the fishermen and imposed no restrictions on sailing. See James Hornell, *Water Transport : Origins and Early Evolution* (Cambridge : University Press, 1946), p. 62. For a fuller account of pearl fishing along the Cape Comorin coast, see Mansel Longworth Dames, trans. *The Book of Duarte Barbosa* (London : The Hakluyt Society, 1921), II, p. 123.

7. Some scholars hold that some kings of South India, coming to appreciate the destabilizing influence of the emigrating Brahmins, found ways to have them quit their respective kingdoms and, indeed, India itself and to move overseas to what today

is called the South Pacific area. Thus Austin Coates has written' "As Buddhist power was maintained during the Ku-shan period by the arrival of more and more non-Indians from across the North-West Frontier the Brahmins' position (in the North) became worse, and thus evidently began first a move-ment in search of employment and asylum in the Hindu King-doms of South India and ultimately a movement overseas which the kings of the South encouraged, presumably because they found this the safest and most profitable way of dealing with these influential refugees from the North if they were to be prevented from taking control of the southern kingdoms. The first overseas migration started in the second century A.D. and led to the foundation of small Hindu colonies in the coastal areas of southern Burma, Siam and Cochin-China." *Invitation to an Eastern Feast* (New York : Harper and Bro-thers, nd), p. 157. While Coates' rationale for the spread of Hinduism throughout the South Pacific regions appears to be sound, the Brahmins who did settle permanently in the South without question did begin championing their religious and cultural values as well as the social system that insured their elite status.

8. For a discussion arguing that Hippalus' discovery took place no latter than 90 B.C., see George Fadlo Hourani, *Arab Seafaring* (Beirut : Khayats, 1963), pp. 23-25. Also see William Vin-cent, *Commerce and Navigation of the Ancients in The Indian Ocean* (London : T. Cadell and W. Davies, 1807), II, pp. 49-59. He concluded that 126 A.D. was the date of the voyage.

9. Wilfred H. Schoff, trans. *The Periplus of the Erythraean Sea* (New York : Longmans, Green, 1912), p. 45. However, Panikkar maintains that Indian navigators had successfully sailed directly across the Arabian Sea about two hundred years earlier. See *India and the Indian Ocean,* (London : George Allen and Unwin Ltd., 1945), pp. 24-25.

10. Consequently, A. L. Basham appears to be correct when he notes that "Certain over-enthusiastic Indian scholars have perhaps made too much of the achievements of ancient Indian seafarers, which cannot compare with those of the Vikings, or of some other early maritime peoples. Much of the merchandise ex-ported from India was carried in foreign bottoms . . . ." *The Wonder that Was India* (New York : Grove Press, 1954), p. 226.

11. Duarte Barbosa, a sixteenth century European traveller noted that only members of the lower castes on the Malabar coast made their livings on the sea either as sailors or fishermen. See *The Book of Duarte Barbosa,* trans. Mansel Longworth Dames (London : The Hakluyt Society, 1921), II, p. 63.

12. J. W. Cohoon and H. Lamar Crosby, trans. *Dio Chrysostom* (Cambridge : Harvard University Press, 1940), III, p. 413.

13. Basham, for example, states that Indians first reached China by sea during the reign of Huang Ti, who ruled between 167 and 147 B.C. "Notes on Seafaring in Ancient India," *Arts and Letters* (London : Royal India and Pakistan Society, 1949), Vol. XXII, No. 2, p. 63. Almost certainly, those that manned these vessels were Buddhists.

14. F. Max Muller, ed. *Sacred Books of the East,* Vols. XXXV and XXXVI : *The Questions of King Milinda,* trans. T. W. Rhys Davids, (Oxford : Clarendon Press, 1890).

15. *ibid.,* XXXVI, p. 269.

16. E. B. Lowell, ed., *The Jataka,* 4 vols. (Cambridge : Cambridge University Press, 1895). The Jataka tales are generally associated with Buddhist life in the second century B.C.

17. *ibid.,* p. 91.

18. *ibid.,* III, p. 302.

19. *ibid.,* p. 170.

20. *ibid.,* pp. 86ff.

21. The descriptive material in this section is largely drawn from K. A. Nilakanta Sastri, *A History of South India,* 3rd ed., (London : Oxford University Press, 1966), pp. 173-206.

22. Concerning this decision, Majumdar has written, "According to the Chola records, the conquest of Kalinga and the whole eastern coast up to the mouth of the Ganges was completed before the overseas expedition was sent. The mastery over the ports of Kalinga and Bengal gave the Chola king well-equipped ships and sailors, accustomed to voyages in the very regions which he wanted to conquer. The naval resources of the whole of the eastern coast of India were thus concentrated in the hands of Rajendra Chola, and it was enough to tempt a man to get possession of the territory, which served as the meeting ground of the trade and commerce between India and the Western countries on the one hand, and the countries of the Far East on the other. The geographical position of the Sailendra empire enabled it to control almost the whole volume of maritime trade between western and eastern Asia, and the dazzling prospect which its conquest offered to the future commercial supremacy of the Cholas seemed to be the principal reason of the overseas expedition undertaken by Rajendra Chola. But it is the conquest of the eastern coastal regions of India that alone brought such a scheme within the range of practical politics." *Hindu Colonies in the Far East,* 2nd ed., (Firm K. L. Mukhopadhyay, 1963), p. 39. Also see Romila Thapar, *A History of India* (Baltimore : Penguin, 1966), p. 196.

23. O. H. K. Spate and A. T. A. Learmonth, *India and Pakistan : A General and Regional Geography,* 2nd ed., (London : Methuen and Company, 1967), p. 184.

24. Quoted in James Hornell, *Water Transport : Origins and Early Evolution* (Cambridge : University Press, 1946), p. 230.

25. *ibid.,* Another quotation attributed to him is that "the sea was a huge beast which silly folks ride like worms on logs."

26. For a discussion of the change in Arab values regarding the sea and maritime travel, see James Hornell, *Water Transport : Origins and Early Evolution* (Cambridge : University Press, 1946), pp. 230ff.

27. C. Northcote Parkinson, *East and West* (Boston : Hughton Mifflin Company, 1963), p. 141.

28. The early Moghuls also ignored India's attractive maritime location and the opportunities it offered for the enhancement of state power. Although not burdened by the Hindus' anti-sea taboos, a long series of Moghul rulers were indifferent to sea power and the benefit accruing to a polity with a strong maritime fleet. Like the Turko-Afghan invaders of India who preceeded them, the Moghuls were a land-oriented people; their skill in employing cavalry troops to attack enemy positions is legendary.

One incident which took place during the reign of Aurangzeb (1658-1707) succinctly illustrates the Moghuls' attitude toward the sea and the importance of naval power in Moghul strategic thinking. At the time the following incident occured, Moghul control of India was well over one hundred years old. Their conquests of both coastlines of India, from the north to the south, were complete. Furthermore, they had learned to live and prosper in the subcontinent in spite of a number of strongly held, traditional attitudes which for a time impeded their acculturation in new land.

Developing naval power and training young Muslims to be capable seamen remained a problem for the Moghuls. Having been repeatedly humiliated at sea by the superior ships of the Europeans, Aurangzeb decided in 1661 that it was necessary to compete with his enemies on the basis of equality. He ordered his chief administrative assistant Jafar Khan, to begin immediate construction of an armada of sufficient tonnage to defeat any force attempting in the future to challenge his rule. Jafar Khan, according to an eyewitness who later related the incident, responded to Aurangzeb's order by stating that the Moghul empire was sufficiently wealthy to afford the type of fleet the king wished. It also possessed the necessary raw materials needed to complete such a major project. What was not available were both sailors to man the vessels and gunners capable of firing whatever armament that was installed on the decks.

Aurangzeb was unimpressed with his minister's evaluation. A very wealthy monarch, he said he intended to hire a sufficient number of European mercenaries to carry out the several duties necessary to keep the proposed Moghul fleet in a seaworthy condition capable of fighting at sea. He called Jafar Khan's attention to the fact that on many other previous occasions when the need arose, he had retained foreigners to execute assignments on behalf of his government, particularly when his own subjects lacked the necessary skill or experience.

The report of the incident continues : "But Jafar Khan boldly ... replied that it would not be well to confide to foreigners—fugitives from their own country—a business of such importance. These men might easily abscond. Nor would they think the Moghul soldier, who might man the ships, of any account. And these, not being properly trained, would allow themselves to be completely controlled by these commanders."

Still unconvinced, Aurangzeb decided to become better acquainted with the art of sailing and sea warfare. After having observed some local ships execute several complicated naval maneuvers, Aurangzeb is reported to have said that his idea of establishing a naval fleet was not practical. There was to be no further work done in this regard. "To sail over and fight on the oceans were (sic) not things for people of Hindustan, but only suited to European alertness and boldness," he concluded. See Niccalao Manucci, *Memoirs of the Moghul Court,* ed. Michael Edwardes, (London : Folio Society, nd.), pp. 43ff.

29. General Sir O'Moore Creagh, *Indian Studies* (2nd ed., London : Hutchinson and Company, 1918), p. 20.

CHAPTER VI

HINDUS AS SOLDIERS AND FIELD TACTICIANS

WAR AND MILITARISM IN HINDU LITERARY EPICS

IN CLASSICAL Aryan literature, two schools of thought regarding war and the rationale for fighting emerged. Although the two philosophies were separated by many centuries, both were ultra-aggressive and intensely pro-militaristic, and both regarded long-lasting peaceful status quo condition with tribal adversaries or neighboring states as unnatural and undesirable. According to the literature of both schools, military power was among the highest societal attributes and its employment a lauditory act. The major difference between the two was over the specific ends served by armed combat and, to a lesser degree, the attitude of what today would be called elitist groups toward organized communal conflict.

The older of the two originated in the Vedic period. As mentioned earlier, generations of prehistoric Aryans were forced to struggle for a long period of time in a hostile environment, throughout their nomadic migrations and, following their introduction into northern India, when they displaced the Dravidian population. In order not to be overwhelmed by those opposing their programs of migration and settlement, Aryan leaders are believed to have designated certain men within their community to concentrate on developing martial talents. A *kshatriya* or warrior caste emerged relatively early in Aryan history. From many descriptive passages found in Vedic hymns, it is clear that battlefield tests of strength—either man-to man, or between rival groups of kshatriyas—were common occurrences, as normal as sex or gambling, two other much praised activities in Vedic literature. Warriors were depicted rushing on to the battlefield to demonstrate their personal courage or to prove the superior power of their clan. Likewise, the Vedic gods accorded the greatest respect and devotion were those directly associated with victorious military adventures. In the *Rig Veda,* for example, Indra is the most celebrated deity, a status he attained once he defeated his enemies in battle. Thereafter he was worshipped as

the leader within the Aryan pantheon. By the same token, there
is little or no discussion in the literature of the period about the
avoidance of war by bilateral negotiations or other diplomatic
techniques.   From their failure to develop ideas of peaceful
accommodation between hostile forces one must conclude that
the early Aryan community favored the use of military power
over its avoidance, and that those who actually engaged in the
combat, the *kshatriyas,* looked upon killing an opponent in battle
as divorced from moral or ethical considerations.

The *Mahabharata,*[1] the foremost Vedic epic and one of the
most extensive statements defining the correct role of military
heros and anti-heros of any civilization, is rich with incidents
illustrating what has been called the war—is sport school of
Aryan militarism.   Its main theme is the involved, bitter rivalry
between the Pandavas and their cousins, the Kauravas.   In the
Bhismaparva (Sixth Book) there is a long dissertation that pro-
claims the righteousness of war in Aryan life.   Equally stressed
is the duty of the *kshatriya* caste to destroy his tribal enemies.
At this point in the *Mahabharata,* the Pandava-Kaurava war was
imminent.   Two great armies had assumed their carefully prepared battlefield positions, and each warrior understood the dire
consequences awaiting the defeated side.   Arjuna, the hero of
the epic, and one of the five Pandava brothers, speaks to his
charioteer of his deep remorse that he may be forced to slay
close relatives and teachers, men eminently worthy of his respect and good feeling. He questions the ethical justification of
his position and confides his preference for turning away from
the fight. The charioteer, in fact, is the god Krishna, who
thereupon talks to Arjuna at length about the proper attitude
a *kshatriya* should have concerning warfare.   He also elaborates
on the merits of a life of action in contrast to a life of avoidance.
With great conviction he argues that Arjuna, because he is of
the *kshatriya* caste, must perform his *dharma* without deviation.
Fighting is Arjuna's assigned and expected role in life. He
must conduct himself according to *kshatriya* norms which require him to take his opponent's life with pride and willingness.
Krishna rather lightly dismisses Arjuna's doubts concerning the
moral impropriety of slaying dear kinsmen on the battlefield. The
essence of their dialogue is as follows :

Arjuna said,—Beholding these kinsmen, O Krishna,

7

assembled together and eager for the fight, my limbs become languid, and my mouth become dry. My body trembles, and my hair stands on end. *Gandiva* slips from my hand, and my skin burns. I am unable to stand any longer ; my mind seems to wander. I behold adverse omens, too, O Kecava ; I do not desire victory, O Krishna, nor sovereignty, nor pleasures ! Of what use would sovereignty be to us, O Govinda, or enjoyments, or even life, since they for whose sake sovereignty, enjoyments, and pleasures are desired by us, are here arrayed for battle, ready to give up life and wealth, viz., preceptors, sires, sons, and grandsires, maternal uncles, fathers-in-law, grandsons, brothers-in-law, and kinsmen. I wish not to slay these though they slay me, O slayer of Madhu, even for the sake of the sovereignty of the three worlds, what then for the sake of this earth ? . . . It behoveth us not to slay the sons of Dhritarāshtra who are our own kinsmen. How, O Mādhava, can we be happy by killing our own kinsmen ? . . . Alas, we have resolved to perpetrate a great sin, for we are ready to slay our own kinsmen from lust of the sweets of sovereignty. Better would it be for me if the sons of Dhritarāshtra, weapon in hand, should in battle slay me, myself unavenging and unarmed ! . . . . . .

Krishna said—Thou mournest those that deserve not to be mourned. Thou speakest also the words of the so-called wise. Those, however, that are really wise grieve neither for the dead nor for the living. It is not that I or you or those rulers of men never were, or that all of us shall not hereafter be. Of an embodied being, as childhood, youth, and decrepitude are in this body, so also is the acquisition of another body. The man that is wise is never deluded in this . . . There is no objective existence of anything that is distinct from the soul ; nor non-existence of anything possessing the virtues of the soul. This conclusion in respect of both these hath been arrived at by those that know the truths of things. Know that the soul to be immortal by which all this universe is pervaded. No one can compass the destruction of that which is imperishable . . . The embodied soul, O, Bhārata, is ever indestructible in every one's body. Therefore, it behoveth thee not to grieve for all those creatures ! Casting thy eyes on the prescribed duties of thy order, it behoveth thee not to waver, for there is nothing else that is better for a Kshatriya than a battle fought fairly. Arrived of itself and like unto an open gate of heaven, happy are those Kshatriyas, O Pārtha, that obtain such a fight ! But if thou dost not fight such a just battle, thou shaft then incur sin by abandoning the duties of thy order and thy fame ! . . . Therefore, arise, O son of Kunti, resolved for battle ! Regarding pleasure and pain, gain and loss, victory and defeat, as equal, do battle for battle's sake and sin will not be thine . . . Thy concern is with Work only, but not with the fruit of work ; nor let thy inclination be for inaction.[2]

As the Aryan community consolidated and expanded its position in northern India, some of Krishna's ideas about warfare changed. His theme that combat should be treated as an accepted feature of life, particularly by *kshatriya,* and his commitment to battle for battle's sake was replaced by more politically mature concepts. The shift reflected the new political arrangements of the Aryan people. In the process of establishing themselves in India, the Aryans gradually abandoned tribal society. For the first time in Aryan history, rulers appeared who controlled kingdoms of a specific size and location and were fighting for additional territory. The transformation of Aryan society from a tribal organization to one more closely resembling today's political divisions was also accompanied by new ideas concerning the proper employment of military force and the correct goals of a king's policies.[3] Leading spokesmen now maintained that a military challenge to an adversary state was but one of several policy options a ruler had in the governance of his land. They were less eager to go to battle, although they did not abandon Krishna's stress on a life of action. Aryan kings were advised to seek a military solution only after they had thoughtfully equated the various unpredictable consequences of warfare with the political-military goals they sought. Kings were cautioned to initiate combat only after alternative measures had been tried and found wanting. Declaring war and striving to destroy an enemy's army had come to be recognized as a perilous course of action a government could choose. The ultimate goal of warfare no longer was to demonstrate *kshatriyas'* personal courage, their physical agility or to resolve tribal disputes. In Indian society of approximately the third century B.C., warfare was sanctioned only when the military security of a rulers's kingdom and his aggressive policies required the elimination of an enemy state, or when its material wealth and physical resources were appreciably increased by annexing the conquered territory. On the other hand, should royal advisers conclude that a military victory was unlikely, the local king was advised to concentrate on enhancing the state's military capabilities and improving its security. If and when such efforts were successful and the would-be aggressor king no longer was the weaker power—when his political-military strength was judged superior to his rival's—he was encouraged to attack his enemy forthwith, destroying neighboring defenses and incorporating the territory into his own realm.

Kautilya, whose *Arthasastra* has been cited earlier, was the leading exponent of the new philosophy of warfare and militarism. His analysis and comments concerning the inter-dynamics between political action and military opportunism is even to this day remarkably sophisticated and perceptive, and his influence on Indian theories of statecraft has been enormous and long-lasting.

Kautilya viewed warfare in an amoral, highly opportunistic, practical manner. A king's first responsibility, he wrote, was to seek power and to attain happiness for those he ruled. Whenever a situation was fluid and the attainment of his policies was in doubt, the ruler was advised to employ non-military means to obtain his objectives. Espionage, sabotage, spying, assassination and other similar actions designed to weaken, if not destroy, an enemy's kingdom were highly recommended by Kautilya, provided their use helped achieve local dominance and increased power. Kautilya justified such chicanery by arguing that "When the advantages derivable from peace and war are of equal character, one should prefer peace; for disadvantages, such as the loss of power and wealth, sojourning and sin, are ever attending upon war."[4] In essence, the political commentators of early India no longer advocated armed combat as the preferred way to resolve local conflicts. Rather, they warned that inter-state conflicts should not be undertaken recklessly and that power politics permitted base actions. However, if a dynamic, would-be aggressor king acquired an overwhelmingly superior power position, Kautilya maintained he should march against his enemy. "Whoever is inferior to another shall make peace with him ; whoever is superior in power shall wage war,"[5] is an often quoted aphorism of Kautilya.

Kautilya concluded from his analysis of inter-state relations among local kings that peace was a transitory condition. Repeatedly he stated that peace was to be a policy chosen because of the existing imbalance of power between two rival states. It was an arrangement to be discontinued whenever one of the rulers decided that his improved resources would lead to the destruction of his enemy. If a king concludes, "that by marching my troops it is possible to destroy the works of my enemy ; and as for myself, I have made proper arrangements to safeguard my own works,"[6] he is well-advised to launch a war. One additional idea of Kautilya deserves mention because it, too, helped define India's traditional ideas about inter-state relationships. Several times in the *Arthasastra* Kautilya expressed his belief that wars and promises between rulers were free of ethical or moral considerations and influence by the religious-philosophical values of the society. For example, he states "whoever is rising in power may break the agreement of peace."[7] Another passage reads "no king shall keep that form of policy which causes him the loss of profits from his own works, but which entails no such loss on the enemy. That is deterioration."[8]

It was from writings such as the *Arthasastra,* advocating a highly utilitarian, amoral approach to inter-state relations and the use of military power, that the Hindu people established their traditional political-military norms. As will be seen, such norms exacerbated local tensions as well as placing a high premium on military power. No ruler in pre-Moghul India could feel secure since he had to acknowledge the transitory nature of his position and the threatened condition of his state. A neighboring king, whether currently a steadfast ally or a non-belligerent, was likely to be an implacable enemy as soon as he acquired sufficient strength to upset the status quo. Aggrandizement was the recognized duty of a king, and the manner of accumulating power was of no great importance. Consequently, aggression by Hindu kings was all but continuous. Internecine warfare occurred regularly generation after generation. Hindu kings consistently scorned policies that would have helped pacify the subcontinent or establish some measure of cooperative relations among their kingdoms. The overall record of India's pre-modern leaders is one of consistently rejecting opportunities that might have facilitated a modicum of good feeling or led to a diplomatic resolution of their innumerable conflicts. Except for the Edicts of Ashoka,[9] it was not the practice of rulers or literati to vigorously condemn wars as either politically destabilizing or morally reprehensible. The *Arthasastra* not only prescribed political-military behavior in pre-modern India, but Kautilyan philosophy became India's model for relations among local states.

MILITARY MYTHS AND MILITARY REALITY

Hindu society has frequently been portrayed as one that traditionally abhored warfare, eschewed militarism and deplored aggressive activities. Such observations were especially prominent in the writings of British authors of the eighteenth and nineteenth centuries. In 1780, Robert Orme, a British officer who researched the military history of the Indians, concluded that Hindu soldiers were inferior to troops from Central Asia and Europe :

> An abhorrence to the shedding of blood, derived from his religion, and seconded by the very great temperance of a life which is passed by most of them in a very sparing use of animal food, and a total abstinence of intoxicating liquors (makes him ineffectual). He shudders at the sight of blood, and is of a pusillanimity only to be excused and accounted for by the great delicacy of his configuration. This is so slight as to give him no chance of opposing with success the onset of an inhabitant of more northern regions.[10]

Mountstuart Elphinstone, depending heavily on Muslim sources, characterized Hindu national character in 1841 as being "effeminate," "timid," "indolent," and "dreading to be involved in trouble." He then added :

> Their great defeat is a want of manliness. Their slavish constitution, their blind superstition, their extravagant mythology, their subtilities and verbal distinctions of their philosophy, the languid softness of their poetry, their effeminate manners, their artifice and delay, their submissive temper, their dread of change, the delight they take in puerile fables, and their neglect of rational history, are so many

proofs of the absence of the more robust qualities of dispo-
sition and intellect throughout the mass of the nation.[11]

Such inaccurate characterizations of the military behavior of
the Hindu people were advanced by Muslims and later by Europeans to serve their narrow ends. The features of Hindu society
they stressed were, in fact, not present in the subcontinent prior
to Muslim domination, when the Hindus became a conquered and
subjugated civilization.

A more accurate and historically correct way of character-
izing the pattern of the military behavior of Hindus, particularly
those who lived in the northern areas, would emphasize numerous
independent kingdoms, interminable internecine wars, incorrigible
militarism, and a general lack of sympathy and support given by
the masses to its armies. Countless invasions of the subcontinent via the northwest passes of the Himalayas and the unima-
ginative performances of Hindu military leaders in defense also
typified the Hindus. Finally, some mention would have to be
made of the stagnant nature of traditional Hindu armaments, contrasting this outmoded equipment with that of the invaders.

As a matter of historical truth, few, if any pre-modern societies either in the East or West compiled as warlike a record as
the Hindu people. They engaged in military competition with
friends and foes alike, striking with almost unbelievable frequency,
all the while displaying what appears to be an unusual fondness
for combat. The writings of Nirad C. Chaudhuri have contributed much to correct these misconceptions about the Hindu
people. "The current belief," he wrote in *The Continent of
Circe,* "is that the Hindus are a peaceloving and non-violent people, and this belief has been fortified by Gandhism. In reality,
however, few human communities have been more warlike and
fond of bloodshed."[12]

The dichotomy between the portrayal of the Hindus as a
pacific, war-abjuring society and their record of military aggressiveness is not the most unusual aspect of their military history.
Equally striking is the fact that Hindus, in spite of the many
times they resorted to arms, never attained high distinction either
as fighting men or as field tacticians. Hindu troops were not
notably proficient officers or soldiers on the battlefield. The tactics their officers employed were never distinguished, and generally not even commendable. In the post-Christian era, Hindu

armies steadfastly employed field maneuverers and resorted to battlefield formations long archaic in other areas of the world. One Indian military historian has argued, for example, that Hindu infantry never outgrew its subsidiary position in the thinking of local kings and generals. From the fourth century B.C. until the close of the twelfth century A.D., Chakravarti observes, there was no continued or systematic attempt in any part of India to use infantry as the kernel of the army, or to develop it into solid, defensive units like those in Greece and Rome. Throughout some sixteen centuries Hindu armies retained their original dominant characteristic : a conglomerate mass of men without notable capabilities for either defensive or offensive operations.[13]

A final feature of traditional Hindu militarism is perhaps the most illuminating. In spite of the many battles the Hindus fought, the Hindu community never produced a single man whose battlefield performance or written commentaries on the art of war rank him among the world's foremost military analysts. No matter how diligently one searches through the annuls of Hindu military history, there is no Alexander the Great, SunTzu, or Caesar.[14] No Hindu officer ever devised novel ground tactics or an overall strategic battle plan that improved the subcontinent's security position, or even able to protect one area of the subcontinent from the disruptive invasions that regularly took place. Early in their history, the Chinese built the Great Wall to ensure the Middle Kingdom's isolation and protect the people from invasion. Despite the fact that the northwest passes of the Himalayas were the traditional routes taken by a long line of invading armies, the Hindu military made no comparable response.

In brief, fighting and marital activities were an important feature of traditional Hindu society, but their armies were poorly equipped and led by officers whose military skill and imagination were not of a high order.[15]

The Hindu military tradition unconventional and deficient in so many respects, is distinguished in one regard, nevertheless. Unlike most other armies of the pre-modern world, Hindu troops (with the exception of the Cholas) were not sent abroad to seize territory or subdue alien people. The most prominent mission of the Hindu military throughout the ages was to engage a neighboring army and try to bring its area under their rule. No Hindu army was sent abroad to invade, conquer and rule a neighboring people living beyond the borders of classical India. The Hindus' abnegation of foreign adventures impressed many of India's invaders and visitors. In reciting the campaigns of Alexander the Great, Arrian noted in his *Anabasis of Alexander* that "no Indian ever went outside his country on a warlike expedition, so righteous were they."[16] Approximately one thousand years later, in 851 A.D., Suleiman the Merchant reported :

> The Wars they wage with the neighboring Princes, are not usually undertaken with a view to possess themselves of the adjoining Dominions; and I never heard of any, but the People bordering upon the Pepper Country (India—ed.) that have seized on the Possessions of their Neighbours after a Victory. . . .[17]

The chapters that follow will concentrate on three distinctive aspects of the pre-modern political-military record of the Hindus. The first relates to north India in the early medieval period when the Rajputs' political and military authority was at its zenith. It focuses on the chronic refusal of the Hindu leaders (Rajputs) to form military alliances when threatened by a common, more powerful enemy from abroad. The second deals with the problem of morale in Hindu military services and in Hindu society in general. This section reviews practices of Hindus that could have weakened the resolve of the Indian people to fight Muslim aggression in a more determined fashion. The third aspect, largely pertaining to south India of the late medieval period, bears upon the repeated reliance of Hindu leaders on war elephants rather than on horses and cavalry troops in battlefield situations.

REFERENCES

1. Protap Chandra Roy, trans., *The Mahabharata* (Calcutta : Bharata Press, 1887).
2. *ibid.*, pp. 76-83.
3. There is an extensive literature on the art of war in ancient India. See, for example, V. R. Ramachandra Dikshitar, *War in Ancient India* (London : Macmillan and Company, 1944); Gustav Oppert, *On the Weapons, Army Organization and Political Maxims of the Ancient Hindus* (London : Trübner and Com-

pany, 1880); Major Gautam Sharma, *Indian Army Through the Ages* (Bombay : Allied Publishers Private Limited, 1966).

4. Kautilya, *Arthasastra,* trans. R. Shamasastry (Mysore : Mysore Printing and Publishing House, 1961), p. 296.

5. *ibid.,* p. 293.

6. *ibid.,* p. 293.

7. *ibid.,* p. 343.

8. *ibid.,* p. 294.

9. See supra, see Chapter II.

10. Robert Orme, *A History of the Military Transactions of the British Nation in Industan* (London : John Nourse, 1780), p. 196, and quoted in Percival Spear, *The Nabobs : A Study of the Social Life of the English in Eighteenth Ceneury India* (London : Oxford University Press, 1963).

11. Mountstuart Elphinstone, *A History of India* (London : John Murray, 1841), p. 374.

12. Nirad C. Chaudhuri, *The Continent of Circe* (New York : Oxford University Press, 1966), pp. 97-98. Also see K. M. Panikkar, *Essential Features of Indian Culture* (Bombay : Bharatiya Vidya Bhavan, 1964), pp. 16ff. K. M. Panikkar is equally firm. "Ahimsa," he wrote, "is no doubt a great religious creed, but India rejected it when she refused to follow Gautama Buddha. The Hindu throne at all times, especially in periods of historic greatness, was one of active assertion of the right, if necessary, through the force of arms ... Krishna (does not) stand for non-violence, 'Wake, be thyself, scourge they forces is the manly teaching of the Gita ..." *Essential Features of Indian Culture* (Bombay : Bharatiya Vidya Bhavan, 1964), p. 16.

13. P. C. Chakravarti, *The Art of War in Ancient India* (Dacca : University of Dacca, nd.), pp. 15ff.

14. One explanation for the absence of great Hindu military theorists was suggested by Strabo, the first century A.D. Greek historian and geographer. Quoting from Onesicritus' observations, Strabo wrote of the Indians that "they make no accurate study of the sciences ... for they regard too much training in some of them as wickedness; for example, military science and like ..." *The Geography of Strabo,* trans. Horace Leonard Jones, (New York : Putnam and Sons, 1930), VII, 61.

15. In discussing the military profession of India, Abbe Dubois wrote, "... But however much the Hindus may have honoured the profession of arms, and however full their national histories may be of wars, conquests, sieges, battles, victories, and defeats, it is nevertheless remarkable that no nation has shown at every epoch in its history so little skill in military science ... The readiness with which they (Hindus) bent their independence, proved how inferior they were in courage and discipline to the proud Tartars who invaded and conquered them." Abbe J. A. Dubois

and Henry K. Beauchamp, *Hindu Manners, Customs and Cere-monies*, 3rd. ed., (Oxford : Clarendon Press, 1906), pp. 668-9.

16. Arrian, *Anabasis Alexander*, trans. E. Iliff Robson, (London : William Heineman, 1929), II, p. 333.

17. Eusebius Renaudot, *Ancient Accounts of India and China by Two Mohammedan Travellers* (London : Sam Harding, 1733), p. 33.

CHAPTER VII

THE LORDS OF THE ELEPHANT

The Horse and Elephant in India's Military History

THE ORIGIN and prehistoric evolution of the horse are still unknown. Leading authorities believe that horses first appeared
in Babylonia as early as 2000 B.C., and were introduced to Egypt
some time during the seventeenth century B.C. From these two
locations their dispersion throughout most other areas of the
world was only a matter of time. It is reasonable to assume that
the first contact the Aryan people had with the animals came
during the migration to the subcontinent. Each wave of Aryans
arriving in northwest India probably brought with them horses
along with their cattle and other possessions. From Vedic literature it is known that the Aryans who settled the Indus Valley
had considerable experience in using horses to pull chariots in
war-time operations, but did not ride bareback. Passages in the
Rig Veda, for example, contain "some of the finest lines on the
horse in the world's literature," as A. L. Basham points out.[1]
The divine horse Dadhikra is pictured in battle as follows :

> Rushing to glory, to the capture of herds,
> swooping down as a hungry falcon,
> eager to be first, he darts amid the ranks of the chariots,
> happy as a bridegroom making a garland,
> spuring the dust and champing at the bit.

> And the victorious steed and faithful,
> his body obedient [to the driver] in battle,
> speeding on through the mêlée,
> stirs up the dust to fall on his brows.

> And at his deep neigh, like the thunder of heaven,
> the foemen tremble in fear,
> for he fights against thousands, and none can resist him,
>   so terrible is his charge.[2]

Another animal frequently cited in Vedic literature is the
elephant. This animal was not known to the Aryans prior to
their arrival in the subcontinent. In her study of India, Romila

Thapar states that the earliest Aryan immigrants regarded the elephants they first saw with great curiosity,[3] and she is unquestionably correct. The name they gave to these unfamiliar beasts
suggests their novelty : *mrigahastin* or, literally, the animal with
a hand. As the years passed and Aryan settlements spread over
an ever-larger area, the Aryans' contacts with elephants became
more frequent and the uses to which the animals were put, more
extensive.[4] The extraordinary strength of elephants made them
ideal beasts of burden for people determined to establish themselves in northern India and to open the land for agriculture.
From *Veda* citations, it seems certain that horses were considered
more suited for the battlefield than for menial tasks.

Other important characteristics of elephants led to their prominence in Aryan affairs. Elephants are not only indigenous to
India, but they flourish there. The climate is ideal for their
development. Local plant life, with grasses and fruits growing
in profusion provided the beasts with ample food. Moreover,
elephants have a long life-span. They are not readily susceptible
to many crippling or fatal diseases. On the other hand, horses
were not native to India and never thrived in the country. They
required grains not available there, and were stricken with crippling or fatal diseases soon after they arrived.

In due course, the Aryans turned increasingly to elephants
instead of horses to support their military programs. This major
strategic innovation possibly was adopted after observing the
battles aboriginal men had fought, but it is equally plausible that
an imaginative *kshatriya* himself hit upon the idea of mounting
an elephant. No *Vedas* refer to the use of elephants in war, so
this development must have occurred in the post-invasion period
of Aryan history. In any event, military leaders of the Aryan
society started to train elephants to carry *howdahs,* or cabs, containing three or four soldiers armed with javelins or bows and
arrows. These elephant troops were given the mission of leading
the attack on the enemy's position, and the horse-drawn chariots
of the Vedic period were gradually eliminated from the battleline formations. By the fourth century B.C., elephants played a
primary role in the military engagements of all Hindu armies.
Horses were not totally eliminated, but their assigned mission
was supportive and of secondary importance.[5] Cavalry units

never occupied the front ranks in the organization of Hindu armies.

Kautilya's *Arthasastra* offers a detailed picture of how the views of Mauryan kings on the martial merits of the elephant and the horse. Many passages in the work stress the elephant's superior abilities to execute military tactics of an offensive nature. He states, for example, that it is the elephant contingents that should advance on an established enemy position or charge onto a battlefield and overwhelm an all but impregnable installation. In another section Kautilya advises that soldiers riding atop elephants would be able to disrupt enemy formations, trampling down their attacking troops and throwing panic into their reserve formations. Finally, he suggests the elephant corp could be employed to destroy an enemy emplacement that enclosed or protected a primary fortification, such as the palace of the king.[6]

The recommended duties given to horses and cavalry troops in the Mauryan army were largely related to defensive operations : exploration of occupied positions, holding strategic positions, protection of the sides (flanks) of the army, and of the rear commissariat, and chasing and rounding-up timid (panic-stricken ?) troops.[7]

Kautilya's *Arthasastras* in due course became the leading military manual of ancient and medieval India and his strategic and tactical ideas prevailed in Hindu India. His judgments concerning the proper development of elephant troops and horse troops became firmly entrenched in the military thinking of India's kings and generals. As subsequent sections of this study will illustrate, elephant troops were positioned in crucial battlefield locations and called upon to execute offensive movements even when it should have been obvious that the beasts were incapable of the missions. India's pre-modern military leaders, exaggerating the true military worth of war-elephants and disregarding their persistent failures on the battlefield, persisted in placing great faith in front line elephant formations. This misplaced trust and poor military judgment was the result of a number of internal factors, all deeply rooted in the cultural values of the Hindus.

The material that follows attempts to explain why the Hindu military traditionally referred to themselves as *gajapatis* or Lords of the Elephant, while their adversaries were designated as *aswapatis* or Lords of the Horse.[8] To acquaint Westerners with the pro-ele-

phant mentality of Hindu leaders, a summary of two crucial
battles in India's military history is given. These engagements
took place approximately nineteen hundred years apart and in
different regions of the subcontinent. The first marks the beginning of Western intervention in India's affairs; the second
crushed the last effective Hindu army in southern India. Of particular relevance to this study is the fact that the Hindus' tactical
reliance on elephants in 1565 at Talikota was not too unlike the
elephant formations their ancestors had used in 326 B.C. at
Arbela on the Hydaspes. Elephants figured prominently in nearly every important battle in India's pre-modern history, but never
with results that justified the vital role assigned them.

THE BATTLE OF HYDASPES (326 B.C.)

The first decisive battle between horse and elephant troops
in Aryan military history took place in 326 B.C. on the Hydaspes.
This incident was the occasion when Alexander the Great and his
army out-maneuvered and out-fought the army of Porus, the king
of Pauravas, whose territory was situated directly in the path of
Alexander's planned invasion route to India. Historians and
military analysts have commented extensively on Alexander's tactics, battle formations, imaginative use of his cavalry and, in
general, his brilliance in seeking out and attacking his enemy's
weak points. At Hydaspes, the key elements in Alexander's force
were his horse cavalry and his infantry troops. According to
reports compiled from a group of narratives written centuries after
his death, Alexander's cavalry was of a superior breed, expertly
trained and ridden by men painstakingly drilled for battle.

King Porus was not Alexander's equal in imagination or
competence, and his army was inferior both in equipment and
training. He placed his reliance on a contingent of two hundred elephant troops plus an additional force of four thousand
cavalry troops, thirty thousand foot soldiers and three hundred
war chariots. Arrian's summary of the military situation immediately prior to the decisive battle, reported that Porus directed
the movements of his troops while mounted on one of the largest
elephants in his stable and that he was surrounded by an "array
of elephants." Alexander, Arrian points out, was required to discontinue his original battlefield strategy because the defenders
had so many elephants on their front lines that novel tactics were

necessary to counter-balance the enemy's seemingly greater power.[9]

Arrian relates how Porus planned to use his elephant troops to crush Alexander:

> ... When he [Porus] found a place where he saw there was no clay, but that the ground from its sandy nature was all flat and firm, and suited for the movements of cavalry whether charging or falling back, he then drew up his army in order of battle, posting his elephants in the front line at intervals of at least 100 feet, so as to have his elephants ranged in front before the whole body of his infantry, and so to spread terror at all points among Alexander's cavalry. He took it for certain besides that none of the enemy would have the audacity to push in at the intervals between the elephants—not the cavalry, since their horses would be terrified by these animals, and much less the infantry, since they would be checked in front by his heavy-armed foot soldiers falling upon them, and trampled down when the elephants wheeled round upon them. Behind these he drew up his infantry, which did not close up in one line with the elephants, but formed a second line in their rear, so that the regiments were only partly pushed forward into the intervals. He had also troops of infantry posted on the wings beyond the elephants, and on both sides of the infantry the cavalry had been drawn up, and in front of it the chariots.[10]

Alexander, however, anticipated Porus' tactics and devised a plan to avoid the awaiting trap. "When he had observed how the Indians were arranged," it is reported, "he made up his mind not to advance against the centre, in front of which the elephants had been posted, while the intervals between them had been filled with compact masses of infantry, for he feared lest Porus should reap the advantage which he had calculated on deriving from that arrangement."[11] By holding the attack until his cavalry force was most advantageously positioned, Alexander gained command of the field and threw Porus' men "into confusion with storms of arrows and charges of their horses".[12]

The unequal—even impossible—situation that Porus' elephant troops found themselves in is summarized in Arrian's history. "The Indians, unable to withstand the charge of Alexander's cavalry, broke from their ranks and fled for shelter to the elephants as to a friendly wall."[13] The following massacre ensued :

> ...the drivers of the elephants urged these animals forward against the cavalry; but the Macedonian phalanx itself now met them face to face, and threw darts at the men on the elephants, and from one side and the other struck the elephants themselves as they stood around them. This kind of warfare was different from any of which they had experience in former contests, for the huge beasts charged the ranks of the infantry, and wherever they turned went crushing through the Macedonian phalanx though in close formation; while the horsemen of the Indians, on seeing that the infantry was now engaged in the action, again wheeled round and charged the cavalry. But Alexander's men, being far superior in personal strength and military discipline, again routed them, and again drove them back upon the elephants, and cooped them up among them... The elephants being now cooped up within a narrow space, did no less damage to their friends than to their foes, trampling them under their hoofs as they wheeled and pushed about. There resulted in consequence a great slaughter of the cavalry, cooped up as it was in a narrow space around the elephants. Many of the elephant drivers, moreover, had been shot down, and of the elephants themselves some had been wounded, while others, both from exhaustion and the loss of their mahouts, no longer kept to their own side in the conflict, but, as if driven frantic by their sufferings, attacked friend and foe quite indiscriminately, pushed them, trampled them down, and killed them in all manner of ways... the Indians, who were in the midst of the animals, suffered far more the effects of their rage. When the elephants, however, became quite exhausted, and their attacks were no longer made with vigour, they fell back like ships backing water, and merely kept trumpeting as they retreated with their faces to the enemy. Then did Alexander surround with his cavalry the whole of the enemy's line, and signal that the infantry... should advance in phalanx....[14]

The Battle of Arbela not only was the first military engagement between Western and Eastern troops—a significant feature of the conflict itself—but it was historic from the standpoint of military tactics and operations as well. It demonstrated conclusively that elephant troops, no matter how massively emplaced and expertly handled, were totally unable to compete against horse troops. What seems so obvious today, however, was not apparent to almost nineteen generations of Hindu kings and generals who time and time again repeated Porus' battleline formations.

THE BATTLE OF TALIKOTA (JANUARY, 1565 A.D.)

The last major battle between a major Hindu army and its Muslim opponent was fought at Talikota, an outpost town near the Krishna River in southern India. The date was January 23-25, 1565. Almost nineteen hundred years had passed since Alexander's troops had overwhelmed Porus' men and vulnerable elephant corps. Many other invaders from Central Asia had marched through the northwest passes of the Himalayan mountains, and by the fourteenth century these Muslim forces had established themselves inexorably throughout all areas north of the Krishna River. One of the several reasons for the Muslims' repeated military victories was their excellent cavalry and the imaginative tactics they developed for such units. The Hindu military, for the most part, were still relying on elephants and elephant formations for both offensive and defensive strategy,[15] their repeated defeats notwithstanding.

The Hindus' unwavering commitment to elephant units was not because of blind faith in the beasts' military capabilities, nor was it the result of local, culturally induced prejudices against horses. Between the Battle of the Hydaspes and the Battle of Talikota, Hindu kings and their generals did in fact accept that elephants had battlefield disabilities, but they were without power to remedy the situation. The most strenuous and costly campaign to build up cavalry resources and to train horse troops was undertaken by the Vijayanagar empire during the fourteenth-sixteenth centuries A.D. The result was modest. The Vijayanagar leaders did manage to establish many well-equipped horse brigades, but as one sixteenth century observer reported, "the flower of the Vijayanagar army is the terrifying elephant corp."[16] Another Portuguese writer mentioned in his writings that it was a "very beautiful sight to behold" the vast Vijayanagar army led by elephants.[17]

The Vijayanagar empire was the Hindus' last major center of power in India, and its ruin and devastation meant that Hindu

hegemony was ended. The empire had been established in 1336
A.D., when a group of Hindu nobles, unwilling to tolerate further
humiliations from Muslim armies across the Krishna River in
the Deccan, managed to take control of territory that approxi-
mates the erstwhile state of Madras. It prospered, and its early
rulers managed its affairs with considerable skill. Vijayanagar
acquired immense wealth from its exports. Continually threatened by hostile Muslim power across their northern boundary,
each king in the early period of Vijayanagar dominance concentrated on improving the empire's military capabilities so as to
become as effective a combat force as that of the Moghul's. One
observer has commented that the Vijayanagars' empire was
"perhaps the nearest approach to a war state ever made by
Hindu kings and its political organization was dominated by its
military needs."[18] The purchase of horses and the creation of
cavalry units became a prime concern because they understood
the need to become far less dependent on war elephants. The
goal was to import horses and to bring their cavalry units up to
those of the Muslims, but without eliminating war elephant
troops.

For many years before the Battle or Talikota, the Vijayanagar Hindus and the Bijapur Muslims had fought local skirmishes, each attempting, by a variety of ruses and strategies to
out-maneuver the other and thus dominate the southern area.
The Moghul force represented a coalition of four kings who
allied themselves for the sole purpose of crushing the Vijayanagars. It was an army not too different from other Muslim
contingents that had repeatedly defeated their Hindu opposition.
In other words, the Moghul alliance put into the field a balanced
and well-led army, one in which a very strong cavalry contingent was supported by powerful infantry units.

Figures about the size of the typical Vijayanagar army, if
they are to be taken literally, are astounding. Seemingly reliable
sources maintain that on each flank of their line the Vijayanagar
had 100,000 infantry soldiers, another 100,000 cavalry troops
and also a company of two hundred and fifty elephant troops.
In the central sector there are supposed to have been 400,000
infantry, 60,000 cavalry, and a company of several hundred
armed elephant troops.[19] These figures appear to be greatly inflated, but nevertheless, there can be little doubt that the four-

teenth-fifteenth century Vijayanagar army, like other Indian armies from the time Alexander first defeated Porus, relied on a battlefield formation that involved a massive accumulation of men supported by very large herds of war elephants.

The initial skirmishes at Talikota, which began on January 21-22, 1565, were indecisive.[20]   Each side managed to prevail at some point along the extended battle line, but neither could gain local superiority.   Where weaknesses in their defensive formation became evident, the Vijayanagar officers were able to call up replacements and restore the integrity of their line.   The primary objective of the Moghul army was to cross the Krishna River in sufficient strength to secure a beach-head on their enemy's territory.   The Moghuls finally decided to out-flank the Vijayanagar force and raced infantry and cavalry troops beyond the two extremities of the defenders' position.   The maneuver was successful.   During the short period of consolidation that followed, the Hindus tried unsuccessfully to throw back the invaders.   On January 23, having poured sufficient supplies and a large number of men across the Krishna, the Moghuls attacked, thus beginning the last great military confrontation between Hindu and Muslim armies.

The commanding general of the Vijayanagar force was Rama Raya, who was over eighty years old at the time of the battle.   Compounding Rama Raya's folly in assuming personal control of his army at such an advanced age was his insistence on personally directing the operation from the cab of one of his largest elephants.   Despite the warnings of his immediate staff that his position was unnecessarily exposed and the animal too slow and clumsy, the king refused to alter his decision.   When a horse was offered him, Rama Raya ordered it away.   His third error of judgment was to station himself along with his senior advisers and leading military aides at the very center of the line and as far forward as it was possible to ride.   It is important to recall that when Porus met Alexander he, too, directed his troops from an elephant and assumed a position in a comparable sector of the line.   No one reviewing the military record of India's most notable Hindu kings will ever fault them for inconsistency or lack of dedication to military traditionalism, defeat after defeat notwithstanding.

Both sides fought with the determination that invariably

appears between adversaries with a prolonged political rivalry and bitter religious hostility. The Hindus, furthermore, were acutely aware of the awful consequences of defeat.

For several hours the battle continued, but with inconclusive results. At some point, the Moghul command decided to commit cavalry and infantry forces from the central sector of their line to launch an all-out attack. They struck the advance units in Rama Raya's defense line with the full impact of their power. Perhaps surprising even themselves, the Moghul troops found the Vijayanagar defense crumbling and many of the enemy in retreat. A small unit of Moghul horse troops raced forward so as to maintain their tactical advantage, and found themselves literally with the command headquarters of Rama Raya and his senior generals. The Vijayanagar staff was panic-stricken as they sought to escape from the trap in which they found themselves. In the ensuing confusion and excitement, only those Hindu leaders astride horses had any chance of fleeing to a less perilous position. Rama Raya did not have such an opportunity : his massive elephant, unable to move swiftly, became the central point of the Moghuls' attack. Dozens of arrows hit the beast from all sides and Moghul spears ripped open his hide. Attempts to calm the elephant so that the king could leave the cab and mount a nearby horse were futile. Moghul soldiers rushed to the area and pounced on the defenseless king. One cavalryman, sword in hand, swung at Rama Raya and decapitated him. Ecstatically the Moghuls raised the general's head aloft so that his troops could see that their leader was dead and their defensive line smashed. It is reported that once the news circulated among the great body of the Vijayanagar army, large numbers of men broke ranks and fled the battlefield in complete disarray. With the collapse of Hindu forces at Talikota, Moghul supremacy throughout the subcontinent of India was assured. Until India's independence in 1948, the Hindus throughout the country were a conquered people, defeated in battle, forced to accommodate themselves to an inimical religion and unable to develop their cultural preferences.

Since the Battle of Talikota, many Hindu military historians have analyzed the Vijayanagar defeat. Two are especially pertinent to the theme of this chapter. Sir Jadunath Sarkar, writing in 1960, concluded that the crushing defeat of the Vijayanagars was the result, inter alia, of "their leaders riding on elephants instead of swift horses of the best breed."[21]   A second contemporary author, P. C. Chakravarti, placed his analysis of the defeat within a wider frame of reference—the Hindus' use of the elephant as the primary weapon in military strategy. Summarizing events since the battle of Arbela, he says :

> In succeeding centuries the importance of elephants went on mounting higher and higher in Indian military estimation. Elephants, though dangerous, were of real value in war. Used with caution, and as a subordinate army, they sometimes turned the scale of victory at the desired moment. The Hindus erred not in the use of elephants but in the emphasis they put on them.[22]

The Hindus' Efforts to Develop Cavalry

In many respects the pre-modern military history of Hindu India was shaped by failure of local kings and generals to modernize their armies and to adopt the more efficient battlefield tactics employed by their invaders. Hindus remained committed to elephants, continued to rely very heavily on the beasts in their front-line operations,[23] and failed to reorganize their armies around cavalry troops. Some Hindus were very much aware of the reasons for their chronically poor showing on the battlefields and, more particularly, the tendency of elephants to flee from a skirmish when frightened and to move painfully slowly when speed was crucial. These men expended considerable time and enormous wealth striving to develop a creditable Hindu cavalry. Throughout the earliest period of their settlement in India, and with increasing intensity until their final sixteenth century defeat by the Moghuls, the ruling class of several kingdoms sought to build up horse herds to improve the position of their troops on the battlefield. All failed to attain their goal. The intractible problem for each ruler was the same : horses were not native to India, imported steeds fared very poorly in its climate and on its terrain. Most significantly, the Hindu people as such failed to develop the requisite skills necessary for the proper care of horses.

Exactly when the Hindus first imported horses from modern Arabia either for military or non-military purposes is unclear. There is very little specific information concerning such trade before the thirteenth century although a number of scholars have examined the problem. Professor Warmington in his study of *The Commerce Between The Roman Empire and India,* for example, concluded that Persian horses were brought into the Indian ports as early as the first part of the sixth century A.D.[24] Other authors place the onset of India's import trade in horses at a somewhat later time. In any event, horses, originally a minor item in early West-East trade relations, eventually became India's primary import product.

Marco Polo's thirteenth century journal gave Westerners the first factual statement of the impressive dimensions of India's import of horses, but his observations were confined to the Hindu kingdoms in the southern section of the subcontinent. (Northern India had long since come under the domination of various Muslim invaders and whatever horses these kings imported, were because of Muslim military needs.) After having visited the southern port city of Malabar, including its active dock area, Marco Polo wrote in his journal that the local royal family imported so many shiploads of horses each year that the annual revenue of the entire kingdom "or a greater part of it, is spent in the purchase of horses." He was explicit :

> In this country no horses are reared, and hence the greater part of the revenue is employed in obtaining them from foreign regions. The merchants of Curmos, of Quisci, of Dufar, of Soer, and of Aden, whose provinces contain many steeds of fine quality, purchase, embark, and bring them to the king and his four princely brothers, selling them for 500 sagi of gold, worth more than 100 marcs of silver. I assure you, this monarch buys annually more than 2,000 [horses] . . .[25]

Throughout the fourteenth and fifteenth centuries, the various Vijayanagar emperors worked determinedly to use their cavalry troops with greater skill and imagination. Regularly threatened by Moghul military power and frequently defeated in local skirmishing, they had good reason to be concerned about the fighting capabilities of their troops, particularly the inferior performance of the cavalry units. By this time, the riding proficiency of the Moghul soldier, as well as his courage and espirit de corp, had become legendary throughout India. Nevertheless, the Vijayanagars persisted. In 1442 A.D., for example, the then reigning ruler, Devaraya, called a general council of his leading nobles and military advisers to determine the specific causes of their defeats on the battlefield.[26]   According to reports, the king in the course of the discussion compared the power capabilities of his kingdom with that of his enemies.   He noted that the area of land he controlled was larger.   His manpower reserves were greater, and the annual revenue of Vijayanagar far exceeded those of the Moghuls.   If the size of the two armies were compared, he continued, the Vijayanagar force was by far numerically superior to the opposition's.   What, then, caused his men to be defeated so regularly in battle ?   Why had Vijayanagar men fought so poorly when called upon to protect their territory ? Why should his court be required to pay tribute to Moghul kings when the reverse should have been the case ?

The king's staff offered but one explanation for their threatened military situation : the inferior strength of Vijayanagar cavalry.   The Muslim horses were described to the king as "strong and able to bear more fatigue than the weak, lean animals [that Vijayanagar men were forced to ride]."[27]

War councils and staff discussions such as the one Devaraya directed led to ambitious efforts to strengthen and improve Vijayanagar cavalry resources.   Invariably the main thrust of such efforts was directed at importing larger and larger supplies of horses from abroad rather than trying to build up local reserves.   For cultural reasons, the Vijayanagars not only were unable to care properly for the animals they purchased but also were prevented from building up herds of horses born on Indian territory.   The only practical solution was to enlarge their imports.   Since Arab ships and crews all but dominated the subcontinent's trade with countries exporting horses, Vijayanagar kings were not always able to locate sufficiently large quantities of horses from abroad at anything but an enormous cost. Arab traders profited handsomely.   For decade after decade the Vijayanagars struggled to bolster their cavalry strength, but without noticeable results.

When the Portuguese arrived in force in southern India during the early decades of the sixteenth century, the Vijayanagars' military situation should have changed.   The Portuguese colonists and the Vijayanagars shared a common hatred for Muslims and for Muslim political-military dominance of the subcontinent. If for no other reason, both were united in wanting to end Mus-

lim pressure on southern India and ought to have developed close
cooperation. For their part, the Vijayanagars should have understood it was in the interest of local Portuguese to end (or at
least reduce) Vijayanagar dependency on imported Arabian
horses for their cavalry units. They should have realized, as
well, that Portuguese maritime strength, demonstrated by their
growing power along the Western coast of India, could be utilized
by local rulers freely. The Vijayanagars, however, either failed
to grasp the logistical opportunities resulting from the Portuguese
presence or their political analysis was impaired by a limited,
imperfect understanding of the world beyond their shores. Whatever the reason, the Vijayanagars neglected to seize the initiative,
and it was the Portuguese who first approached the Hindus.

In 1509, Albuquerque, who had become viceroy of the
Portuguese settlements in the south, found that his military position was threatened by a local Muslim army. If Vijayanagar
troops joined in his planned counter-attack, however, Albuquerque
thought there was an excellent chance that the combined forces
would be able to defeat the Muslims. He sent a lengthy letter
to the king of Vijayanagar : His order from Lisbon called for his
armies to wage war against Muslims, but his king had only
friendly feelings toward the Hindus. If Vijayanagar would ally
itself to the Portuguese, Albuquerque was well situated to offer
a number of strategic advantages to the Hindus. One item concerned the importation of cavalry horses. If the Hindus agreed
to cooperate, Albuquerque stated that he would ensure that Por-
guese merchants would supply the Vijayanagar empire with sufficient Arab and Persian horses to satisfy their needs, and in addition, he promised to deny all such animals to the Muslims. In
effect, in concluding a Portuguese-Vijayanagar alliance, Albuquerque was guaranteeing the Hindus an end to their dependence on
Arab merchants and Arab ships for their cavalry needs.[28]

For reasons never explained, the Vijayanagar court failed
to respond to the Portuguese overtures, and so failed to establish military ties with them against their common enemy, the
Muslims. In late 1510, after Albuquerque had captured Goa for
the second time, the king of Vijayanagar did send an ambassador
to Albuquerque. His "anxiety was to secure horses." Explaining the shift in Vijayanagar policies, Sewell states :

He must have thought little of this foreign settlement on the coast as a political power, but what he wanted was horses, and again horses, for his perpetual wars against the Adil Shah[29] (his Muslim enemy—ed.).

In reply, Albuquerque notified the king that the Portuguese would not only supply the Hindus with horses but would deny them to the Muslims.

In due course, a treaty was concluded between the two rulers, and for a time the importation of horses to the Hindus increased but without giving them a monopoly. Portuguese traders, however, apparently established contacts with several Muslim courts and began selling them, also, significant quantities of cavalry mounts. The traders by this time well knew the enormous profits from supplying both Muslims and Hindus with horses to continue their respective military activities. In 1514 A.D., the Vijayanagar king formally notified Albuquerque that he was prepared to pay L.20,000 for the exclusive right to buy the horses the Portuguese landed at Goa.[30] The offer, first refused, was a short time later renewed. Local Muslims made similar offers to Albuquerque, thus enabling him to advance the military programs of one side and, conversely, weaken those of the other. For some time the Portuguese profitted from their position, but ultimately decided it was in their country's interest to favor the Hindus over the Muslims, the profits from auctioning imported in the open Goa market notwithstanding. On September 19, 1547, a new Treaty of Friendship and Commerce was signed. Article II stated :

> The governor of Goa will allow all Arab and Persian horses landed at Goa to be purchased by the king of Vijayanagar on due notice and proper payment, none being permitted to be sent to Bijapur.[31]

The Hindus' demand for horses had become all but insatiable as they approached the climax of their conflicts with the Muslims. The memoirs of one European traveller in Vijayanagar territory reported the Hindus were so desperate for mounts that they willingly paid for animals that died at sea rather than alienate the Portuguese merchants who had shipped them. The importer, it was said, had only to present the tail of the dead horse to the proper Vijayanagar authority and he would be reimbursed at the same rate as paid for animals that had managed to endure the sea voyage.[32] The Portuguese were no less imaginative and eager for profits. One decree of the period stated that vessels plying the Portuguese flag and arriving from Ormus, then a main trading center in horses, would be permitted to dock at Goa without paying regular custom duties only if they carried aboard at least twenty horses apiece. Ships berthing without horses were required to pay the customary eight percent duty on the entire cargo.[33] Needless to say, few Portuguese traders neglected to take full advantage of the decree.

One would have thought that the Vijayanagar's long and concerted efforts would have resulted in quality stables and first-rate cavalry units. Given their energetic programs to breed horses and teach their troops to ride and fight as well as the horse-borne troops of their Muslim enemies, the Hindus should have downgraded their war elephants and all but discontinued placing elephant troops in their frontline formations. A reformulation of Hindu battlefield tactics did not take place ; the Hindus remained only a little less committed to the use of elephants than their Mauryan ancestors. "The flower of the Vijayanagar armies," a sixteenth century Portuguese traveller reported, "was its terrifying corp of elephants."[34]

THE HINDUS EQUINE PRACTICES

Only if typical Hindu equine practices are recounted it is possible to understand why Hindu efforts to assemble and support cavalry units were doomed to failure and why their overall battlefield performance was consistently so poor. From the various books, letters and reports of Western travelers to India, a picture of local practices in the care and feeding of the animals emerges. The earliest source dates from the latter part of the thirteenth century A.D., but in all probability describes procedures used in Hindu stables of much earlier eras.[35] A subsequent report was written in mid-seventeenth century, a period considerably later than the chronological termination of this study. This account makes all too apparent the determination (or inability) of the Hindu people not to modify their traditional ideas and prejudices concerning horse care, despite their very long and singularly disastrous record.

By the time Marco Polo arrived in the Malabar area of the Coromandel coast at the end of the thirteenth century, the importation of Arabian horses was a well-established item in India's trade with the West. Having just departed from China, a country that traditionally took great care to ensure the well-being of its herds, he was at once aware of the unfortunate diet and its sorrowful consequences that Hindu horses received from their grooms. In his journal he wrote :

> In this country there grows no grain but rice. It is remarkable that large fine horses in process of breeding produce only ponies with twisted legs, unfit for riding, and good for nothing.[36]

The care of horses by the Hindus underwent no significant changes throughout the fourteenth century, as an increasingly large number of Muslim visitors discovered. The contrast between their high regard for horses and the painstaking attention they gave their animals and the practices of Hindus must have been a source of considerable anguish to them. The classical Arab attitudes toward horses has been summarized by C. Northcote Parkinson :

> The Prophet himself clearly realized the immense importance of horses to his people, as is plain from various passages in the Koran. He declares that the Almighty created horses from a condensation of the south-west wind and he represents God as thus apostrophising that animal : 'Thou shalt be for man a source of happiness and wealth; thy back shalt be a seat of honour and thy belly of riches; every grain of barley given to thee shalt purchase indulgence for the sinner'. Elsewhere, he propounds the comfortable doctrine that the money which one spends on horses in the eyes of God is alms that one makes at one's own cost. 'Every grain of barley given to a horse is entered by God in the Register of Good Works'.[37]

Abdullah Wassaf (Abdullah the Panegyrist), an Arab who entered India in the early fourteenth century, was appalled at the Hindus' chronic deficiencies in servicing their animals. He admits that he was commercially involved in the flourishing Arab-Hindu horse trade then taking place and that the large financial rewards he received from such ventures were attractive to his commercial instincts. As a lover of all horses, however, he was horrified at the treatment they received once they were handed over to local Hindu stable attendants. In his description of the many Hindu misconceptions of proper animal care, he fortuitously revealed the stubborn refusal of Hindus to modify their ideas and practices concerning equine management. At the time of Abdullah's visit, a number of Hindu kings were deeply involved in a campaign to develop cavalry units for their military forces and should have begun revising their attitudes about horses and improving the care given them. Abdullah's comments explain the inability of the Hindu cavalry to compete on an equal basis with the troops from abroad :

> ... It is a strange thing that when these horses arrive there, instead of giving them raw barley, they give them roasted barley and grain dressed with butter, and boiled cow's milk to drink.

Warming to his subject, Abdullah wrote the following poem :

> Who gives sugar to an owl or crow ?
> Or who feeds a parrot with a carcase ?
> A crow should be fed with a dead body,
> And a parrot with candy and sugar.
> Who loads jewels on the back of an ass ?
> Or who would approve of giving dressed
>   almonds to a cow ?

He continued :

> They (the Hindu grooms—ed.) bind them for forty days in a stable with ropes and pegs, in order that they may get fat; and afterwards, without taking measures for training, and without stirrups and other appurtenances of riding, the Indian soldiers ride upon them like demons. They are equal to Burák (the legendary horse Mohammed rode up to heaven—ed.) in celerity, and are employed either in war or exercise. In a short time the most strong, swift, fresh, and active horse becomes weak, slow, useless, and stupid. In short, they all become wretched and good for nothing. In this climate these powerful horses which fly swiftly without a whip .. become exceedingly weak and altogether worn out and unfit for riding. There is, therefore, a constant necessity of getting new horses annually .... [38]

Some three hundred and fifty years after these comments were written, Westerners continued to compare the Hindus' care of horses with what Abdullah had seen in both philosophy and details. They still were shocked at the insensitivity Hindus displayed in attending to the basic needs of their animals. One such traveller was Jean Baptiste Tavernier, a French jeweller, who made six extended trips to India between 1641 and 1666, and reportedly resided in the country for some ten years. His chronicle is accepted as a trustworthy account of local life and Hindu practices. In the course of his narrative, Tavernier discusses the stables of local Hindu kings and the horse population of the country :

> . . . The horses imported into India, whether from Persia or Arabia, or the country of the Usbeks, have a complete change of food, for in India they are given neither hay nor oats. Each horse receives for its portion in the morning two or three balls made of wheaten flour and butter, of the size of our penny rolls. There is much difficulty in accustoming them to this kind of food, and often four or five months pass before it can be accomplished. The groom is obliged to hold the horse's tongue in one hand, and with the other he has to force the ball down the throat. In the sugar-cane or millet season they are given some of them at mid-day; and in the evening, an hour or two before sunset, they receive a measure of chickpeas which the groom has crushed between two stones and steeped in water. It is these which take the place of hay and oats. As for the stables of the king. . .they are poor places, badly built, and do not deserve to be mentioned.[39]

Later in his work Tavernier provided more details :

> . . . As neither barley nor oats are to be had in this country, the cattle are fed on certain large and hard peas, which are first crushed between two grindstones and then allowed to steep for half an hour, for they are very hard and consequently difficult of digestion. The horses are given some of these peas every evening, and in the morning they receive about two pounds of coarse black sugar, which is almost like wax, kneaded with an equal weight of flour and a pound of butter, of which mixture the grooms make pellets or small balls, which are forced down the horses' throats, otherwise they would not eat them. Afterwards their mouths are washed, especially the teeth, which are covered with the paste, this gives them a dislike of this

kind of food. During the day the horses are given some grass which is torn up in the fields, roots and all, and is most carefully washed so that no earth remains.[40]

INDIA'S EQUINE DISABILITIES : A THEORY

The preceding material has demonstrated the heavy dependence of Hindus on elephant warfare for nineteen hundred years. The more complex and challenging issue is what prevented Hindus from adapting the horse-oriented military tactics of India's various invaders. Specifically, what precluded Hindus from importing an adequate supply of studs and dams to breed an on-going healthy horse population for their cavalry units ? Was India's long dependence on war elephants a blind, irrational and self-imposed limitation of the Hindu people or did cultural pressures in the subcontinent make it impossible for the Hindus to raise strong, spirited animals and to train their cavalry to ride and fight as skillfully as their adversaries ?

The centuries-old failure of the Hindus to sponsor horse-breeding projects and their lack of success in cavalry tactics were the result of two inter-related factors. The first was India's topography and climate. The second was the cultural values and prejudices of the Hindu people. These forces, each reinforcing the other, doomed from its inception every project to develop horses that Hindu kings sponsored, and frustrated the aspirations of their generals and field tacticians to acquire skilled and accomplished cavalry units for their armies.

INDIA'S CLIMATE AND TERRAIN

The fact that horses are not indigenous to any region of the subcontinent of India, directly or indirectly, altered the course of India's political-military history. Starting with the earliest Aryan tribesmen, every succeeding generation of warriors was compelled to import larger and larger herds of Arabian steeds and, simultaneously, to encourage horse farming in a country not at all suited for such efforts. The tens of thousands of animals that came from abroad fared poorly, if at all, in about ninety percent of the countryside. Only in selected areas of the north and west were horses successfully raised. As the Hindu people acquired control of lands to the west and then moved south, the opportunity for their soldiers to become expert cavalrymen diminished.

One major obstacle was India's climate. For several months of the year the subcontinent was subjected to monsoon rains, and its immigrant horse population was subjected to damp or enervating humidity. During the remaining months of the year, India was exceedingly hot and dry, also conditions that do not produce equine stamina and vitality.

Horses are susceptible to a variety of respiratory and circulatory diseases, and when exported and relocated, find it difficult to adjust to their new surroundings. In India's pre-modern period, thousands of horses were imported from Arabia only to die soon after their arrival in India because they had no resistance to local infections. Those few that managed to survive never regained their stamina and well-being.

The Hindus' efforts to breed horses successfully was also hindered by India's agricultural limitations. To raise to maturity herds of strong, spirited riding horses—animals that could be used in combat situations—it was essential to provide a proper diet of nutritious fodders. Horses, as is today common knowledge, thrive on grains such as oats, barley, maize, and gram supplemented with an adequate ration of hay or grass. In pre-modern India, many of these crops were not raised because of soil conditions, rainfall patterns, and other natural features of the land. The grains indigenous to India were not the customary diet for horses and difficult, if not impossible, for them to digest. Hindu grooms experimented with various exotic combinations of local nutrients. Horses were forced to eat the concoctions of boiled, sweet mush and either became poor, weakened replicas of their former selves[41] or became ill and died. The Hindus in fact, had no alternative—the land of India could not produce their customary, wholesome fodder.[42]

HINDUISM AND HORSE BREEDING

The second reason for the Hindus' sorry record of equine management is speculative. It involves traditional caste society and the prevailing values of Hindus concerning occupations. Only if this additional reason is included, can the Hindus' great lack of talent be explained adequately.

Horses are highly prone to a variety of illnesses and require considerable personalized attention if they are to thrive. Wherever bred, they need attendants who take a personal pride in their well-being, and who are knowledgeable and skillful in attending to their illnesses. Grooms, trainers, stable attendants, and veterinarians—like sailors and ship captains—must be men committed to their work. Most important, the attendants must be prepared to learn how to improve the general well-being of the animals.

There is no evidence that veterinary medicine in pre-Moghul India was either a respected occupation or even of concern to upper caste Hindus. Some writers claim that the early Indians had an advanced and sophisticated knowledge of animal diseases and their cure, but specific details concerning animal pathology are not offered. A distinction should be made, however, between the Buddhist-Jain community and the Hindus. When Buddhists and Jains had their greatest cultural impact in India (6th century B.C. until the 6th century A.D.), they not only cared for all animals in an enlightened and humane fashion, but also, according to some, established animal hospitals to minister to sick and disabled horses.[43] Their dedication to the principle of *ahimsa* without question influenced them. No reports, however, say anything about the attitudes and efforts of the Hindu community toward veterinary medicine. The omission is not accidental. Long before the Hindu people became the most prominent community in India and determined its dominant values, they scorned occupations related, directly or indirectly, to animal care. Hinduism did not specifically teach its practitioners to dislike animals or to be insensitive to their needs, but classical Hindu society did not hold veterinarians (or grooms and other horse-stable personnel) in high esteem. The interest that Hindus traditionally exhibited in animal affairs was of a different nature, and for goals unrelated to the physical well-being of the animals.

Hindu society did produce specialists in what today is known as the science of animal lore (*pasu-vidya*). Their efforts and experimentations, however, were neither medicinal nor therapeutic. Believing that the prolonged study of animals would provide them profound insights into the mysteries of the universe and endow them with special magical powers, many dedicated their lives simply to observing animal behavior or examining the distinguishing characteristics of one creature, such as snakes, lizards, or monkeys. Hindu literature praises the occult powers that stemmed from these studies, but there is no encouragement of serious animal pathology. Veterinary science made little progress in premodern Hindu India.

The origin of these adverse societal pressures (once again) was the caste system and its standards of proper behavior. Traditionally, Hindus studiously avoided coming into contact—even the most casual association—with animal blood, dirt, or excrement.[44] It was a cardinal principle of Hinduism that these were demeaning experiences that were to be avoided by all twice born men if at all possible.[45] Any work requiring a Hindu to become bloody or soiled was anathema. It was placed at the bottom of the Hindus' work scale.[46] Only those without caste, the poorest and the least educated were available for the care of animals. The orthodox, well-situated Hindu would not be attracted to this work because it would automatically jeopardize his caste status and expose him to severe societal sanctions.

Attending to the daily needs of horses, studying their sicknesses and prescribing medication must have been rejected outright by the best educated, socially prominent groups of the Hindu community. It was work regarded as mean and debasing, and it clashed with Hindu cultural values. As a consequence, Hindu India failed to produce veterinarians technically equipped to maintain the health of its imported herds, and the cavalry units of Hindu armies were deprived of the opportunity to match their opposition in strength, ability and endurance.

The thirteenth century observations of Marco Polo support these conclusions. In describing the sorry conditions that imported horses were subjected to in Malabar, he commented that the local residents "have no veterinaries." With obvious reference to the financial rewards the exporters realized from trading in horses, he added, "You can take it from me that the merchants who export them do not send out any veterinaries or allow any to go."[47]

CONCLUSIONS

Alexander's decisive victory at Hydaspes should have suggested to local warriors (and their Hindu successors) that traditional battlefield tactics were no longer adequate to meet military threats from abroad. His brilliant employment of cavalry troops, repeated with identical results so many times throughout succeeding generations, ought to have been a signal throughout India to eliminate war-elephant corps and to strengthen the more powerful and efficient cavalry troops. Hindu kings and their generals failed to apply one of the oldest and most basic military axioms: when one force has achieved victory through a novel weapons system or an imaginative tactical formation, the defeated army must duplicate this tactic or instrumentality. Stubborn fidelity to outmoded battlefield practices, blind adherence to military customs—no matter how prized or how successful in earlier periods —is a sure recipe for defeat and humiliation. Faced with situations all but identical to that of the Hindu people, most non-Indian civilizations were flexible enough to adopt their enemy's weapons systems and/or to imitate his battlefield formations. Indian generals learned nothing from their reverses.[48]

As the material presented in this chapter has shown, the Hindus were incapable of acting in such a manner. Even under the most propitious circumstances, traditions and customs are never easily overturned among the Hindu people. In emulating Western-style horse and cavalry units, however, discontinuance of the Hindus' time-honored reliance on war elephants was reinforced by exceedingly powerful caste prejudices and sanctions, both of which were reinforced by India's inhospitable climate and topography. Wave after wave of foreign invaders, consequently, sacked Indian cities, looted temples and shrines, and ultimately conquered the subcontinent.

REFERENCES

1. A. L. Basham, *The Wonder That Was India* (New York : Grove Press, 1954), p. 36. On the role of horses in pre-modern India generally, also consult V. R. Ramachandra Dikshitar, *War in Ancient India* (London : Macmillan and Company, 1944), pp. 174-9.

2. *Rig Veda,* IV, 38, 5-6; and quoted in A. L. Basham, *The Wonder That Was India* (New York : Grove Press, 1954), p. 36.

3. Romila Thapar, *A History of India,* I, (Baltimore, Md., Penguin Books), p. 35.

4. Within this prehistoric period the Aryans also increasingly honored the elephant in daily prayers. The *Rig Veda* contains a pas-

sage in which the head of a household places his elephant side by side with his son as object to be prayed for. See Mrs Manning, *Ancient and Medieval India* (London : Allen and Company, 1869), II, p. 351.

5. For an extended discussion of the pre-modern Hindu military system, see Abbe J. A. Dubois and Henry K. Beauchamp, *Hindu Manners, Customs and Ceremonies,* 3rd ed., (Oxford : Clarendon Press, 1906), pp. 667-84. Concerning Hindu cavalry, they simply state that "the cavalry formed the third division (of the Hindu military line). Indian generals in ancient times, however, did not rely much on this arm," p. 673.

6. Kautilya, *Arthasastra,* trans. R. Shamasastry, (Mysore : Mysore Printing and Publishing House, 1961), p. 399.

7. *ibid.,* pp. 398-399.

8. Noted in K. M. Panikkar, *Problems of Indian Defence* (New York : Asia Publishing House, 1960), p. 66.

9. Arrian, *Anabasis of Alexander,* trans. E. Iliff Robson, (London : William Heinemann, 1929), p. 59. Also see Megasthenes' comments concerning the use of elephants in war in early India, *Indica,* trans. E. Iliff Robson (London : William Heinemann, 1929), II, pp. 341-9.

10. John W. McCrindle, *The Invasion of India by Alexander The Great,* 2nd ed., (Westminster : A Constable, 1896), pp. 102-3.

11. *ibid.,* p. 104.

12. *ibid.*

13. *ibid.,* p. 105.

14. *ibid.,* p. 105-107.

15. Reporting of conditions in the middle of the ninth century A.D. Suleiman wrote of a local king that "When he goes out to battle, he is followed by 50,000 elephants." H. M. Elliot and John Dowson, *The History of India as Told by its Own Historians* (London : Trübner and Co.,1871), I, p. 25.

16. The quote is by Duarte Barbosa and cited in Donald F. Lach, *India in the Eyes of Europe* (Chicago : University of Chicago Press, 1968), p. 380.

17. This comment was written by Fernao Lopes de Castanheda and also is cited in Lach, *ibid.*

18. K. A. Nilkantha Sastri, *A History of South India from Prehistoric Times to the Fall of Vijayanagar,* 3rd. ed., (London : Oxford University Press, 1966), p. 305.

19 .For discussion concerning the size of Vijayanagar armies, including the number of elephant troops used, see Robert Sewell, *A Forgotten Empire* (London : Swann Sonnenschein, 1900), pp. 147-51 and p. 201.

20. The details of the Battle of Talikota are taken from K. A. Nilkantha Sastri, *A History of South India,* 3rd ed., (London : Oxford University Press, 1966), pp. 294-6.

21. *Military History of India* (Calcutta : M. C. Sarkar, 1960), p. 15.

22. P. C. Chakravarti, *The Art of War in Ancient India* (Dacca : University of Dacca, nd.), p. 47.

23. This point was regularly noted by Muslim invaders of India in their writings. Thus, Timor, the late fourteenth century conqueror of India, wrote in his autobiography, "It has been constantly dinned into the ears of my soldiers that the chief reliance of the armies of Hindustan was on their mighty elephants; that these animals, in complete armour, marched into battle in front of their forces, and that arrows and swords were of no use against them; that in height and bulk they were like small mountains and their strength was such that at a given signal they could tear up great trees and knock down strongly built walls; that in the battle field they could take up the horse and his rider with their trunks and hurl them into the air. Some of the soldiers, in the doubt natural to man, brought some little of what they had heard to my attention, so when I assigned their respective positions to the princes and *amirs* of the right and left wing and of the centre, I enquired of the learned and good men that accompanied my army . . . where they would like to be placed in the day of battle. They had been with me in many campaigns, and had witnessed many a great battle, but the stories about the elephants of India had so affected them that they instantly replied that they would like to be placed with the ladies while the battle was in progress .. .." Sir H. M. Elliot and John Dowson, *The History of India as Told by Its Own Historians* (London : Trübner, and Co., 1869), III, pp. 437-38.

24. E. H. Warmington, *The Commerce Between the Roman Empire and India* (Cambridge : University Press, 1928), p. 150 and pp. 262-3.

25. *The Travels of Marco Polo,* ed. Hugh Murray, (New York : Harper and Bros., 1845), p. 260. Also see R. A. Jairazbhoy, *Foreign Influence in Ancient India* (New York : Asia Publishing House, 1963), pp. 171ff.

26. The account of the meeting is found in Firishtan's *History of the Rise of Muhammedan Power in India* and is quoted in Robert Sewell, *A Forgotten Empire* (London : Swann and Sonnenschein, 1900), p. 72.

27. Quoted in Robert Sewell, *A Forgotten Empire* (London : Swann and Sonnenschein, 1900), p. 72.

28. Robert Sewell, *A Forgotten Empire* (London : Swann and Sonnenschein, 1900), pp. 123-4. Also see K. A. Nilakantha Sastri, *A History of South India,* 3rd ed. (London : Oxford University Press, 1966), p. 279, and *India in the Eyes of Europe,* ed. Donald F. Lach, (Chicago : University of Chicago Press, 1965), p. 370.

29. See Robert Sewell, *A Forgotten Empire* (London : Swann and Sonnenschein, 1900), p. 126.

30. *ibid.,* p. 186.

31. Robert Sewell, *A Forgotten Empire* (London : Swann and Son-nenschein, 1900), p. 186.

32. *The Chronicle of Fernao Nuniz* states that the Vijayanagar king "caused horses to be brought from Oromus and Adeem into his kingdom and thereby gave great profit to the merchants, paying them for the horses just as they asked. He took them dead or alive at three for a thousand *parados,* and of those that died at sea they brought him the tail only, and he paid for it just as if it had been alive." Included in Robert Sewell's *A Forgotten Empire* (London : Swann and Sonnenschein, 1900), p. 307.

33. These details are from the writings of a late sixteenth century Venetian merchant who visited India, Cesare de Fredrici, and are noted in Donald F. Lach, *India in the Eyes of Europe* (Chicago : Univ. of Chicago Press, 1965), p. 470.

34. Quoted in Donald F. Lach, *India in the Eyes of Europe* (Chicago : Univ. of Chicago Press, 1965), p. 380. "These colossal beasts when prepared for war are covered with copper trimmings and their trunks are similarly protected. On their tusks are fastened great two-edged swords with which they kill many of the enemy by rampaging through their ranks. Wooden towers are strapped to the backs of the leading elephants from which as many as eight archers launch their arrows against the enemy."

35. There are, of course, much earlier observations of Western visitors concerning India's lack of horses. In the ninth century A.D. Suleiman the merchant stated without further elaboration that "The Indians have but few horses..." Eusebius Renaudot, *Ancient Accounts of India and China by Two Mohammedan Travellers* (London : Sam Harding, 1733), p. 37.

36. *The Travels of Marco Polo,* ed. Hugh Murray, (New York : Harper and Bros., 1845), p. 262.

37. C. Northcote Parkinson, *East and West* (Boston : Houghton Mifflin Co., 1963), p. 137.

38. H. M. Elliot, *The History of India as told by its own Historians,* ed. John Dowson, (London : Trübner and Co., 1871), III, pp. 33-4.

39. Jean Baptiste Tavernier, *Travels in India,* 2nd ed., trans. V. Ball, (London : Macmillan and Co., 1889), I, p. 103.

40. *ibid.,* p. 283.

41. An early nineteenth century traveller stated that no horses breed "on the whole western side of the peninsula; or if by accident a foal is dropped, it is worth nothing." William Vincent, *The Commerce and Navigation of the Ancients in the Indian Ocean* (London : T. Cadell and W. Davies, 1807), II, p. 510.

42. Hindu grooms of the nineteenth century continued to feed their horses a similar diet. See Mountstuart Elphinstone, *The History of India* (London : John Murray, 1841), I, pp. 14-15. He notes that Indian horses were fed a diet of boiled pulse, wheat straw, grass and large amounts of sweet jowar and bajra.

43. Major Sharma argues that "Veterinary science was very advanced (in ancient India)." *Indian Army Through the Ages* (Bombay : Allied Publishers Private Limited, 1966), p. 23. However, he cites examples that deal with the feeding off horses, work that is generally thought to be reserved for grooms and stable attendants. Nothing in his treatise suggests Hindus were notably distinguished in studying the physical ailments of their charges. Also see Franklin Edgerton, trans., *The Elephant-Lore of The Hindus* (New Haven : Yale Univ. Press, 1931), passim.

44. This feature of Hindu behavior remains unaltered even in the contemporary period. Robert Montgomery Martin, for example, noted in 1858 that ". . . even the touch of dead bodies (was) deemed the extreme *of pollution*", *The Indian Empire* (London : The London Printing and Publishing Co., 1958), I, p. 46.

45. The comments of the late Jean Dubois are relevant. Discussing general condition in south India during the early nineteenth century, he wrote : "There are several kinds of animals, especially dogs, to touch which would defile a Brahmin. It is very interesting to watch their movements, and the care they will take to avoid the familiar caresses of these faithful companions of man. If, in spite of their efforts, the dog really does touch them, they are obliged to hurry off immediately and plunge with all their clothes on, into water, and thus remove from both their person and their garments the stain which they had involuntarily acquired by the touch of one of these unclean animals." Abbe Jean A. Dubois, *Hindu Manners, Customs and Ceremonies,* Henry K. Beauchamp, trans., 3rd ed., (Oxford : Clarendon Press, 1906), p. 185.

46. In discussing this feature of Hindu society, K. C. Chakravarti states that, ". . . . the higher caste Hindus were forbidden to dissect human or animal bodies. This practically meant a serious handicap for the development of the science of medicine. The prejudice was so strong that when the Calcutta Medical College was started in the thirties of the last century (i.e. the 1830's—ed.) high caste Hindu students were not forthcoming . . ." *Ancient Indian Culture,* 2nd ed. rev. (Bombay : Vora and Co., 1961), p. 272.

47. Quoted in Romila Thapar, *A History of India* (Baltimore : Penguin Press, 1966), p. 208.

48. Major Gautam Sharma, *Indian Army Through the Ages* (Bombay : Allied Publishers Private Limited, 1966), p. 20. P. C. Chakravarti sadly notes that "(As) in the 4th century B.C., so in the 11th and 12 century A.D., the superiority of foreign horsemen once again decided the fate of India." *The Art of War in Ancient India* (Dacca : Univ. of Dacca, nd.), p. 36.

Chapter VIII

THE MORALE OF HINDU ARMIES

The Tradition

Beginning with their earliest accounts of Muslim-Hindu military engagements, Muslim historians repeatedly described the dishonorable battlefield behavior of their opponents. Hindu soldiers, they wrote, deserted their positions whenever the fighting became particularly fierce or as soon as it appeared that the invaders had won a major military advantage. One of the most frequently described situations in Muslim literature of the period is of a massive Hindu army fleeing in total disarray when a pivotal outpost had been overrun, when its defense perimeter had collapsed, or when a king had been killed or seriously wounded during the fight. Such misfortunes, they wrote, were the signal for the Hindu army to give up the contest and accept defeat. Only infrequently did the Muslim historians mention a Hindu counter-attack or a regrouping of remaining Hindu troops to re-challenge the enemy.

The deplorable behavior of the Hindu military did not stop here, according to the Muslim writers. When a prisoner of war was captured by a victorious Muslim army, Hindu men (along with their wives and other female companions) were said to have converted to the Islamic religion with no decent concern for their Hindu heritage or cultural traditions. The defeated Hindu king was often pictured as the most eager to convert, rushing to accept his captors' invitation to turn to Mohammed as the true God and abandon the religious, cultural and the social traditions that represent Hinduism.

Muslim historians who wrote about India during the years of Islamic triumphs were not, however, objective reporters of these battles or what followed when the fighting ended. Muslim writers deliberately exaggerated the manly and martial qualities of their royal patron and his troops because their reputations and possibly their lives depended on a lauditory exposition of Islamic strategy and battlefield conduct. Their accounts were also influenced by their religious heritage. In the classical Koranic tradition, any Muslim soldier who died on the battlefield while fighting the enemy of Allah was considered a martyr and promised eternal life in paradise without trial on resurection and judgment day.[1] Furthermore, the Muslim historian could not be expected to be dispassionate when writing about the Hindus since their idolatrous and despised religion was an anathema to the observant Mohammedan.

It is, nevertheless, reasonable to conclude that Muslim reporting in general is an accurate summary of the Hindu military and civilian population's personal behavior in battle and when they came under Muslim control. When Hindu military units lost the initiative and it appeared that their positions would be overwhelmed by Muslim power, they probably did desert their posts and flee to avoid capture. They may have been unwilling to re-form their units and return to the fight, but they may have been motivated by cultural factors, not by fear. Hindu prisoners of war—kings, troops and their camp followers—as well as behind-the-line civilians may well have embraced Islam with some eagerness, agreeing to accept the Koran and adopt the Islamic way of life. But they may have converted to Mohammedanism because their experiences had hopelessly compromised their standing as orthodox Hindus, rather than because of fear of immediate physical punishment or worse. In other words, it may have been cultural pressures that drove Hindus away from their heritage.

Can such a theory be supported in fact? Can culturally rooted behavior norms explain the Hindus' performance? The subsequent sections will examine the effects of Hindu beliefs and day-to-day practices on Hindu troops as well as on the population in general.

THE EVIDENCE : HINDUS AS FRONTLINE SOLDIERS

During the reign of Subuktigin, Turkish armies began their first noteworthy invasion of Hindu India. The campaigns continued periodically until Islamic power was firmly and permanently installed throughout the northern regions of the subcontinent. Subuktigin's initial raid took place in 986-7 A.D.; *the* so-called Slave Kings, the first Islamic rulers to be established in Delhi, assumed sovereignty in 1206 A.D. During these nearly three centuries, various Hindu armies struggled to throw back the Turks

and re-gain their lands. They applied what must be regarded
as traditional Hindu military strategies and tactics, fighting with
customary Hindu vigor and determination.

The pre-Slave King era was the last period of Indian history
when the mass of Hindu people could observe the various forms
of their religion without strong Muslim interference and conduct
their personal lives and caste affairs unmolested by a competing
group. A selective review of the narratives written by Muslim
historians between 986-1206 A.D., and subsequently during the
Moghul period, provides us with a picture of the field behavior
of Hindu troops and their conduct upon being taken prisoner by
the Muslim Turks. What follows are three chronologically
separate instances when Hindu troops fled the battlefield en masse
immediately after experiencing a military reverse, but long before they were irrevocably defeated.

One of Subuktigin's earliest raids was directed at the important Hindu city of Lamgham, which one Muslim historian described as "celebrated for its great strength and abounding in
wealth."[2] The local Hindu ruler at Lamgham decided to fight
rather than surrender his capital and its resources. He is reported
to have collected and positioned an army of more than one hundred thousand men, stationing them at key locations about the
periphery of the city. Subuktigin, in turn, brought up an equally
impressive battle force. After some initial skirmishing, the two
great armies joined in battle. The initial victory—but not one
that appears to have been calamitous for the Hindus—was won
by Subuktigin's men. Thereupon, the Hindus left their other
perimeter defense positions, and most, if not all, of the Hindu
troops fled Lamgham. They abandoned their arms, provisions,
and even their animals as they rushed to separate themselves from
the now triumphant Turks. Al'Utbi, who chronicled the battle,
stated :

> The Hindus turned their tails towards their heads like
> frightened dogs, and the Raja was contented to offer the
> best things in his most distant provinces to the conqueror,
> on condition that the hair of the crowns of their heads
> should not be shaven off. So the country in that neigh-
> bourhood was clear and open before Amir Subuktigin, and
> he seized all the wealth which was found in it. . . .[3]

Mahmud of Ghazni was the next Turkish ruler whose raids

disrupted the peace of northern India, and he was no less determined than his predecessors to prevail over the Hindu defenders. In the campaign he waged in 1018 A.D., he marched his troops against a leading prince, Kulchand. According to Muslim sources, Kulchand had defeated many of his fellow Hindu rulers in the years prior to Mahmud's attack. His capital city consisted of "much power, great wealth, many brave soldiers, large elephants, and strong forts, which were secure from attack and capture."[4] What happened at this fort, Al'Utbi writes, was a repetition of the debacle at Lamgham. The preliminary skirmishes between a relatively few of the total forces outside the city's gates were won by the attacking Muslims. Large numbers of Hindu troops still manned peripheral locations and the fort itself. There is no reason to assume that Kulchand, at some point, did not order a counter-attack to relieve pressure at points where his troops were suffering losses, but the entire Hindu army crumbled almost immediately after the first perimeter position fell. The following is the account left by Al'Utbi :

The infidels, when they found all their attempts fail, deserted the fort, and tried to cross the foaming river which flowed on the side of the fort, thinking that beyond it they would be in security; but many of them were slain, taken, or drowned in the attempt, and went to the fire of hell. Nearly fifty thousand men were killed and drowned, and became the prey of beasts and crocodiles. Kulchand, taking his dagger, slew his wife, and then drove it into his own body.[5]

Three centuries later when Babur and his Moghul troops sought hegemony in northern India,[6] Hindu troops behaved in much the same manner as their forebears. Following the defeat of Rana Sanga's armies before Kanwah, only one significant center of Rajput power remained, commanded by Medini Raj at Chanderi. The contest between the invaders and Medini's men was not long in coming : on January 28, 1528 A.D., the two armies met. On the second day of the seige, the king concluded that further resistance to Moghul power was without purpose, and decided to abandon the fight. All Hindu women within the fortress were killed by Medini's men, acting on orders of their ruler. Medini himself and his entire force removed their clothing and rushed naked into the lines of Babur's blood-thirsty men. For these faithful Hindu warriors, death was preferable to capture and humiliation by Muslim jailors.[7]

THE EVIDENCE : HINDUS AS PRISONERS OF WAR

Muslim historians report that captured Hindus, military as well as civilians, enthusiastically embraced Islam and willingly rejected Hinduism. In reading such reports—and there are many descriptions of such situations—one is not favorably impressed with the religious dedication of the Hindu people, not with their allegiance to its cultural beliefs. Hindu kings, princes, their battle troops, and the civilians caught up in the endless wars fought in India all were prepared to turn their backs on Hinduism as a way of life and convert to Islam. Most Muslim writers explain the absence of Hindu martyrs either as the Hindus' wish to remain alive or, (and this reason is given far greater emphasis) their realization that Hinduism was a false and degrading religion.

A typical episode reported in Muslim histories occurred in 1018 A.D., when Mahmud of Ghazni laid waste the Indian landscape. By this time Mahmud had already led eleven earlier raids against the Hindus, and the looting and plunder of his troops had brought great suffering to everyone in their path. The military objective of his twelfth campaign was the Hindu city of Baran, ruled by Herdat, a powerful Hindu king. The two armies ultimately met and engaged in a hotly contested battle before Herdat's forces, at last overcome by Muslim power, were forced to surrender. The king was taken prisoner and confined in a jail. There he was pressed to convert. Al'Utbi described the result :

> Herdat reflected that his safety would be secured by conforming to the religion of Islam, since God's sword was drawn from the scabbard, and the whip of punishment was uplifted. He came forth, therefore, with ten thousand men, who all proclaimed their anxiety for conversion, and their rejection of idols.[8]

A THEORY TO EXPLAIN HINDU MILITARY ROUTS AND RELIGIOUS CONVERSIONS

In all major civilizations of the world the return home of a soldier who has been held prisoner of war has traditionally been an occasion of great happiness and prolonged celebration by his family and friends. The town in which the man was raised and oftentimes the state to which he owed political allegiance have shared in the festivities. If the soldier or civilian had managed to escape from a prisoner of war camp, the community has been all the more exuberant.

Hindu prisoners of war who managed to escape from a Muslim jail and return to their homes, however received a far different welcome. There were no celebrations of any sort. The members of his immediate family, particularly those who were pious Hindus, were likely to resent his reappearance and almost certainly refused to embrace (or even touch) him. The members of his caste group were no less hostile and aloof, and probably were considerably more destructive. He was likely to be denied most, if not all, of his caste privileges and rights. Everywhere he turned it is probable that former friends and relatives were all too ready to humiliate, ostracize and villify him. His future within the only societal unit he had known from birth was indeed bleak.

While there are only a few detailed reports available that discuss such prisoner of war treatment among Hindu people prior to the sixteenth century, they are sufficiently precise to provide a clear picture of the reception such a man would receive.

Alberuni's eleventh century chronicle of his travels throughout India is the principal source of this information, and he is particularly graphic. In introducing his observations, and possibly preparing his reader for the material that follows, Alberuni states that Brahmins living in northern India had repeatedly told him that they regarded a returning prisoner of war as a threat to their religious and cultural purity. The soldiers not only embarrassed their family and their particular caste, but also endangered the standards of cleanliness of both.

The Hindu escapee, Alberuni continued, was not joyfully received; instead, his return brought great pain and sorrow. From the moment of his capture, the soldier had become an out caste to all observant Hindus, civilians and military alike. Those at home assumed he had associated with Muslims while in captivity, and the fact that this association was involuntary was immaterial. The captive had eaten and drunk according to Muslim standards, not the norms of the Hindus. Although during imprisonment he lived with other Hindus, he did not adhere to the caste precepts of segregation and isolation. He did not perform the obligatory daily Hindu rituals, particularly bathing, and he failed to observe the Hindus' strict dietary code. Every morsel of food and every drop of water the prisoner received from his Muslim jailors was regarded as contaminated because non-Hindus were associated with its collection, preparation and serving. Here, too, the involuntary nature of the man's predicament was of no significance.

These standards, Alberuni relates, applied to both men of high caste and lesser "twice born" soldiers. There was one distinction, however, between the treatment accorded Brahmins and non-Brahmins. For the latter group, there was the possibility of expiation for the defilement acquired in captivity. Even for the non-Brahmins, however, the process of regaining caste purity and re-establishing caste status was a dreadful, denegrating experience. It was a rite so vulgar that the basic dignity of the individual, let alone a hero-soldier, could hardly survive. Alberuni describes the cleaning process :

> ... the Hindus order that they (the returning prisoners of war—ed.) should fast by way of expiation, that they bury them in the dung, stale, and milk of cows for a certain number of days, till they get into a state of fermentation. Then they drag them out of the dirt and give them a similar dirt to eat, and more of the like.[9]

This sorded atonement was available only to lesser caste members. Returning Brahmins were prohibited from such rituals. They were doomed to be treated forever as defiled, impure and disgraced men, isolated socially from other Brahmins of good standing. They were a lost group, and powerless to remove the stain of contamination. Again quoting from Alberuni's account :

> [The returning Brahmin] is never allowed to return into the condition of life in which he was before he was carried off as a prisoner. And how should that be possible ? If a Brahmin eats in the house of a Sudra for sundry days, he is expelled from his caste and can never regain it.[10]

The Hindus also had special rules for kings captured by their enemies : Kings were spared the humiliating experiences of other captured Hindus, but their fate was not much better. When Jaipal was defeated on the battlefield by Mahmud of Ghazni in 997 A.D., Mahmud specified that Jaipal must make a yearly payment of booty and accept Mahmud as his overlord. It was so agreed, and Jaipal was allowed to return to his palace to carry out his obligations under the agreement. "There is a custom among these men," Alberuni wrote, "that if any one is taken prisoner by an enemy, as in this case Jaipal was by the Musalmains, it is not lawful for him to continue reign."[11] Alberuni reports :

> Jaipal, therefore, saw that he was captive in the prison of old age and degradation, he thought death by cremation preferable to shame and dishonour. So he commenced with shaving his hair off, and then threw himself upon the fire till he was burnt.[12]

CONCLUSIONS

Because there were no pre-modern Hindu historians, it is difficult either to support or refute Alberuni's description of local treatment of returning prisoners of war. Assuming, however, that Alberuni was an accurate reporter and that Hindus were not heroic fighters and hastily fled the battlefields, who can blame them ? Capture by an invader was akin to a sentence of death. If the captive was a Brahmin, he realized his religious standing and his societal role—the quintessence of his life—were forfeited forever. A lower caste soldier knew that when he regained his liberty he would be compelled to undergo a purification ritual as offensive as any ceremony in Hindu literature. The circumstances of capture made no difference. The decisive event that irretrievably sealed his fate—was being made captive of the Muslim enemy, forced to live according to daily practices and values he believed to be an anathema. As Leitch Ritchie has observed, "after a defeat, the soldiers had no resources to fall back upon, no allies to fly to, no recruits to muster, and it was hopeless to rally."[13]

Muslim historians judged Hindu troops by wholly inappropriate Muslim religio-military standards. The standards of two peoples differed on the battlefield and in many places. Had the Muslims been more aware of the dreadful stigma that capture signified to the Hindus, their strident comments might have been more temperate.

REFERENCES

1. Majid Khadduri, *War and Peace in the Law of Islam* (Baltimore : Johns Hopkins Press, 1955), pp. 55-6.
2. Sir H. M. Elliot and John Dowson, *The History of India as Told by its Own Historians* (London : Trübner and Co., 1869), p. 22.
3. *ibid.*, p. 23.
4. Sir H. M. Elliot and John Dowson, *The History of India as Told by its Own Historians* (London : Trübner and Co., 1869), p. 43.
5. *ibid.*
6. See supra, Chapter II.
7. The following is in part Babar's account of the collapse of Chanderi : "The citadel was attacked on all sides . . . Though the Pagans exerted themselves to the utmost, hurling down stones from above, and throwing over flaming substances on their heads, the troops nevertheless persevered . . . (They) scaled the walls in two or three places. The Pagans, who were stationed in the covered way, took to flight, and that part of the work was taken. They did not defend the upper fort with so much obstinacy, and were quickly put to flight; the assailants climbed up and entered the upper fort by storm. In a short time the Pagans, in a state of complete nudity, rushed out to attack us, put numbers of my people to flight, and leaped over the ramparts . . . The reason of this desperate sally from their works was, that, on giving up the place for lost, they had put to death the whole of their wives and women, and having resolved to perish, had stripped themselves naked, in which condition they had rushed out to the fight . . ." Sir H. M. Elliot and John Dowson, *The History of India as Told by its Own Historians* (London : Trübner and Co., 1869), IV, p. 277.
8. Sir H. M. Elliot and John Dowson, *The History of India as Told by its Own Historians* (London : Trübner and Co., 1869), p. 42.
9. Edward C. Sachau, ed., *Alberuni's India* (London : Trübner and Co., 1888), I, p. 162.
10. *ibid.* At another point in his study, Alberuni stated "(T)hey never desire that a thing which once has been polluted should be purified and thus recovered, as, under ordinary circumstances, if anybody or anything has become unclean, he or it would strive to regain the state of purity." See *ibid.,* I, p. 20.
11. *ibid.,* I, p. 21.

12. Sir H. M. Elliot and John Dowson, *The History of India as Told by Its Own Historians* (London : Trübner and Co., 869), II, p. 27. Another Muslim historian, Hamdu-lla Mustaufi, in his study of the same period, *Tárikh-I Guzída,* summarized Jaipal's position as follows : "It is a rule among the Hindus that a king who has been twice made prisoner by Musulmans ought no longer to reign, and that his fault can only be purged by fire. Jaipal, therefore, made the kingdom over to his son and burnt himself ...." See *ibid.*, III, p. 64.

13. Leitch Ritchie, *A History of the Indian Empire* (London : W. H. Allen, 1948), I, p. 16-17.

CHAPTER IX

THE HINDUS AND THEIR MILITARY ALLIANCE POLICIES

THE TRADITION

INDIAN MILITARY annals report very few occasions when a group of neighboring Hindu kings joined together to form an alliance to fight an invading army.[1] Repeatedly Hindu princes and their aides were defeated in decisive engagements when, if they had pooled their military power, they might have saved their respective kingdoms, if not India itself. They chose, however, to be crushed in seratim rather than combine forces to better withstand foreign challenges. Indeed, if records are carefully examined, there appears to be only one occasion when a sizeable group of Hindu kings agreed to allow a single command to direct their troops against a common enemy.[2] The prevailing pattern of military behavior throughout the pre-modern era shifted between endless fratricidal wars, irrespective of the severe dangers from invading troops and feeble efforts to form a common front, generally tardily conceived, poorly defined, disorganized and ineffectual.[3] Central Asian invaders struck repeatedly against India. They followed the same general strategic program to defeat a local Hindu prince, eliminate him by death or vassalage, and then use his territory as a base from which to carry out the next phase of their operations, pillage and/or conquest. Sometimes the invaders chose only to raid the northern kingdoms before returning to their base, laden with enormous quantities of booty and prisoners.

Had the Hindu rulers wanted to pool their resources, they would have achieved important military advantages and impressive power. What they lacked was a common purpose. Sharma, for example, points out that "but for lack of foresight on the part of the rulers in north India, these invaders could well have been checked and halted long before they reached the line of the Indus River."[4] Romila Thapar, also notes the unconventional Hindu military behavior, but only hints at the underlying reason(s):

The biggest puzzle is why a conjoint effort of the various Indian rulers was not made, through the centuries, to defend the north-west passes. Time and again various invaders had poured in through these passes, yet little attempt was made to prevent this, the defence of the region lying arbitrarily in the hands of local rulers. Even if the building of a Great Wall was not feasible, the construction of fortifications along the passes was always a possibility. Perhaps there was a basic lack of consciousness of the need for defence.[5]

Here, then, is a pattern of political-military behavior so radically different from the practices of other contemporary civilizations (East or West) that it strongly implies that novel, local pressures and prejudices were operating within the Hindu world.

The absence of alliance politics is especially conspicuous in northern India during the Turkish invasion of Subuktigin and his son, Mahmud. Between 986 and 1026 A.D., these two Ghaznawid conquerors passed through the Himalayan passes at least thirty times and pillaged a wide area of India without triggering the formation of a determined Hindu coalition. By this time the Rajputs had become the dominant group within the Hindu world of northern and western India, and it is their military actions and reactions that will be examined here. They had emerged as the prime defenders of a revitalized Hinduism and accordingly bore the brunt of Muslim aggression, particularly the attacks of Subuktigin and Mahmud. Indian historians oftentimes refer to the Rajputs of this period as the *Pratiharas* or the door-keepers of the country.[6] Their military conduct in a real sense was characteristic of the behavior within Hindu society of the eleventh and twelfth centuries. In discussing the assimilation of the Rajputs, Banerjee says, "there might be foreign elements in the Hindu population of the 'Rajput period,' but there were few recognisable foreign elements in the Hindu society and culture or in the Hindu political system on the eve of the Turkish conquest."[7]

Before settling down in northern India, the Rajputs are believed to have lived for some time in Central Asia. Even there, they acquired a reputation as an ultra-martial people. Their male population, trained from puberty to act aggressively and to regard warfare as the highest expression of masculinity, is reported to have fought regularly with consuming passion and high attention to chivalry.   During the fifth-sixth centuries A.D., various Rajput tribes, after crushing the then existing Hindu military organization of the north, began to settle there permanently, and slowly but steadily entered Hindu society.   By the eighth century A.D., the Rajputs had become the main defenders of India. They not only adopted Hinduism as their dominant religious philosophy, but also assumed the status and duties of the ancient *kshatriya* caste.   The Rajputs' political-military organization was a feudal system that emphasized the clan and the loyalty owed by the mass to clan princes, who in turn, were subject to the king's authority.   The dominant characteristic of the typical Rajput clan system was a passion for fighting and attainment of glory on the battlefield.   Throughout the period of Moghul raids into India, the Rajput clans fought a seemingly endless series of wars against one another.   The victory of one Rajput dynasty settled little politically; instead it lay the groundwork for a future attack by the defeated state.   It was a system, as will be demonstrated, that not only made political unification of the north impossible, but also guaranteed the failure of a common military effort against the invaders.

THE GHAZNAWID INVASION

In an earlier chapter the military invasions of the Muslim Turks from Ghazni were mentioned.   The Ghaznawid armies struck India for the first time in 986 A.D. Over the next thirty-nine years these armies periodically invaded the northwest area and, indeed, utilized the same invasion routes time and time again.   They devastated the land, leveled cities and destroyed farms, annihilated the men, women and children they captured, and stripped the countryside of some of the most revered religious treasures of Hinduism.   Most histories of India recount in elaborate detail the prolonged successes of the Ghaznawids, particularly their most brilliant sultan, Mahmud of Ghazni. What is absent from such chronicles, however, is any description of the weak military responses of the Hindu kings and their sorry efforts to defend themselves and their lands. Never once did the local Hindus organize an effective defense of the country.

Any analysis of this period of Indian history, it must be noted, is dependent on accounts prepared by Muslim writers,

and all were hopelessly biased. Muslim prejudices notwithstanding, it appears that the combined military strength of the
several Hindu kingdoms that suffered most grievously during the
forty years of Ghaznawid attacks equalled—if not exceeded—
the troop strength of the attacking Muslims. Furthermore, the
Hindus held other important advantages. Their lines of com-
munication were shorter, supplies were available locally, and
they had intimate knowledge of the terrain. The various Hindu
armies that clashed with the Ghaznawid forces, it is important
to make clear, were not so poorly directed that defeat in every
battle was a foregone conclusion. Even a few Muslim writers
concede that some Hindu troops conducted themselves with distinction in battle. What the Hindus failed to develop at any
time in the pre-modern period was a unified defense strategy
that would offer them a reasonably good chance of halting invasions from the northwest. They were still as disunited and
eager to battle one another as when they first arrived in India,
at least two thousand years earlier. Throughout the Ghaznawid period, mutual jealousy, suspicion among the ruling elite,
and a policy of plotting one's neighbor's demise combined with
indifference to the fate of neighboring Hindus and a surprising
disregard for the sanctity of Hindu temples and religious shrines.
Each helped produce a pathetically weak, all but uncoordinated
defense system.

The first Ghaznawid invasion of India began in 986 A.D.,
when Subuktigin marched his troops into Hindu India. The
raid was so successful that a second attack was launched the
following year. This time, according to some reports, Jaipal, a
Rajput king in the path of the invasion, made an effort to rally
other local rulers similarly threatened. He called on them to
form a league that would unite for the common defense the
several armies the kings commanded, but his proposal does not
seem to have progressed beyond the most elementary stages of
discussion. Accordingly, Subuktigin defeated all the Hindu
armies he encountered in seratim, and sacked a wide area of
the north before returning to his capital at Ghazni.

Some contemporary authorities on Rajput history dispute
the story that a confederacy was attempted. Thus Banerjee
writes of the parochialism of Rajput princes :
   . . . It would be going too far if we assume that the

Rajput princes of the tenth century realised the gravity of the Turkish menace and offered their support to the Shahis (Jaipal's clan) in defending the north-west. It was more natural for them to look upon the crisis of the Shahi kingdom as a purely local affair and to pursue their own schemes of conquest nearer home.[8]

In 997 A.D., Subuktigin's son Mahmud of Ghazni (literally Mahmud the Infidel Slayer) succeeded to the throne and resolved to continue his father's policy of raiding Hindu territory. Mahmud was so confident of his military power and acumen that he is alleged to have decided to attack the Hindu kingdoms to the south every year that he was able to direct a campaign. Between 1000 and 1027 A.D., he led seventeen separate invasions of India. Mahmud's armies usually entered the subcontinent in September or October when the weather and terrain were propitious for marching and fighting. Once in India proper, they would pillage and destroy the territory they conquered with utter ruthlessness before returning to Ghazni the following spring. The rapiousness of one campaign was exceeded only by the excesses of the next. Dozens of Hindu shrines and temples, some among the most venerated within the Hindu world, fell under Mahmud's control and were stripped of everything of value before being reduced to dust and rubble. Hindu religious objects and treasures worshipped for centuries became part of the booty Mahmud seized and shipped back to his royal treasury or distributed to his men. Thousands of local residents caught up in the wars were slaughtered or taken prisoner. Hindu women were used by the Muslim troops for their immediate pleasures.

Few invading armies in history ever depended less on the element of surprise and new strategies in attacking enemy strongholds. Each invasion route passed through the same Himalayan passes as the preceding, and the troops forded the same rivers and marched along the same main roads as the year earlier. When they returned to their home base in Ghazni, the Muslim troops, whether because of general military circumstances or because they were creatures of habit, retired from India in the same, ordained manner.

During the twenty-five years of attacks and raids led by Mahmud, fragmentary reports mention only five occasions when local, quarrelling Hindu kings attempted to combine their military forces. Each of these efforts occurred under circumstances that all but guaranteed failure. Usually the scenario found one or two Rajput kings facing certain defeat from the onrushing, more powerful Ghaznawid army and *in extremis* appealed to a neighboring Hindu king to help prevent their impending ruin. Never once throughout the quarter century was there a judiciously planned meeting of local Hindu (Rajput) rulers to try to develop an integrated coalition that might deal with the next Muslim attack more proficiently. Political responsibility, according to fixed Rajput ideas, did not extend to territory outside a king's governing control. Hopelessly divided and rent by decades of the most bitter internecine fighting, the Hindu-Rajputs could hardly have been a weaker adversary for the invaders.

Not even the destruction of the most venerated Hindu shrines was sufficiently provocative or loathsome to bring about a collective Hindu response. Whether the people of northern India were indifferent to the desecration of their shrines, were poorly informed about the pillage, or were intimidated by the Muslims' power to seek retribution, they did accept the invaders' plunder.

The Hindus' reaction to the leveling of the holy city of Mathura is typical of their response throughout the period of the brutal Ghaznawid attacks. Even Muslim historians acknowledge the city was a place of awesome beauty. Al'Utbi states that one of its buildings was an "exquisite structure, which the inhabitants [believed to have] been built, not by men, but by Genii" (Gods—ed.)[9]. The most impressive structure was its main temple :

> In the middle of the city there was a temple larger and firmer than the rest, which can neither be described or painted. The Sultan thus wrote respecting it :—'If any should wish to construct a building equal to this, he would not be able to do it without expending an hundred thousand red dinars, and it would occupy two hundred years, even though the most experienced and able workmen were employed'.[10]

Another Muslim source identifies the temple as "the birthplace of Krishna . . . whom the Hindus venerate as an incarnation of God."[11] Mathura also has been called one of the most celebrated seats of the Hindu religion and learning of the time.

Given such great significance, the response—or lack of it—

from the several Hindu kings and population in general is astounding. "When the Sultan reached the city," Nizam-ud din Ahmad states, "no one came out to oppose him. The Sultan's army plundered the whole city and set fire to the temples."[12]

Mahmud's men's conduct toward Hindu women and girls was more rapacious and predatory than most of the early invaders of India. At the end of one especially hard-fought seige, it is stated, the Ghaznawids captured 200,000 Hindu females. Eventually most of them were sent back to the harems in Ghazni, marched there over many miles of Hindu-controlled territory. Muslim historians report several other similar events. While the numbers of Hindu women seized seems inflated, there can be little doubt that the Muslim armies, acting as victors in a manner peculiar to those times and location, stripped many local kingdoms of an appreciable portion of their young girls and women. Nevertheless, the fathers, brothers and husbands of those captured appear never to have counter-attacked the Muslim train as it moved northwards.

THE DESTRUCTION OF SOMNATH (JANUARY, 1026 A.D.)

Mahmud's most devastating attack on a Hindu holy city was at Somnath, situated near the present day town of Patan at the southern tip of the Kathiawar peninsula. The battle there and its aftermath is the most revealing display of the Hindus' centrifugal attitudes vis a vis politics and religion, their individual passivity, and their leaders' inability to establish a working military alliance. This attack, it should be repeated, occurred after nearly forty years of Ghaznawid invasions and pillage.

The city and temple of Somnath had been sacred to Hindus for about one hundred and fifty years when Mahmud decided to destroy it. From surviving descriptions, Somnath, located on the very shores of the Arabian Sea, must have been a place of extraordinary beauty, enormous wealth and profound mysticism. The temple itself was dedicated to Soma, the diety representing Siva as the Moon God. The principal relic in the temple was a massive *linga,* probably the most treasured object of its kind in the entire Hindu world. It was made of stone and positioned so that it faced the waters of the sea. As the tides rose, the waves gradually immersed the *linga,* and when the waters receded, the shrine would reappear. A staff of some 1000 Brahmins allegedly dedicated their lives to caring for the idol and the temple. Every day a detachment of temple servants brought water from the Ganges River—at least a thousand miles away—to Somnath in order to bath the *linga* according to Hindu rites. Other attendants regularly gathered fresh flowers in Kashmir, some 600-700 miles away, and delivered them to the temple so the idol could be decorated in a befitting fashion. The monetary resources of the temple were probably as great as those of any shrine throughout the subcontinent, for it is reported that some 10,000 villages were pledged to help defray the expenses for the proper upkeep of Somnath.[13]

In the fall of 1025, Mahmud decided to strike at Somnath and destroy the *linga* and the temple. This campaign, he is reported to have said, would be the culmination of his military career against the Hindus and the most illustrious victory ever attained by a Muslim army against these much despised people. According to Muslim historians, Mahmud decided to strike against Somnath after learning what the Brahmins of the temple were claiming that the Ghaznawid armies' victories in their earlier attacks against Hindu shrines were only because the gods' displeasure with the idols located at these sites and that the *linga* of Somnath was so pleasing to Siva and the other deities of the Hindu pantheon that it was militarily invincible. No matter what type of force the Muslims were able to muster against Somnath, the Somnath leaders bragged, it was divinely protected and secure.

On October 18, 1025, Mahmud left Ghazni and headed south once again; it was the beginning of his sixteenth raid on the subcontinent. He was accompanied by an army of some 30,000 cavalry troops and hundreds of foot soldiers, baggage carriers and other attendants. The line of march to the temple covered 1,000 miles, and required that his troops cross some very difficult terrain.

The first leg of the invasion was from Ghazni to the city of Multan where a sizeable Muslim fortress was located. Here Mahmud decided to re-group, replenish his supplies, and repair any damaged equipment. There was little, if any, opposition from the townspeople.

Mahmud's stay at Multan was sufficiently long and his military objective so apparent that several local Hindu kings met to discuss how best to deal with the threat. Each ruler's territory lay in the path of Mahmud's march to Somnath, some 600 miles to the south. Although they exchanged ideas and initiated preliminary steps for a combined Hindu military operation, their efforts were of only nominal consequence. There was no Hindu attack on Mahmud's armies while they were re-grouping at Multan.

Once the Muslims resumed the invasion march, individual Hindu kings offered limited resistance. A few sued for peace after token shots were fired, others even earlier. At a key location, some two hundred miles before Somnath, a sizeable Hindu army surrendered en masse because the generals were convinced that the Hindu troops at Somnath, divinely blessed and protected by Soma, would annihilate Mahmud and his entire force. Defending the area, they decided, was fool-hardy and unnecessary for an ultimate Hindu victory. This Hindu army reportedly was slain to a man.

In the city of Somnath, thousands of Hindu soldiers and civilians awaited the attack. They lived in a world of fantasy, disregarding the perilousness of the situation and giving little attention to the forthcoming battle. Nohing was done to develop the city's defenses; no battle plan was devised. The Hindu gods would produce a miracle : the invaders would be killed and the sanctity of the city and the temple preserved intact.

When the Muslims ultimately reached the perimeters of the fortress and began storming the gates of the temple itself, the Hindus continued trusting their gods. Wave after wave of unarmed Hindus threw themselves against the attackers, and they were duly slaughtered. Others who were armed tried to stem the attack, but they, too, fell without slowing down Mahmud's troops. Somnath's defenses collapsed and finally the temple stood unguarded.[11]

On January 8, 1026, Mahmud and his troops marched into the innermost sanctuary of the temple. Standing before the *linga,* he ordered it destroyed. Within minutes, his troops had the revered *linga* on the ground and smashed to pieces. The victors thereupon broke or carried off everything of value and then burned all the temple buildings. The city of Somnath was similarly looted and gutted; thousands of Hindus were slaughtered wherever they were found When the Muslims finally withdrew from Somnath, one of the most honored and holy sites of Hinduism was no more.[15]

Although the Hindu defenders inside Somnath were crushed, other Hindu armies in the general area of the city remained intact. These troops had not been committed to the battle and possessed the military capability to launch a counter-attack. They did not move. Likewise, there does not seem to have been any great outpouring of popular Hindu indignation or demand to punish those who sacked the great shrine. The indifference of the civilian population of India to the battles taking place in their midst, it should be noted, was not unusual. Thirteen hundred years earlier, Megasthenes found it noteworthy to mention in his writings that he had witnessed *kshatriyas* fighting the troops of Alexander the Great even as local farmers placidly continued tilling their fields.[16]

The Hindus' passivity is all the more surprising, considering that the Muslim troops withdrew slowly because of long baggage lines and the need to cross a desert. At one point, they ran short of water for themselves and their horses and had difficulty getting fresh supplies. Mahmud and his troops left India unchallenged.

Mahmud himself died soon after returning to his palace in 1026, probably a contented leader since he had fulfilled his lifetime goal of leading a holy war against the infidels to the south. He and his troops executed one of the most destructive (and profitable) raids against a major Hindu shrine without facing united Hindu opposition. The Hindus' military response, at best, was disjointed and sporadic. The civilian population was equally lethargic. Of greater significance, Mahmud's numerous raids produced no dramatic changes of strategy among Hindu leaders: no contingency plans were formulated to create military alliances of local rulers in the event of future Muslim attacks, and Hindu generals devised no plan to guard the north-west passes.[17]

In the remaining decades of the eleventh century and continuing to the beginning of the twelfth, a succession of Muslim armies did invade the Punjab. Ultimately Muslim political-military power declined sharply, and some commentators believe the Hindus could have regained their lost territory. They failed to respond. Banerjee writes :

The time was ripe for sustained efforts on the part of the

Rajput dynasties . . . to liberate the Punjab from the rule of the alien princes lacking roots in the soil. Here the Rajputs failed in their great historic task. When the situation called for aggression against the Turushkas they remained steadfastly loyal to the weak policy of defense. Their territorial ambition was directed against their Hindu neighbours and their warlike zeal exhausted itself in mutual quarrels which contributed in the long run to the permanent success of the Turushkas in engulfing them all in common ruin.[18]

HINDU MILITARY PAROCHIALISM CONTINUED

The next major invaders of northern India originated in Afghanistan. In the last quarter of the twelfth century the Ghor campaigns opened a new phase in the Islamic conquest of India. The invaders were the Ghoris, led by Muhammad of Ghor, and their aggressive campaigns resulted in the collapse of a number of Rajput kingdoms. In the late fifteenth century the Ghoris, in turn, were succeeded by the Moghuls who took up the challenge and marched south against India. In both periods, the Hindus of the north experienced approximately two hundred years of Muslim subjugation and humiliation yet, conducted themselves as they had done in earlier centuries. They remained individualistic, aloof and non-cooperative with one another. And they continued clan warfare. Rather than recall the details of Rajput parochialism, we shall summarize the events surrounding two crucial, catastrophic Hindu defeats on the battlefield which took place in different periods of Indian history. Both illustrate the fatuousness of classical Hindu military analysis and operations and that the Hindus might have been spared pain and indignity had they been willing to relinquish their prejudices against local military cooperation and work out a functional alliance of local armies.

BATTLE OF TARAIN (1192 A.D)

In the last part of the twelfth century A.D., the Turkish-Muslim dynasty of Ghor had become the dominant military power in Afghanistan. Muhammad, leader of the Ghor forces, was as covetous of India's wealth as Mahmud of Ghazni had been, and no less determined to force the Hindus to discontinue their idolatrous ways. The first Ghor invasion took place in 1191, when Muhammad and his men attacked territory ruled by Prithviraj, a Rajput prince whose capital was located at Delhi. The attack failed, but the following year Muhammad returned with a larger contingent and again challenged Prithviraj. The resulting battle took place at Tarain, a strategically located position, and has been called one of the conclusive military engagements in the history of the world because it helped decide the fate of India.[19]

When Muhammad first appeared, Prithviraj was involved in a series of petty, inconsequential wars with two neighbouring Hindu rulers. The hostility between Prithviraj and the most powerful of these kings was particularly intense and bitter since somewhat earlier Prithviraj had kidnapped and later married his rival's daughter. As the tensions resulting from these romantic escapades were peaking, Muhammad and his troops appeared. Realizing that his power was inferior to the invader's and possibly anticipating the disastrous consequences that would follow defeat, Prithviraj tried to create a grand coalition of local Hindu armies in the threatened sector.[20] The other powerful kings, including one whose daughter had been abducted chose to remain detached, and not unite and together fight to eliminate the common foreign menace. Prithviraj and his men stood all but alone at Tarain and were defeated soundly. Within a matter of weeks every other Hindu king in the area was also soundly defeated, thus extinguishing Hindu power throughout northern India. Summarizing general Hindu military practices throughout the twelfth century, Dr B. N. S. Yadava has noted that "Prithviraj was the most outstanding hero of the age but could not realize that with the Turks at the gates of his northern frontier, the policy of war with his neighbours . . . was suicidal."[21]

The Hindus' own evaluation of the defeat at Tarain is revealing. The battle has been memorialized in a Rajput epic poem, *Prithviraj Raso* (The Chronicle of King Prithi), thought to have been composed by Chand Bardai. It is a poem frequently called the most distinguished literary work of medieval India, and one that epitomizes the idealized Hindu resistance hero. Many stanzas of the poem are given to excoriating the barbarous battlefield tactics of the invading Muslims. Local Buddhists are subjected to great abuse because their pacific philosophy of life, it is claimed, helped destroy the Hindus' traditional martial attitudes. Prithviraj, too, is criticized for his overly generous chivalry on the battlefield. What one fails to find in *Prithviraj Raso* is some appreciation that the Hindu people might have averted defeat and Muslim occupation had they been less intransigent and more willing to join their respective military forces against their common enemy. As de Riencourt[22] observed, the underlying tone of the poem is self-pity and self-indulgence.

BATTLE OF KANWAH (MARCH, 1527 A.D.)

The most notable example of Hindu alliance politics and possibly the only instance of genuine military cooperation among beseiged Hindu rulers took place in the early decades of the sixteenth century when India again faced invasion. This time Moghul troops challenged the status quo.

The most capable military force able to challenge the Moghuls and prevent them from acquiring dominion were the Hindu troops of the Mewar kingdom. Since the early part of the fourteenth century, the Mewars had been ruled by a line of aggressive, militarily-skillful Rajput chiefs, each engaging in frequent hostilities against his fellow Rajput rulers to extend his control over a larger area of Rajasthan. In 1526, prior to the Moghul invasion, Rana Sanga, the sixth in his line, had organized a coalition. Because of his many local campaigns, he was recognized leader by "seven Rajas of the highest rank, nine Raos, and one hundred and four chieftains bearing the titles of Rawul and Rawut...." An additional group of twelve more Rajput princes did him homage, served him as tributaries or held of him in chief.[23] As Tod notes, Rana Sanga was ascending to the pinnacle of distinction when the Moghuls struck, and even held promise of bringing all Hindu territory under his control. While his leadership ability and military skills were of an unusually high order, it must be emphasized that the coalition army he commanded resulted from his pre-Moghul campaigns, and it was not a response of independent sovereigns who rallied together when danger threatened.

The leader of the Moghul attack was Babur, a direct descendent of Timur, who in turn had been related on his mother's side to Ghangis Khan. Babur led a preliminary raid across the frontier in 1517, and two years later launched a second exploratory attack. A six year lapse followed while Babur secured his base on the shores of the Oxus and Jaxartes Rivers. In the spring of 1526, Babur marched in strength against India. At Paniput, a strategically important location at the edge of the Gangetic plain, the Moghuls gained a relatively easy victory over the local sultan. Babur then occupied Delhi and Agra, completing his conquest of the Punjab.

It was soon apparent that Babur planned to settle permanently in India. This decision was of the greatest importance for Rana Sanga, since the Moghul's territorial ambitions were bound to clash with those of the Rajput leader. The earlier relationship between these two courts had been friendly and cooperative, and at one period Rana Sanga had hoped to use Babur's power to help crush local opposition. When Babur established himself at Delhi, however, the Rajputs could no longer deny the immediate danger to their continued autonomy and their future freedom to be Hindus.

Rana Sanga issued the call for joint Hindu action, and according to Tod, "almost all the princes of Rajasthan" responded. Tod also reports that a Rajput confederation, consisting one hundred and twenty chieftains and their troops, soon moved against Babur, all under the command of Rana Sanga. Other writers disagree. According to Professor Banerjee, "Rana Sanga . . . found at Khanua that the Rajput clans could not serve under a common banner even against a common foe.[24] The king, Banerjee argues, failed because he was trying to impose on the Rajput states a type of unity which went against the traditional political-social organization of these clans.[25]

The crucial engagement between the Moghuls and the Hindus took place near the village of Khanua, about forty miles from Agra, on March 16, 1527. The fighting lasted ten hours and cost hundreds of lives on both sides. Ultimately Babur's troops prevailed, due in part to their superior tactics, imaginative use of their matchlock artillery, and great personal loyalty to their leader. When it was obvious that the Rajputs would be crushed, Rana Sanga fled the battlefield. He died some months later broken-hearted and in disgrace. Thus ended a battle that has been characterized as "one of the decisive battles in Indian history."[26] Its consequences were monumental because "the last hope of the Rajputs to restore Hindu supremacy in North India"[27] ended at Khanua.

A Theory Concerning Hindus' Military Unilateralism

In the eleventh century A.D., Alberuni wrote that Hindu ethnocentralism was a prime cause of their poor military record. Having spent thirteen years travelling among the Indian people and visiting most areas in the north, he characterized Hindus as "haughty, foolishly vain, self-conceited, and stolid." Warming to his evaluation, he continued :

> According to their belief, there is no other country on earth but theirs, no other race of man but theirs, and no created beings besides them have any knowledge or science whatsoever. Their haughtiness is such that, if you tell them of any scholars in Khurasan and Persis, they will think you to be both an ignoramus and a liar. If they travelled and mixed with other nations, they would soon change mind . . .[28]

While such portrayals are not without some historical interest, they do not help explain the persistent refusal of Hindu kings to combine their respective armies when a foreign invader, inimical to their religious and cultural values, threatened India. Forming a united military front in the face of an invasion threat is one of the oldest responses known in the world's political literature. The state of Ch'in during the Warring State Period of early Chinese history. (c. 5th century B.C.— 221 B.C.),for example, favored policies which led to a centralized military force. Also, Thucydides' *History of the Peloponnesian War* reveals how frequently concerted military action was instituted when the Greek city-states were endangered by an aggressive power. Machiavelli's *Discourses* also contains many thoughtful comments regarding the expediency of military alliances as well as the specific conditions favoring their formation. Why, in contrast, did generations of Hindu leaders manage their military crises so differently ? Why did India not establish tradition of combined military cooperation particularly when raids and invasions from Central Asia threatened Hindus ? What local ideas, domestic pressures, or cultural norms caused Hindus to rely on military unilateralism when joint action might have been far more utilitarian ?

THE BIG FISH—LITTLE FISH THEORY OF STATECRAFTS

In Indian political literature, the leading treatise on state-craft encouraged policies of independence, emphasized unilateralism, and stressed the transitory nature of joint efforts between states. Kautilya's *Arthasastra,*[29] the earlier noted fourth century B.C. analysis of inter-state relations, was a work that suceeding generations of Hindu leaders regarded as the most enlightened, accurate study of statecraft produced in India. It was a work that advised kings to work zealously for their individual aggrandizement while criticizing policies that might bring about permanent cooperation with local rulers or long-lasting alliances. At the formative stage in India's political-military evolution, Kautilya wrote an analysis of inter-state conduct and military strategy that came to dominate India's political-military thinking until the Moghul period. Here Kautilya argued for ideas that resulted in generations of Hindu leaders discounting military cooperation with other similarly threatened Hindu states, denegrating the value of political centralism, and tirelessly seeking ways to gain power and incorporate smaller states into their empire. This last concept is best known as the *matsyanyaya,* or a great fish swallows a small one.

In Kautilya's study the basic idea that determines inter-state relations is the *mandalla,* or, literally, the circle of neighbouring states. This idealized pattern of statecraft became the prototype of a king's policies.[30] It was an elaborate exposition of how a ruler determined which neighboring kingdoms were enemy states and which were friendly or potential allies. When presenting his ideas concerning expansion and conquest, Kautilya offers kings a basic, simplistic formula to reach policy decisions concerning all important issues about when to wage war and when to seek peaceful accommodations with local rulers.

According to the *mandalla* concept, it was axiomatic that states sharing a common geographical boundary were implacable enemies. Geographical proximity, in other words, resulted invariably in political-military enmity and ultimately a war would take place. The loser forfeited its independence and was compelled to abandon aspirations for local hegemony, or until he was able by cunning or deception to resume his drive for conquest. The victor was advised in the *Arthasastra* either to kill the defeated ruler or at the very least force him to become a vassal. He also was expected to use his newly acquired power base (territorial and otherwise) to launch an attack against his new neighbor-enemies. As a general rule, every king who adhered to Kautilya's philosophy was advised to work tirelessly to build up and improve his power, increase the armed forces, strengthen the kingdom's perimeter defenses, improve battlefield formations and tactics, and lastly, augment the treasury with as much regularity as "fruits are gathered from a garden as often as they become ripe."[31] The cycle of preparing for war or engaging a local kingdom on the battlefield was to be repeated until at some never defined period in the future, a world conquerer (*cakravartin*) would rule.[32]

Having analysed the power resources of the kingdom and the techniques to augment them, Kautilya turns to the operational mechanics of the *mandalla*. There is extended discussion of the nature of alliances and their dynamics. Kautilya concluded that natural allies were separated from one another by at least one intermediary kingdom Rulers who shared a common boundary were natural enemies. Once the intermediary kingdom was defeated and its territory divided between the two allies, or a vassal state was established, the alliance was terminated. The two winning kings, having smashed the common threat, each now continued his respective struggles for power and wealth. Each allied himself with the kingdom on the opposite flank of the new enemy, his former ally. In Kautilya's words, "one shall make an alliance with a king who is stronger than one's neighboring enemy . . . there can be no greater evil to kings than alliance with a king of considerable power, unless one is actually attacked by one's enemy."[33]

It is important to call attention to the fact that Kautilya never projected a situation in which a group of Hindu states allied themselves to defeat a common Hindu enemy. The *Arthasastra* postulates many conflict situations and specifies the correct response to such crises, but never considers the need for local sovereigns to put aside their interminable struggle for hegemony and to join together in joint military ventures. More germane to this study, Kautilya never examined the possibility that several Indian states, contiguous or non-contiguous, would mutually benefit from forming a military alliance to defeat a common challenge from a non-Hindu invader whose conquest and pillage in the north threatened them all. Because Kautilya's appreciation of inter-state relations was limited, the principal text on political-military affairs in pre-modern Indian literature omitted any discussion of the efficacy of military cooperation and compromise in what became the country's principal crisis situation, namely, how to defeat a foreign invader.

The Clan System of the Rajputs

Kautilya's philosophy of war and peace must have pleased the Rajputs once they began settling permanently in India. His analysis of power politics, and particularly his ideas of independent kingdoms using force to attain local superiority free of moral restraints, expressed concepts the Rajputs appear to have followed in their pre-Indian period. Or did the Rajputs implement Kautilya's "big fish-little fish politics" only after they had become the dominant Hindu group in north India, and had accepted the traditional Hindu pantheon, Hindu literature and its social organization? Much is unknown about Rajput development. A case in point is the extent of their indebtedness to Kautilya's writings. An argument for such a connection has been made.[34] Of greater relevance to this study is some understanding of how these two forces—the philosophy of the *Arthasastra* and the Rajput clan system—complimented one another.

Every traditional state represented one clan. The most humble farmer of a state as well as its ruling class considered themselves sons of the same father and enjoyed their patrimony by the same right. The land that made up a Rajput state was not held to belong to the king personally, but to the clan as a whole. It was territory all hoped to enlarge, make more affluent and powerful, and, of course, more secure from outside threats. The primary responsibility of the ruler was to favor policies that produced such results; it mattered little if success was achieved at the cost of a neighbor's land, wealth or security. For Rajputs, the highest good in relation to political-military activity was conceived in terms of the state.

The Rajput clan-state system resulted in two political-military consequences. First, it blocked any eventual possibility for far reaching unification. Each state was an end in itself. Each Rajput government was disinterested in promulgating policies designed to stimulate voluntary merger, central military authority, or any form of close association with other Rajput kingdoms. The political-military crises of another kingdom, including foreign invasions or threats from abroad, were of little or no concern to other Rajputs. They were certainly not a valid reason to work jointly for the removal or defeat of a common enemy.

Secondly, the system did exacerbate local pettiness, perpetuate clan hatreds, and both sanction and encourage frequent resort to military force. A thirteenth century Hindu play, *Hammiramada-mardona*, characterized the period as "the all-pervasive and ruinous discord among the kshatriyas which was responsible for their internecine wars, their proud isolation and their fall before the Muslim invaders like dry leaves in autumn."[35] In fighting among themselves, consequently, Rajput power was foolishly spent. To again quote from Professor Banerjee's study :

> They could not rise above the parochialism on which the clan system was based. They could not think of India as a whole. They could not place themselves in the wide perspective of history. Deeply rooted in the past, stagnant in ideas as well as in methods, they lost those glittering prizes which history offers to rulers and peoples who can plunge into the unknown in pursuit of large plans and great visions.[36]

CONCLUSION

By never learning how to act in a unified manner, the Hindu people throughout their history wasted innumerable opportunities to defeat their foreign enemies jointly and prevent the subjugation of Indian territory. Militarily, a long list of Hindu kings and generals conducted themselves over several millenia in as short-sighted and parochial fashion as is possible to conceive. They never learned to build up coordinated military forces or to set up a unified defence system in the northwest area. Hindus were anything but pacific people, but fighting became the responsibility of one caste, and they neglected to keep abreast of military developments in other lands. What today would be called collective security alliances were all but ignored, although joint efforts might have been kept the invaders beyond the Himalayan mountains. The mass of Hindus were indifferent to the wars taking place in their midst as well as the destruction of the prized temples and relics of their faith. The country became a warren of rigidly divided, intensely antagonistic kingdoms. At no time in pre-modern India were there strong centripetal pressures, or what might today be called inchoate patriotism. What was nurtured throughout the subcontinent was a culture that encouraged political instability and military unilateralism.

From Kautilya they learned that waging war was not only socially acceptable, but the only duty of a spirited leader. The idealized hero-king was a conqueror who plotted to extend his realm to the maximum of his talents and deviousness, invariably at the expense of his weaker neighboring states and without a noticeable regard for moral and ethical considerations. Internecine fighting at an early period became the approved standard of conduct.

The Rajputs continued to follow a similar political-military philosophy. Although soldiering and fighting were exhalted, their efforts were wasted fighting one another for trivial reasons rather than joining together against Muslim invaders.

In recent years as independent India initiated several in-depth studies of its early history, a number of its contemporary scholars have written in detail of the country's marked anti-alliance prejudices. One of the most astute analyses is a study of Indian military history written by Sir Jadunath Sarkar. In reviewing the chronic invasion threats that Hindus living in the northwest area regularly faced, Sir Jadunath concluded :

> .... there was constant feuds between clan and clan, king and king, and Hindu powers could offer no united opposition to foreign invaders, except on rare occasions and then their confederated forces were too ill-knit and too slowly mobilized to win decisive successes.[37]

An equally vivid, if somewhat more critical analysis of pre-modern India's military incompetence is found in the conclusions of Major Gautam Sharma's study, *Indian Army Through the Ages* :

> During the first thousand years or so of the period before the Moghul take over of India/it will be observed that in spite of the foreign impact the army organization in the country was not changed to a great degree. Lessons of

Hydaspes were forgotten soon after and the armies continued to be flooded with large masses of untrained infantry, cumbersome chariots and the unwieldy elephants. ... The north western passes thus came to be neglected. There is the absence of a frontier policy all through the succeeding years [post early first century A.D.—ed.]. During the Muslim inroads the rulers in the border areas held their own for a short while and at times formed confederations but in the absence of a unifying force, central command and well-organized armies they were defeated by the invaders . . .

. . [The armies] were ignorant of developments abroad and made no attempts to improve their organizations in the light of changed conditions. There was no unifying force and the internecine warfare and operations that went with them were a great drain on the country, in the destruction of the best youth of the day and then the devastation of vast areas of land which brought about shortages of food and famine . . . .[38]

At least three other factors present within classical Hindu society reinforced the non-alliance tradition. First, Hindus, unlike the Jews, Christians and Muslims, never conceived of themselves as a community of co-religionists whose future prosperity demanded unity and cooperation. Rather, the Hindus have regularly shown a weak sense of identification with others who followed the social-ethical precepts of Hinduism or who worshipped its pantheon of gods and goddesses.[39] Secondly, Hindus failed to champion programs and policies that might lead to political centralism or stimulate trends that could result in the peaceful merger of several kingdoms. In Hindu literature there is extensive discussion about a king who would unify the world (*cakravartin* or a "ruler the wheels of whose chariot roll everywhere without obstruction, emperor, sovereign of the world"),[40] but scant attention is given to a monarch who would produce comparable results within the subcontinent. Finally, the individual Hindu was concerned primarily with religious and philosophical problems associated with everyday life. Here was the real nub of a man's being. Political and military affairs consequently were not accorded the same prolonged, close scrutiny as was the case in other early civilizations.

REFERENCES

1. For a discussion holding that military alliances were known in ancient India, see B. A Saletore, *Ancient Indian Political Thought and Institutions* (London : Asia Publishing House, 1963), p. 96.

2. See infra, pp. 158-60.

3. Typical Hindu efforts to organize joint military ventures took place in 1011 A.D., when Mahmud of Ghazni was upsetting the status quo of the north. His goal was Thánesar, a Hindu centre some one hundred and twenty miles north of Delhi where a much venerated temple was located. Recognizing the threat, Anandpal, the ruler of Delhi, resolved to form an alliance of other Hindu princes in order to stop the invader. He "sent messengers throughout Hindustan to acquaint the other Rajas that Mahmud, without provocation, was marching with a vast army to destroy Thanesar, now under his immediate protection." He warned the other kings that if they did not respond expeditiously "against this roaring torrent, the country of Hindustan would be overwhelmed, and every state, small and great, would be entirely subverted." It was, typically, another instance of Hindu policy decided too late and implemented too slowly. Firishta reports in his account *Tarikh-i-Firishta,* "Mahmud having reached Thanesar before the Hindus had time to assemble for its defense, the city was plundered, the idols broken, and the idol Jagsom sent to Ghaznia to be troden under foot in the street, and decapitated . . ." Quoted in Sir H. M. Elliot and John Dowson, *The History of India as Told by Its Own Historians,* (London : Trübner and Company, 1869), pp. 446-7 and pp. 453-4.

4. Major Gautam Sharma, *Indian Army Through the Ages* (Bombay : Allied Publishers Limited, 1966), p. 48.

5. Romila Thapar, *A History of India* (Baltimore : Penguin Press, 1966), I, p. 238.

6. In contemporary literature, by far the best discussion of Rajput History and their political-military behavior is Anil Chandra Banerjee, *Lectures on Rajput History,* Raghunath Prasad Nopany Lectures, Calcutta University, 1960 (Calcutta : K. L. Mukhopadhyay, 1962). Much of the material in this section is taken from this source. Concerning earlier analysis of Rajput origins and political-military traits in general, see H. G. Rawlinson, *India : A Short Cultural History,* ed. C. G. Seligman, (London : Cresset Press, 1943), pp. 199-202. Also see Martin, who correctly noted that the Rajput feudal system of government led them to fight "not so much in a single great action, as inch by inch, each man fighting for his own chief, and his own hearth and home." Robert Montgomery Martin, *The*

Indian Empire (London : London Printing and Publishing Company, 1858), I, p. 71.

7. Anil Chandra Banerjee, *Lectures on Rajput History* (Calcutta : K. L. Mukhopadhyay, 1962), p. 30.

8. Anil Chandra Banerjee, *Lectures on Rajput History* (Calcutta : K. L. Mukhopadhyay, 1962), p. 61.

9. Quoted in Sir H. M. Elliot and John Dowson, *The History of India as Told by Its Own Historians* (London : Trübner and Co., 1869), p. 44.

10. *ibid.*

11. The quotation is from the writings of Nizamu-d din Ahmad and is cited in Sir H. M. Elliot and John Dowson, *The History of India as Told by its Own Historians* (London : Trübner and Co., 1869), p. 460.

12. *ibid.*

13. The Muslim historian Ibn Asir prepared the earliest known description of Somnath. He wrote, "This idol was the greatest of all the idols of Hind. Every night that there was an eclipse the Hindus went on pilgrimage to the temple, and there congregated to the number of a hundred thousand persons. They believed that the souls of men after separation from the body used to meet there, according to their doctrine of transmigration, and that the ebb and flow of the tide was the worship paid to the idol by the sea, to the best of its power. Everything of the most precious was brought there; its attendants received the most valuable presents, and the temple was endowed with more than 10,000 villages. In the temple were amassed jewels of the most exquisite quality and incalculable value. The people of India have a great river called Gang, to which they pay the highest honour, and into which they cast the bones of their great men, in the belief that the deceased will thus secure an entrance to heaven. Between this river and Somnath there is a distance of about 200 parasangs, but water was daily brought from it with which the idol was washed. One thousand Brahmans attended every day to perform the worship of the idol, and to introduce the visitors. Three hundred persons were employed in shaving the heads and beards of the pilgrims. Three hundred and fifty persons sang and danced at the gate of the temple. Every one of these received a settled allowance daily . . ." Quoted in Sir H. M. Elliot and John Dowson, *The History of India as Told by its Own Historians* (London : Trübner and Co., 1869), pp. 468-9.

14. The oldest account of the Battle of Somnath was also written by Ibn Asir and reads as follows : ". . . He (Mahmud) reached Somnát on a Thursday in the middle of Zi-l Ka'da and there he beheld a strong fortress built upon the sea shore, so that it was washed by the waves. The people of the fort were

on the walls amusing themselves at the expense of the confident Musulmáns, telling them their deity would cut off the last man of them, and destroy them all. On the morrow, which was Friday, the assailants advanced to the assault, and when the Hindus beheld the Muhammadáns fighting, they abandoned their posts, and left the walls. The Musulmans planted their ladders against the walls and gained the summit : then they proclaimed their success with their religious war-cry, and exhibited the prowess of Islám. Then followed a fearful slaughter, and matters wore a serious aspect. A body of Hindus hurried to Somnát, cast themselves on the ground before him, and besought him to grant them victory. Night came on, and the fight was suspended.

"Next morning, early, the Muhammadáns renewed the battle, and made greater havoc among the Hindus, till they drove them from the town to the house of their idol, Somnát. A dreadful slaughter followed at the gate of the temple. Band after band of the defenders entered the temple Somnát, and with their hands clasped around their necks, wept and passionately entreated him. Then again they issued forth to fight until they were slain, and but few were left alive . . . ." Quoted in Sir H. M. Elliot and John Dowson, *The History of India as a Told by its Own Historians* (London : Trübner and Co., 1869), p. 470.

15. Only after regaining their independence in 1947—more than six hundred years after the Somnath debacle...did the Hindus undertake a program of reconstructing Somnath. See Donald Eugene Smith, *India as a Secular State* (Princeton : Princeton University Press, 1963) p. 386.

16. See Supra, Chapter II.

17. The Hindus' military behaviour at this time is in dramatic contrast to that of the Chinese. During the late Chou period states of Northern China began erecting great walls along their frontiers in order to provide for their security in a more efficient manner. See Edwin O. Reischauer and John K. Fairbank, *East Asia* : *The Great Tradition* (Boston : Houghton Mifflin Co., 1958), p. 56.

18. Anil Chandra Banerjee, *Lectures on Rajput History,* Raghunath Prasad Nopany Lectures, Calcutta University, 1960, (Calcutta : K. L. Mukhopadhyay, 1962), pp. 74-5.

19. This opinion is that of Professor Banerjee, *Lectures on Rajput History*, Raghunath Prasad Nopany Lectures, Calcutta University, 1960, (Calcutta : K. L. Mukhopadhyay, 1962), p. 82.

20. See Major Gautam Sharma, *Indian Army Through the Ages* (Bombay : Allied Publishers Private Limited, 1966), p. 57.

21. "Chivalry and Some Aspects of Warfare on the Eve of the Muslim Conquests of Northern India," *University of Allahabad for 1966* (Allahabad : Senate House, 1966), p. 13.

22. Amaury de Reincourt, *The South of India* (New York : Harper and Brothers, 1960), p. 169.

23. James Tod, *Annals and Antiquities of Rajasthan,* rev. ed., (Calcutta : S. K. Lahiri, 1894), I, pp. 277-8.

24. Anil Chandra Banerjee, *Lectures of Rajput History,* Raghunath Prasad Nopany Lectures, Calcutta University, 1960 (Calcutta : K. L. Mukhopadhyay, 1962), p. 111.

25. For a fuller development of this point, see *ibid.,* p. 94.

26. R. C. Majumdar, H. C. Raychaudhuri, and Kalikinkar Datta, *An Advanced History of India,* 2nd. ed. (New York : St. Martin's, 1965), p. 429.

27. H. G. Rawlinson, *India : A Short Cultural History* (New York : Appleton-Century, 1938), p. 290.

28. *Alberuni's India,* trans. Edward C. Sachau, (London : Trübner and Co., 1888), I, p. 23.

29. Kautilya's *Arthasastra,* trans. R. Shamasastry, (Mysore : Mysore Printing and Publishing House, 1961).

30. Of the *mandalla* A. L. Basham has written that this principle of political-military behavior "can be seen throughout the history of Hindu India in the temporary alliance of two kingdoms to accomplish the encirclement and destruction of the kingdom between them." *The Wonder That Was India* (New York : Grove Press, 1954), p. 127. Heinrich Zimmer called it "The principal Hindu formula for the arrangement of foreign alliances and coalitions . . . ." *Philosophies of India,* ed. Joseph Campbell, (Cleveland : World Publishing Co., 1961), p. 114. Professor Charles Drekmeier finds that "a basic proposition of Hindu thought is the inherent unfriendliness and potential enmity of foreign powers and the consequent need for preparedness. Broadly speaking," he continues, "a people is to be feared or disregarded in international policies according to its proximity to the state . . . ." *Kingship and Community in Early India* (Stanford : Stanford University Press, 1962), p. 267.

31. Kautilya, *Arthasastra,* trans. R. Shamasastry, (Mysore : Mysore Printing and Publishing House, 1961), p. 276.

32. Concerning the importance of the idea of a ruler of the world-state, see John W. Spellman, *Political Theories of Ancient India* (Oxtord : Clarendon Press, 1964), pp. 173-4.

33. *ibid.,* p. 296.

34. While it is not possible to prove conclusively that the Rajputs were familiar with Kautilya's philosophy of statecraft, several writers indicate that such was the case. Thus, for example, Professor Banerjee recently observed that the achievements of Chandragupta, Kautilya's patron, "left an enduring impression upon the country and several centuries later the poet of the *Mudra-rakshasa* paid a glowing tribute to the great liberation." See Anil Chandra Banerjee, *Lectures on Rajput History,* (Calcutta : K. L. Mu-

khopadhyay, 1962), p. 52. The late Professor Rawlinson wrote that the Rajputs after settling in North India, "patronised learning, and their courts were filled with Brahmin scholars, poets and dramatists." He also states that the Rajputs enjoyed listening to recitations from the *Mahabharata*. See H. G. Rawlinson, *India : A Short Cultural History* (New York : Appleton-Century, 1938), pp. 199, 201.

35. Dr B. N. S. Yadava, "Chivalry and Some Aspects of Warfare on the eve of the Muslim Conquest of Northern India," *University of Allahabad Studies for 1966* (Allahabad : Senate House, 1966), p. 12.

36. Anil Chandra Banerjee, *Lectures on Rajput History*, Raghunath Prasad Nopany Lectures, (Calcutta : K. L. Mukhopadhyay, 1962), p. 112.

37. Sir Jadunath Sarkar, *The Military History of India* (Calcutta : M. C. Sarkar and Sons, 1960), p. 32.

38. Major Gautam Sharma, *Indian Army Through the Ages* (Bombay : Allied Publishers Private Limited, 1966), pp. 68-9.

39. See infra, pp. 35-36.

40. John W. Spellman, *Political Theory of Ancient India* (Oxford : Clarendon Press, 1964), p. 173. For an extended discussion of the Hindu theory of a world sovereign, see Sir Jadunath Sarkar, *Military History of India* (Calcutta : M. C. Sarkar and Sons, 1960), p. 72. Quoting Kamandaka, a political philosophy of the early ages, Sarkar reports him as holding that the wise ruler should focus on "the aspiration to conquer."

CHAPTER X

THE HINDUS AS OVERSEAS COLONIZERS

THE ANATOMY OF COLONIALISM

COLONIALISM IS not an innovation of the contemporary nation-state, and it has not been restricted to the powerful and dynamic countries of the West. Colonialism along with warfare ranks as one of man's oldest political activities. In every epoch of history, leaders who directed the destiny of their respective states have led campaigns to seize additional territory to create an empire that would enhance their power, add to the majority of the military establishment, and they hoped, secure for their people some type of material benefit. The colonial drives of the Assyrians and the Persians, the Greeks and Romans, the Muslim Arabs, as well as the Chinese, are but a few instances of colonialism's persistence throughout the pre-modern period.

The specific means employed to establish a colonial empire have varied considerably, but a number of common features were evident whenever one state sought to expand its power and assert political-military control over another community. Although none of the characteristics is apparent in every instance of colonialism, the items listed below are a representative picture of the modus operandi of history's leading colonialist powers. In descending importance they are :

(1) A resort to military force to gain control over the territory sought—The frequency with which kings ordered their armies to go abroad and forcefully subdue a hostile indigenous population has been so well documented that additional comment is unnecessary. Rulers advantageously located on sea lanes ordered their armies overseas to establish a non-contiguous empire. Arriving on foreign shores, the invaders proceeded to challenge the defending armies, and if successful, seized the organs of government. Powerful rulers of land-locked, inland states were no less resolute. Lacking ready access to the sea, they were obliged to look elsewhere for areas in which to expand. It was not uncommon for armies to march considerable distances overland, very often under inhospitable conditions.

Once the land armies reached their ultimate destination, their orders were no different from their ocean-borne colleagues in arms : defeat the local forces and assume political control of the area. In short, those seeking colonial empires in the pre-modern period accepted the use of military power as a legitimate means to acquire territory, wherever located.

(2) Establishment of a system of political control—Once the military victory was realized, the classical colonial power introduced a governing system to ensure its dominating role in local affairs. In some instances there was outright annexation, and the foreign territory became an integral part of the metropolitan state. Other times a less politically destructive arrangement was employed, such as the appointment of a resident consul or governor-general, men ruling in the name of the victor, but without eliminating the earlier political system. A third variation was the naming of key advisers to the court of the defeated king and charging them with the responsibility of preserving the new status. No matter what the system, however, the end was the same : conquerors were able to rule their militarily acquired territory with a minimum of internal conflict.

(3) Exploitation of resources and subjugation of the residents—Colonialism is associated with the material exploitation of the dominated territory and with harsh measures to keep the local people in line. It was not uncommon for the most valuable natural resources of the defeated country to be appropriated, in whole or in part, for the benefit of the conquering state. When land was needed or wanted, it, too, was expropriated and payment, when forthcoming, was usually inadequate. Both the civilian and the military in the occupied state were treated in a humiliating way, and many were killed.

(4) Subversion of the local culture and indigenous folkways—Because the typical colonial power believed that the continuance of the traditional religion, customs, folkways and sometimes even the language threatened the permanence of their conquest, its policies were designed to weaken, if not totally obliterate, any manifestations of independence and freedom of expression. A high degree of tolerance and sympathy for indigenous religions, local customs and manners has not been especially notable in the history of colonialism. What is conspicuous are

campaigns to produce as high a degree of cultural synthesis as possible.

The pre-modern colonial policies of the Hindu people[1] and their behavior in lands far removed from India proper were an exception. For nearly fifteen hundred years the Hindus were what today would be called colonists. The area of their overseas dominance covered a broad expanse of the southwest Pacific. Here Hindu culture not only spread but penetrated the local ethos so deeply that Hindu religion, social ideas, art and literature had a permanent influence on the life style of the native communities. It is not the purpose of this study to examine this phenomenon in detail, but a select number of events will be cited to illustrate the atypical behavior of the Hindu people and the political-military roles they assumed in their colonies.

The actions and reactions of the Hindu colonists in Greater India, as well as Hindu kings who ruled mainland states, reflected cultural values and were the logical outgrowth of their mainland traditions.

CHARACTERISTICS OF HINDU COLONIALISM

The style of political behavior of the Hindu colonists was as endemic to their culture as Confucian China's sinicization of its neighboring states or the Muslim's division of the world into the *dar al-Islam* and the *dar al-hard,* or to the European genre of colonialism of the eighteenth and nineteenth centuries. Hindu colonialism allowed Indians to help civilize Southeast Asia by encouraging cultural syncretism and by fostering religious tolerance and social equality without resorting to the use of military power or political conquest.

Without question, the most striking feature of the Hindu colonial era was the almost complete absence of military power either to establish the original sphere of influence or to expand the area. In spite of the Kautilyan tradition of military aggressiveness, Indian kings did not campaign abroad in search of glory, adventure, or the material aspects of conquest. In the fifteen hundred years of Hindu colonialism, on only one occasion did a mainland king order his military forces overseas to overthrow a local ruler and to establish a military presence in Southeast Asia. (See the account of Rajendra Chola, supra). Aside from this incident, there is no evidence that Hindu ships were

used to challenge local naval power or even test their determination to dominate waters adjacent to their territory. The
absence of all forms of militarism from contiguous Burma to the
outermost islands of the Malaya archipelago is the more impressive in view of the Hindus' propensity for military contests and
internecine warfare in India proper. The classical political-
military philosophy of Hindu rulers apparently precluded the
physical seizure of foreign lands or the use of force to compel
alien people to acknowledge their power and majesty. Arrian,
cited earlier, was remarkably astute and prophetic when he noted
in the fourth century B.C., that Indians were too righteous to
carry on war in alien lands.[2] The stay-at-home qualities of the
Hindu military, he observed, became a set feature of their political-military behavior.

A second feature of Hindu colonialism was the absence of
a tangible political linkage between the mainland and the overseas territory under its dominance.[3] None of the various metropolitan rulers most active in Indian history during this entire
period sought to assert dominion by appointing a pro-consul or
a governor-general to rule in his name. Nor did any king incorporate any area of Greater India directly into his state. Both
political annexation and the establishment of overlord-vassal relations were alien to Hindu Behavior. Even when Hinduism
was well rooted throughout the South Pacific, native leaders were
allowed to maintain independent status and to determine their
respective political destinies free from overright from India proper. Local kings were not required to make periodic trips to
India to demonstrate their acceptance of subservient status or
to pay allegiance to their conqueror. When the native elite
from Southeast Asian lands did travel to India, they appear to
have been received in a friendly and hospitable fashion. Nothing suggests that they were treated with contempt, scorned or
belittled. Nor were they obliged to acknowledge the superiority of the metropolitan king at court ceremonies. They were
accorded a reception due their rank and, more revealing, as
men from abroad who were fellow Hindus. In discussing diplomatic relations, Coedes finds that "the exchange of embassies
between the two shores of the Bay of Bengal were made on the
basis of equality."[4]

The third feature of Hindu colonialism relates to the inter-personal relations between the Hindus who emigrated and the local population. Native women were not abused, maltreated, or shipped to the mainland to gratify the sexual desires of Indian men. According to one Chinese report, the marriage of Hindu men to local women that took place were alliances entered into freely, not arranged by force or worse. In a kingdom of the Malaya Peninsula during the fifth century A.D., he wrote, "there are over a thousand Brahmins from India [here]; the people practice their doctrine and give their daughters to them in marriage, so that many Brahmins stay there."[5]

Native men, likewise, seemed to have been treated with remarkable goodwill, sympathy and respect. The master-slave mentality characteristic of the colonial tradition of so many countries did not appear in the thousand years of Hindu colonialism. The Hindus seem to have encouraged excellent relations with natives abroad. As Hinduism spread and Hindu gods were worshipped by the local population, it was not unknown for native men to go to India, visit Hindu shrines and temples, and acquire a deeper knowledge and appreciation of their newly found faith. When they returned home, their dedication to Hinduism was strengthened. Such events can take place in a colonial setting only when there is a healthy interaction between the colonialists and the natives.

Economic exploitation was not practiced by Hindu colonists. When the enormous profits realized in India from the sale of Asian spices and other luxury goods are considered, this feature of Hindu colonialism is exceptional. In the overseas territory in which the Hindus settled, large quantities of such products were either grown locally or imported from countries farther to the East. The medieval seller's market in spice probably is without comparison in history. The Hindu traders and merchants who settled in foreign ports or resided in inland cities must have been well-situated to capitalize on their greater familiarity with commerce and the import requirements of Mediterranean states. No report exists today, however, that even faintly hints at commandeering, robbery, or other forms of imperialistic exploitation. One must conclude that the Hindus who located themselves abroad conducted their trading relations with an unusually high degree of fairness.

Finally, the migration of many Hindus to Southeast Asia

did not bring about the destruction of indigenous religious practices, social forms, or what may be designated as the natives'
previous style of living. They immeasurably enriched and influenced the day-to-day conduct of the local population. Local
leaders came to revere Hindu gods and to adopt Hindu socio-
economic systems. Cultural re-orientations invariably take place
whenever a more advanced, sophisticated people come into prolonged contact with a less progressive society. These exact conditions prevailed throughout Southeast Asia when the Hindus began to locate there; they were in theory able to effect a cultural
revolution that could have overwhelmed the pre-colonial native
ethos in toto. The process of Hindu acculturation, however, was
syncretic in nature. Some of the original native practices remained; others were modified significantly; still others appear to
have been discontinued. To transform so many local societies
in so many ways reflects most favorable on the Hindus' talents
and sensitivities.

The Location and Chronology of Hindu Expansion

Greater India or Farther India, both phrases used to identify the area of Hindu overseas expansion and colonization, consisted of two proximate yet geographically distinct regions of
Southeast Asia. The first comprised the Asian mainland that
flanked the littoral of the Bay of Bengal, the Gulf of Siam and
the South China Sea. It included what today is lower Burma,
most of southern and central Indo-China, and the long, narrow
Malay Peninsula extending down to the Straits of Malacca. During the centuries when Hindus were active here, there were two
leading kingdoms : Fu-nan, located in what is the southern part
of modern Cambodia, and Champa, made up of the region
around the present city of Hué plus the southern region of
Annam. The second area of Greater India, rather than being
part of the Asian land mass, was separated from the Indian
mainland by thousands of miles of ocean. It was made up of
a chain of islands, all of which are currently part of Indonesia
but originally were independent native principalities. Today
this region is designated as the Malay Archipelago, or simply
Malaysia and includes, among others, the islands of Java, Bali,
Madura, Borneo and the Celebes. In the period under discussion emigrating Hindus established themselves in the two dom-

12

inant kingdoms of the area, namely, the kingdom of Srivijaya based on Sumatra and its successor and conqueror, the kingdom of Sailendra whose capital city was located on Java.

Another way to define the sweep of Hindu expansion is to recite the distances between mainland India and the overseas territory. Since archieval material written by Hindu authors is non-existent, the sea lanes Hindu ships followed, or the land routes of their caravans can only be surmised. It is generally agreed that the two leading ports of debarkation were Madras and Tamluk. A voyager who departed from Madras and whose destination was the extreme section of Sumatra, consequently, had to be prepared to sail a minimum of about three thousand nautical miles. If he left from Tamluk and landed in southern Burma, he sailed about one thousand nautical miles. To travel farther east to such lands as Java or the several kingdoms beyond, necessitated an additional journey of at least five hundred miles.

The mileage for overland routes were equally impressive distances. Hindus setting out from one of India's northern cities, perhaps along the Ganges, had to march at least one thousand miles over difficult terrain before reaching a settlement in Burma. Those who preferred continuing to the southern areas of the Malay Peninsula travelled an additional thousand miles.

The earliest period when Hindus began migrating overseas and settling in the East is all but impossible to determine with a high degree of accuracy. Approximate dates are available from a number of sources, however. One popular Chinese legend states that in the first century A.D., a Brahmin helped found the Fu-nan kingdom.[6] A more reliable Chinese source of the second century A.D., notes that by this time the social and political structure of Fu-nan closely resembled a Hindu kingdom in India.[7] Other colonies of Greater India are associated with later periods. Archeological discoveries at Champa, for example, indicate a Hindu community there no later than the fourth century A.D. On what is today the Malay Peninsula, it appears that Hindus had become important leaders of local societies sometime during the second century.

Each of these time periods is an approximation, the reasoned conclusions of scholars who have examined the current evidence. Perhaps the most realistic position, however, was taken by Professor Coedes, who side-stepped the entire issue of pre-

cisely determining when the Hindus first appeared in Southeast
Asia. "It seems to me prudent to say simply," he wrote, "that
Indian colonization was intense in the second and third cen-
turies of our era and came to fruition in the fourth and fifth."[8]

The decline of Hindu colonization, on the other hand, can
be determined with greater accuracy. By the mid-thirteenth
century the Islamic campaign into Southeast Asia had commenced, with the natural continuation of their military successes in
the subcontinent. Having established themselves throughout the
north, Muslim kings steadily moved their armies south until they
ruled India. Their eagerness to proselytize Islam and their love
of fighting did not ebb when they secured Cape Comorin, however. Expansion abroad was the next logical consequence of
their evangelical-martial spirit. Muslim missionaries and traders
appeared in Southeast Asia, eager to mould the behavior of the
local people, convert them to Islam, and re-direct governmental
processes. On the other hand, as Hindus gave up control of
their own country, their earlier enthusiasm for overseas expansion also faded and eventually disappeared. "(T)he downfall of
Hinduism in India," Majumdar notes, "also led to decay of
their colonial supremacy. The fountain head, having dried up,
the streams fed by it were also gradually choked, leading to
their untimate disappearance."[9]

MOTIVATION FOR HINDU MIGRATION

In his analysis of India's colonial expansion, Professor
Coedes raises a question central to the theme of this study.
"How can we explain," he asks, "this maritime drive of a people
who regarded crossing the 'black water' and contact with the
mleccha barbarians as bringing defilement and pollution?"[10]
Other scholars have also been perplexed by the migration of
Hindus because of their abhorrence to overseas travel and their
strong aversion to foreign residence. It is an issue well worth
some attention. How did hundreds (thousands?) of Hindus
justify their departure from India when they had been taught
that such travel was culturally repulsive? What motivated men[11] to leave their mainland homes, travel great distances
under perilous conditions to settle in primitive areas far removed
from the shrines and temples they revered?

Those who have attempted to determine the motivation of

Hindu travelers have proposed a number of hypotheses, but there is little agreement among scholars.[12] One writer, for example, notes without further explanation that the migration of travel-fearing, religious Hindus must be considered "one unique and far-reaching departure from tradition...."[13] Others have tried to be more imaginative and emphasize two reasons for the colonial expansion of the Hindus. The first stresses the part played by Brahmins and minimizes trade and commerce; the second stresses the role of India's mercantile class and their desire to profit from the burgeoning Far East trade and downgrades the prominence of Brahmins.

THE BRAHMIN HYPOTHESIS

During the first two or three centuries of the Christian era, India was politically and culturally in turmoil.[14] The programs of political centralization that the Mauryan kings introduced and their successors sought to establish had collapsed. Insurgent tribes from Central Asia invaded the northwest; some of these tribal people settled permanently in the north and, in fact, had started a process that would ultimately allow them to dominate the Punjab. Each time a new invading horde appeared—and there were many—the orthodoxy of the Hindu community was further weakened and compromised. Upper caste Hindus despaired of coming into contact with the increasingly large number of *mlecchas* who settled in the area and threatened their purity. Classical Brahmanical doxology, it will be recalled, required upper caste Hindus to be free of association with foreigners and uncontaminated by their pollution.

Once the Kushan tribes, the foremost invaders in the post-Mauryan period, dominated the north, the Brahmins' position in society began to deteriorate seriously. The Kushans' presence meant that orthodox Hindus could not avoid frequent and prolonged association with them. The greater the social intercourse, the more immediate was the danger to the Brahmins. Furthermore, Buddhist and Jain missionaries by the early decades of the Christian era were attracting larger and larger numbers of people to their heretical doctrines. The Kushan king, Kanishka's sympathetic understanding of Buddhist beliefs throughout most of his reign (c. 78-144 A.D.) must have further alerted the orthodox to their deteriorating situation. His convocation of the fourth General Council of the Buddhist hierarchy had to have triggered great alarm among the Hindus. The Council's deliberations and decisions revived the missionary features of Buddhism : hereafter Buddha was to be considered a savior-god whose message was to be advanced throughout the world rather than only India.

Each of these several events in north Indian history—the growing Kushan community, Kanishka's sponsorship of Buddhism and the Council's promotion of Buddhism's evangelicism—demoralised the Brahmins. No longer had they unchallenged power to determine the area's cultural standards and direct its religious affairs; their adversaries were gaining power and prestige. Two of the values Brahmins most highly prized, their individual purity and their religious elitism, were in jeopardy.

The first migration of ultra-orthodox Brahmins may have left northern India to seek relief for reasons as fundamental as these. The destination of some emigres probably was south India, the lands where the Dravidians lived. For other Brahmins, however, quitting India completely may not have been too radical a departure from tradition to reassert their cultural superiority and, hopefully regain purity by appropriate rituals. The injunctions against sea voyages and residence abroad may not have been too great a price to pay for such opportunities. Beyond the seas and thousands of miles from the Indian subcontinent, Brahmins could both be free themselves of *mleccha* pressures and also Buddhist-Jain campaigns to subvert their allegiance to Hinduism. Another complementary version of this theory maintains that Hindus were invited to settle the Southeast Pacific region by native leaders who had heard of the Brahmins' superior cultural achievements and strong religious leadership.[15]

THE TRADER-MERCHANT HYPOTHESIS

The second hypothesis sought to explain Hindu colonial expansion and the willingness of Hindus to disregard anti-sea injunctions by emphasising commercial considerations and the enormous profits that were realized from foreign trade. Scholars who favor this position stress the fabled wealth of the Far East, particularly its spices and precious minerals,[16] and the demand for these products throughout Europe. A few renegade Brahmins, they argue, probably accompanied the initial waves of traders who sailed abroad in search of the East's treasures, and Brahmins followed in later periods. They should not be considered as leaders or initiators of India's colonial movements.

Another version of the so-called trade theory involves India's pressing need for gold and its inability to continue importing the metal from Central Asia. It is known that India imported large quantities of gold from what is today known as Siberia until just before the beginning of the Christian era. Native jewelers and other artisans who worked in gold required a steady supply because the women of India enjoyed decorating their bodies with rings, bracelets, ear-rings and the like. Also, the wealthier people of Indian society sought out decorative and utilitarian objects made of gold. After political conditions in Central Asia were disturbed by tribal wars and internecine fighting, however, any caravan crossing the area on its way to India was prey to raiding parties and attacking soldiers. As such raids became more and more frequent, Indians began seeking out other possible sources for their supplies, the theory holds. In time, two new gold sources emerged. The first was the Roman Empire. It is known that India required Roman traders to pay for their purchases of Indian products with gold coin and that much was melted down after being circulated. In time the prolonged export of gold coins to India became a serious concern to Roman authorities. The Empire experienced what today would be designated a severely unfavorable balance of trade. Pliny the Elder, for example, conplained bitterly of the annual drain of gold, "so dearly do we pay for our luxury and our women."[17] During the reign of Emperor Vespasian (69-79 A.D.), a decree was issued which severely curtailed for the first time the amount of gold coin that could be exported yearly from the Empire's treasury. This edict, it is believed, all but ended India's source of gold from the West.

Southeast Asia—the lands that made up Greater India—may have been the second source of gold. There are scholars who maintain that the quest for several precious metals, but notably gold, was the motivating force causing Hindu migration overseas. In support of their hypothesis, they note that early merchants and traders regularly called the Far Eastern lands either *suvarnabhūmi* or *suvarnadvīpa*, that is the land of gold or the islands of gold. One such writer is Sylvain Levi, who declared categorically that "(i)t was gold that attracted India to the Eldorado of the Far East."[18] Other authorities, while not discounting altogether the gold motivation theory, take a more cautious approach. Thus, Professor G. Coedes :

(A)ccording to this hypothesis, Indian culture was spread by high-caste Indians who ventured forth to seek their fortunes in the lands of gold and spices—an idea which cannot be rejected out of hand, but which remains no more than hypothesis so long as no precise facts are found to confirm it."[19]

If, in fact, the leading impetus for Hindu overseas expansion was trade and commerce, it is interesting to speculate on which people might have been attracted by such sailing adventure besides northern Hindus. The Dravidians' conversion to Hinduism and their acceptance of its societal norms, as explained previously, took place only when Brahmins, finding the north a continuing threat to their caste purity, re-located in the south and began to influence Dravidian behavior. This development reached something of a climax during the centuries immediately before the Christian era. It is possible therefore that disgruntled Dravidian sailors, rejecting the Brahmin campaign against deep sea travel, could find ships going to *suvarnabhumi* and *suvarnadvipa* ready to sign them on. Supporting this premise is Coedes' observation that "all the regions of India contributed more or less to this expansion and it is the South that had the greatest part."[20]

THE HINDU SYSTEM OF COLONIALISM

The Hindus who reached Southeast Asia were fortunate in finding conditions ideal for their take over as the region's cultural leaders. The territory was inhabited by diverse peoples, all of whom were far less culturally sophisticated than the arrivals from India. The natives' lives focused primarily on feeding and housing their families. A few basic crops, such as rice, bananas and possibly sugar-cane, were grown. Hunting animals that roamed the forest areas attracted some while others turned to fishing in local waters. In none of the lands that came under Hindu influence was there the rudiment of an emerging religious philosophy or an ethical code of societal behavior. Animism was widely practiced; mysticism also held a powerful attraction. Another factor contributing to the Hindus' colonial success was their ability to use a written language in land that had no such linguistic traditions of their own. Finally, the areas was organized politically into petty although self-governing units. A chief directed the fortunes of the tribe, and he had rights and duties somewhat comparable to rulers in other parts of the world. Because the royal courts were unstructured, the more learned and/or aggressive Hindus found themselves in great demand.

How did emigrating Hindus manage to implant Hindu gods and Hindu social ideas, along with Hindu literature and art forms, so firmly in Southeast Asia that even today the legacy of Hindu presence is much in evidence ? How did Brahmins and other twice born men achieve in a relatively few years such influential positions in the courts of native leaders that they were able to effect a cultural revolution ?

Scholars who favor the colonial theory that focuses on Brahmin emigres stress their role as men of distinguished intellectual talents and the literati of Hindu society. Local kings, having heard rumors (from whom ?) of their learned accomplishments and religious leadership as well as their organizational talents, invited them to re-locate in their respective lands. Once abroad, Brahmins were assigned key positions within the local court structure becuse they were considered superior men. Many soon entered into a close personal relationship with the chief, his immediate court, and to a lesser degree, the larger aristocracy of the area. Contacts between Brahmins and the mass of natives were infrequent, it is believed, and so the lower stratum of Southeast Asian societies were less attracted to Hinduism than the ruling elites. As honored court officials, Brahmins were well placed to influence the life style of the chief and his nobles, the gods they worshipped, the values they preferred and even the political-social-economic organization they chose. In later years when a ruler needed men with military talents or artisans with special skills, *kshatriyas* and artificers from India were invited to relocate. They joined the earlier settled Brahmins and both groups joined in forming a powerful acculturation force.

Not too different a scenario is developed by scholars who argue that Hindu traders and men of commerce were the men who introduced and established Hinduism overseas. Of this group, Professor Majumdar is a leading spokesman, and he has portrayed the acculturation sequence in the following fashion :

"Two or three Indian vessels sailing together reach a coastal town. The new-comers ingratiate themselves into the favor of the local chiefs by costly or curious presents, the real or pretended knowledge or healing arts, and also magical powers to prevent illness or drive away evil spirits. Some of them assume lofty airs as belonging to royal or noble family and possessing immense wealth. All these highly impress the ruling chief as well as the common people who look upon the Hindus as people of superior race. The latter settle down among them, learn their language and marry the local girls. The leaders of the new immigrants naturally select the daughters of the chiefs or at least girls of high family. These wives are soon initiated into the religious and moral ideas and beliefs and social customs of their husbands and become instrumental in spreading them among the indigenous people . . . The native wives of the Indians become the best missionaries for the propagation of Hindu religion and culture. Gradually the new culture spreads from the coastal region to the interior, and from one locality to another. Ultimately, either the king adopts the Hindu faith, or some Hindu immigrant succeeds in winning his favour and marries into royal family, thus assuring the complete triumph of Hindu culture. In some cases the Hindu immigrants, backed by support of Hinduized natives, take advantage of changing political situations to seize the royal power. To explain satisfactorily the thorough-going conquest of Hindu culture in all aspects of life, we must assume that the Hindu immigrants included not only merchants, but also Brahmans and Kshatriyas, as well as people following different arts and crafts. It is not necessary to suppose that they all came together; it is more likely that they represent successive waves of immigration from India, each being encouraged by the good reports about the new settlements carried by the returning emigrants. . . ."[21]

THE HINDUS' ACCULTURATION PROCESS—A THEORY

The Hindus' colonial behavior, as noted earlier, is consistent with a number of strongly-held beliefs and concepts of Hindu society. What philosophical ideas, cultural doctrines and ethical propositions relating to inter-personal behavior motivated Hindus abroad to favor a style of colonialism that was based on cultural leadership rather than one which established political-military domination over the lands and peoples of Southeast Asia ? A theoretical answer to the question begins with an understanding of two features of classical Hinduism, both of which were formulated early in the history of the Hindu people and firmly established in India long before their expansion got under way. These are : (1) an exceptionally high degree of toleration, religious and otherwise, for those who did not subscribe to the Hindu code, and (2) an equally impressive willingness to fuse or reconcile differing groups within their community.

TOLERATION AND SYNCRETISM IN THE HINDU RELIGION

Compared with other leading faiths, Hinduism has been one of the world's most theologically tolerant and accommodating religions. Within Hinduism can be found the broadest panorama of ideas and practices, ranging from spiritual expressions that are little more than simplistic ceremonies of untutored men seeking some divine guidance to ideas about God, salvation and the essence of life that are some of the most profound formulations of any faith. It is widely acknowledged that the flexibility of Hindu religious leaders to accommodate Hinduism to such disparate points of view, accepting men from both perimeters as bona fide Hindus, has been one leading reason for its survival and success in India.

Many other ideas and principles of Hinduism reinforce its attitudes of compassion and adaptability. In Hinduism, for example, there is no suggestion of religious elitism. Hindu doxology does not teach that Hindus are a chosen group of people who are divinely nominated to carry out a special, noble mission here on earth. Hindus do not look upon their ethical code as superior to others. Also, there is no missionary theme in Hinduism : Hindus never considered it their earthly duty to undertake programs aimed at the conversion (forcible or peaceful) of their immediate neighbors, nor did they journey abroad to save men from the consequences of their ignorance. Their leaders never preached a doctrine that the human condition would improve and Man would move toward spiritual perfection if non-Hindu doctrines and practices were eliminated. They did not engage in holy wars, military conversions of unbelievers, or other such programs so commonly practiced by other religious groups. Lastly, Hinduism never formulated a central dogma held to be immutable or which claimed to represent the eternal, unalterable truth. From the earliest formulation of Hinduism, a quite different doctrine was taught. In the *Rig Veda,* for instance, are found passages that encouraged diversity and plurality. Thus :

> They call him Indra, Mitra, Varuna, Agni, and he is heavenly nobly-winged Garutman.
> To what is One, sages give many a title : they call it Agni, Yama, Matarisvan.[22]

Sarvepalli Radhakrishan, before he became President of India, summarized the toleration theme of Hinduism :

> (It) affirms that the theological expressions of religious experience are bound to be varied . . . Hinduism repudiates the belief resulting from a dualistic attitude that the plants in my garden are of God, while those in my neighbor's are weeds planted by the Devil which we should destroy at any cost. On the principle that the best is not the enemy of the good, Hinduism accepts all forms of belief and lifts them to a higher level. The cure for error is not the stake or the cudgel, not force or persecution, but the quiet diffusion of light.[23]

In applying Hindu doctrine to the world at large, Hindu leaders concluded that the human mind is finite and limited : no man is able to grasp and understand the nature of the total reality of anything so complex and intricate as Man's spiritual enlightenment. Those who represented the most theologically esoteric sect of Hinduism no less than those who made up its lesser expressions had differing personal experiences. But each of these many approaches to the attainment of oneness with the Absolute Spirit has a place within Hinduism, their leader preached, and each approach traditionally has been considered valid. In this way, the Hindu religion, a grand assortment of deities and forms, stressed diversity and plurality.

Many aspects of the high toleration found in Hinduism are well illustrated in its long competition with Buddhism. In the Western tradition, when two or more antithetical religious movements struggled for primacy and for allegiance from the people at large, particularly when one theology was extremely old and well-tested and the other was restless with youthful impatience, the resulting tensions produced a bitter contest and not infrequently, a long-lasting military conflict. The frequency and duration of the Catholic-Protestant wars in Europe over the last several hundred years is a case in point. The Hindu-Buddhist confrontation, on the other hand, did not follow a similar pattern. For approximately twelve hundred years (c. 600 B.C.—600 A.D.), Hindus and Buddhists competed for the allegiance of the Indian mass. It was a contest energetically pursued by both sides. Neither side, however, raised an army of zealot-soldiers, hoping by the power of its arms to crush those who opposed its doctrines. They also did not seize and persecute those who rejected their preachments. Ultimately Hinduism prevailed throughout India, and Buddhism gradually declined in the land where it originated. For purposes of this study, the crucial point is the Hindus' victory was realized without bloodshed or the other sordid characteristics of Western religious rivalry.

Furthermore, the Hindu-Buddhist confrontation did not end with the latter group in disgrace throughout India. Many of the basic tenets and early features of classical Buddhist theology were incorporated into the Hindu credo and profoundly affected it. The concept of *ahimsa* or non-violence frequently associated with contemporary Hinduism, for example, originated with the early Buddhist monks and nuns. Another instance of the Hindus' doctrinal tolerance is the concept of *dharma* or duty. This idea, too, appeared first in the teachings of Siddhartha Gautama, but centuries later emerged in Hinduism and became a vital part of its credo. Perhaps the most salient example of Hindu toleration is the incorporation of Buddha himself into the Hindu pantheon. Temples that early Buddhists built in India were taken over by the Hindus who, thereupon, began worshipping Buddha, and ultimately Buddha came to be identified as an incarnation of Vishnu himself.

Hindus also displayed great toleration toward Islam when the two creeds first encountered one another. Arab historians report that when their armies began settling parts of the Sind in the early decades of the eighth century A.D., they were able to prosper and were allowed a high degree of religious freedom by local Hindus. They were permitted to construct mosques, establish trading centers and generally live according to their Muslim laws and customs in spite of the fact that they were vastly different from those favored by Hindus.

TOLERATION AND SYNCRETISM IN THE HINDU SOCIAL ORDER

The willingness of Hindus to accept local gods into the Hindu pantheon was equalled only by their readiness to incorporate local tribes and alien invaders into the caste system and to supply them with caste geneologies. Today it is believed that some of these caste histories are spurious and were produced by Brahmin leaders to facilitate the absorption and general acceptance of foreign groups into the Hindu community. Liberal policies such as these could never have succeeded if early Hindus had not rejected in toto the idea of a closed, restricted society.

The key to an understanding of mobility and syncretism within Hindu society is the operation of the caste system. It has never been a closed arrangement. Rather, throughout history the caste system has demonstrated great plasticity, that is, it has been an open-ended division of society in which non-Aryan peoples and groups (i.e. non-Hindus and non-caste oriented) were permitted to join and in a relatively short time were accepted as bona fide Hindus. In general, the incorporation of the new-comer group was accomplished without destroying all their earlier established social attitudes and folkways. What resulted from the process were non-Aryan Hindus who fitted nicely into an appropriate caste group, had religious equality, and who were not discriminated against because they continued to follow some of their indigenous usages and customs.

According to a recent study, Hindu syncretism is in evidence as soon as the first waves of Aryans invaded the subcontinent. In R. K. Choudhary's opinion, these groups found that some of the areas they wished to settle were occupied by the *vratya* people, a prehistoric community of India about which almost no specific, verifiable information is available. The early Aryans and the *vratyas* are thought to have clashed because of fundamental religious and social differences. Tensions rose to great intensity. The *Mahabharata,* for example, castigates the *vratyas* profusely and groups them with pimps, prisoners, abortionists, drug-addicts, drunkards, illegitimates, and other low regarded groups of society. When the *vratyas* refused to succumb to Aryan campaigns of humiliation and discrimination, Aryan leaders

decided to alter their tactics.   According to legend, it became
Aryan policy to bring the   *vratya* population   directly into the
mainstream of Aryan life.   An Aryan sponsored fiction was circulated that *vratyas* were a group of errant Brahmins who had
discontinued practicing the prescribed rites of the twice-born but
who deserved the respect and honor of Brahmins.   There does
not appear to be a scintella of evidence to support such a claim.
In any event, the Aryans, by resorting to a program of acceptance
and toleration of a dissenting minority, were able eventually to
incorporate the *vratyas* into the larger Hindu community.[24]

The absorption of the Dravidian people into Hindu society
is another case in point.   By the time Brahmins migrated from
the north and began settling in south India, the Dravidians had
established a society with a life style that complemented their
customs, values, and religious practices.   Dravidian society was
not as advanced or elaborate as the culture of the   re-locating
Brahmins, but they were industrious and capable.   The Dravidian
language was well-developed; the community was prosperous because of its trade and local fishing; local gods and goddesses were
worshipped, and polyandry and matriarchy were   well-accepted
social institutions.   The Brahmins, therefore, had to be considerably more tolerant of alien customs and a minority point of view
here than in the north, and they were.   A cultural synthesis between the Dravidians and Hindus did take place in south India,
but it was a highly   selected one.   To quote from   Rawlinson's
study, it resulted in northern Hindu influence remaining a "mere
veneer."[25]   Yet by tolerating essential features of the Dravidians'
culture, the Hindus managed to integrate the Dravidian people
into their society.   As centuries, past, Hindus continued to be
champions of a philosophy of toleration and synthesis.[26]   They
also remained willing to produce imaginary geneologies to facilitate the integration of an alien group into Hindu life. Since the
Rajput-Hindu assimilation has been summarized elsewhere in this
study,[27] it need not be repeated here.   What is relevant to re-
emphasize are the means the Hindus employed to   accomplish
their end.   Once Rajput men began settling permanently in India,
some were attracted to women from the Hindu community.   At
this point, the syncretic practices of Hindu thought and the willingness of the Hindu community to tolerate diversity   became
important.   Brahmin leaders, rather than concluding that Rajput

marriages to Hindu women violated the norms of pollution, decided to sanction such unions.   To bring about a more peaceful
accommodation, Brahmins created fictitious geneologies for the
would-be Rajput bridegrooms as well as those yet unbetrothed.
They decreed that Rajput priests were of the Brahmin caste and
that Rajput princes belonged to the *kshatriya* caste, both findings
without any factual basis whatsoever.   The men were initiated
into the religious community of the twice-born and granted all the
rights and privileges of true-born Brahmins and *kshatriyas*.

Conclusion

In analyzing the colonial period of India's history and the
accomplishments of Hindus in Southeast Asia, Professor Coedes
emphasizes how well prepared they were to establish themselves
in local societies.   He notes :

> . . . the Indianization of Indochina does not differ essen-
> tially from that of the   Dravidian countries in India itself.
> As has been well said by de la Vallee Poussin, it is no more
> than 'the extension overseas of the process of Brahminiza-
> tion which started long before the time of Buddha, and
> which, from its area of origin in North West India, has
> spread and   still continues to spread in   Bengal and the
> south.' I should be inclined to go farther and to add that
> perhaps the   only difference between the   Aryanization of
> Bengal and the Dravidian countries and that of South East
> Asia is that the first, being a process which took place over
> an inland area, occurred so to speak by osmosis, whereas
> this was not the case when the same process took place
> overseas . . .[28]

In world history, many expansionist societies have located
themselves abroad and found themselves dealing with a culturally
inferior, indigenous population.   Few societies, if any, succeeded
as well as did the Hindu emigres.   They implanted leading features of Hindu culture permanently in Southeast Asia life, but
their acculturation efforts were free of military force or punative
means. Theirs was a process that insured a high level of cooperation between Hindus and the local people while preserving the
autonomy of both.   If the Hindus who sailed to and settled in
Southeast Asia had not been taught by their   religion to prize

diversity and respect dissent, it is most unlikely that India's colonial ventures would be so highly regarded.

REFERENCES

1. There is considerable disagreement among scholars as to whether Hindus or Buddhists played the greater role in the colonization of Southeast Asia. Understandably, Hindu scholars frequently minimize the activities of the Buddhists and the permanence of their missionary efforts. For example, Dr R. C. Majumdar states, "(I)t is a well-known fact (sic—ed.) that compared with Brahmanical religion, Buddhism had a very feeble hold in South-East Asia ... The discovery of early Buddhist images does not prove the contrary, or even that the first colonists were Buddhists ... In South-East Asia ... the archeological remains clearly prove the dominance of Brahmanical religion. It is true that Buddhism had very important centres and played an important part in the spread of Hindu culture in this region, but there is no evidence that it had supplied the chief stimulus to the Hindu colonization there. If we have to give credit to any particular religion, it rightly belongs to both Brahmanical and Buddhist sects and, on the whole, the balance would probably incline to the former." *Ancient Indian Colonization in South-East Asia* (Baroda : Maharaja Sayajirao University of Baroda Press, 1963), p. 16. Also see Austin Coates, *Invitation to an Eastern Feast* (New York : Harper and Bros., nd), pp. 157-8; and D. P. Singhal, *India and World Civilization* (Lansing, Michigan : Michigan State Univ. Press, 1969), II, pp. 80ff.
    Despite Majumdar's strong beliefs, which are supported by other historians, the Buddhist community of India played a key role in the colonial period and in the acculturation of the Far East. Since throughout this study a distinction has been made between Hindus and Buddhists, the focus of this chapter concerns only the former.

2. See supra, Chapter VII. An earlier translation of this same passage by Edward Jones Chinnak (London : George Bell, 1893) reads, "But none of the Indians ever marched out of their own country for war, being actuated by a respect for justice."

3. The feature of Hindu colonialism also distinguishes it from that of China. Coedes' writings emphasize the striking contrast between Indian and Chinese colonialism. He wrote that "... we are struck by the fundamental difference of the results obtained in the countries of the Far East by the civilizing activity of China and India.

"The reason for this lies in the radical difference in the methods of colonization employed by the Chinese and the Indians. The Chinese proceeded by conquest and annexation; soldiers occupied the country, and officials spread Chinese civilization. Indian penetration or infiltration seems almost to have been peaceful; nowhere was it accompanied by the destruction that brought dishonor in the Mongol expansion or the Spanish conquest of America . . . .

"The Indians nowhere engaged in military conquest and annexation in the name of a state or mother country." *The Indianized States of Southeast Asia,* ed. Walter F. Vella, (Honolulu : East-West Centre Press, 1968), p. 53.

In *The Making of South East Asia* Coedes wrote that "Indian culture (was not) ever introduced for political purposes, as was the case with the sinicization of Viet-nam, which was conquered by China and then administered for several centuries as a province of the empire; whereas none of the Indochinese States of Indian type was ever a dependency of an Indian metropolitan power." G. Coedes, *The Making of South East Asia,* trans. H. M. Wright, (Berkeley : University of California Press, 1966), p. 50.

4. G. Coedes, *The Indianized States of Southeast Asia,* ed. Walter F. Vella, (Honolulu : East-West Centre Press, 1968), p. 34.

5. Quoted in G. Coedes, *The Making of South East Asia,* trans. H. M. Wright, (Berkeley : University of California Press, 1966), p. 52.

6. The ancient Chinese legend states that ". . . there was a person called Huen-chen of Ho-fu. He was a staunch devotee of a Brahmanical god who was pleased with his piety. He dreamt that the god gave him a divine bow and asked him to take to sea in a trading vessel . . . Then he embarked on a trading vessel and the god changed the course of wind in such a manner that he came to Fu-nan . . ." R. C. Majumdar, *Hindu Colonies in the Far East,* 2nd ed., (Calcutta : Firma K. L. Mukhopadhyay, 1963), p. 177.

7. G. Coedes, *The Making of South East Asia,* trans., H. M. Wright, (Berkeley : Univ. of California Press, 1967), p. 58.

8. *ibid.,* pp. 50-1. Also see the same conclusion in his *The Indianized States of Southeast Asia,* ed. Walter F. Vella, (Honolulu : East-West Centre Press, 1968), pp. 18-19.

9. R. C. Majumdar, H. C. Raychaudhuri and Kalikinkar Datta, *An Advanced History of India* (New York : St. Martin's Press, 1965), p. 522.

10. G. Coedes, *The Indianized States of Southeast Asia,* ed. Walter F. Vella, (Honolulu : East-West Centre Press, 1968), p. 19.

11. It generally is agreed that almost all Hindu travellers were men, and Hindu women remained at home.

12. For a summary of the debate, see G. Coedes, *The Making of South East Asia,* trans. H. M. Wright (Berkeley : Univ. of Calif. Press, 1966), pp. 51-2, and also his *The Indianized States of*

13

Southeast Asia, ed. Walter F. Vella, (Honolulu : East-West Centre Press, 1968), pp. 19-21. Most worthwhile in this connection is J. C. van Leur, *Indonesian Trade and Society,* 2nd ed., (The Hague : W. van Hoeve, 1967), pp. 89-143.

13. Austin Coates, *Invitation to an Eastern Feast* (New York : Harper & Brothers, nd), p. 156.

14. See supra, Chapter II.

15. Van Leur assigned Brahmins the key role in spreading Indian civilization not only through the subcontinent proper, but also into Southeast Asia. Thus he wrote, "In it (the caste system) the position of the ancient Aryan priesthood, the Brahmins, became an all-dominating one . . . This Aryan occupation did not expand further than to the plains of northern India as colonization. The Deccan Plateau and the Southern Indian coastal regions remained Dravidian, traditional and indigenous (sic) in their whole complex of ethnic structure and regal authority. Indian civilization, however, continued to move further southwards. The chief disseminator of the process of 'Indianization' was the Brahmin priesthood; the aim of the "Brahmin mission" was not the preaching of any revealed doctrine of salvation, but the ritualistic and bureaucratic subjugation and organization of the newly entered regions. Wherever the process of 'Indianization' took place, 'religious' organization was accompanied by social organization—division in castes, legitimation of the ruling groups, assurance of the supremacy of the Brahmins. The colossal magical, ritualistic power of the Brahmin priesthood was the most characteristic feature of early Indian history . . . .

"Under such conditions Indian civilization expanded over southern India . . . (It was a process) going on for southern India around the beginning of the Christian era. It continued through the centuries . . .

"Southern India was the trading region for Indonesia; the shipping to the east went especially from the southern Indian shipping, the Indonesian rulers and aristocratic groups came in contact with India, perhaps seeing it with their own eyes. In the same sort of attempt at legitimizing their interests involved in 'international trade' . . . and .... organizing and domesticating their states and subjects, they called Indian civilization to the east—that is to say, they summoned the Brahmin priesthood to their courts." *Indonesian Trade and Society,* 2nd ed., (The Hague : W. Van Hoeve, 1967), pp. 96-8.

16. Panikkar in *Asia and Western Dominance* notes that the spice trade with the East was "one of the great motivating factors of history and one which yielded the largest profits to merchants as commodities in universal demand . . ." He then quotes an unnamed author who wrote that 'pepper may not mean much to us, but in that age it ranked with precious stones.

Men risked the peril of the deep and fought and died for pepper.'
See p. 22ff.

17. Quoted in A. L. Basham, *The Wonder That Was India* (New York : Grove Press, 1954), p. 229.

18. Quoted in G. Coedes, *The Indianized States of Southeast Asia*, ed. Walter F. Vella, (Honolulu : East-West Centre Press, 1968), p. 20. Levi at one point also states that "I would like to stress the role played by the search for gold in the Indian expansion in Further India . . ."

19. G. Coedes, *The Making of South East Asia*, trans. H. M. Wright, (Berkeley : University of Calif, Press, 1951), p. 51.

20. Quoted in H. G. Quaritch Wales, *The Making of Greater India*, (London : Bernard Quaritch, 1951), p. 22.

21. R. C. Majumdar, *Ancient Indian Colonization in South East Asia*, 2nd ed., (Baroda : Maharaja Sayajirao University of Baroda Press, 1963), pp. 8-9. Also see Gabriel Ferrand's description of the colonization of Java in Coedes, *The Indianized States of Southeast Asia*, ed. Walter F. Vella (Honolulu : East-West Centre Press, 1968), p. 22.

22. *The Hymns of the Rigveda*, trans. and ed. Ralph T. H. Griffith, (Benares : E. J. Lazarus and Co., 1925) I, p. 227.

23. "A Vision of Hinduism" and quoted in *The Hindu Tradition*, ed. Ainslie T. Embree (New York : Vintage Books, 1966), p. 345.

24. See R. K. Choudhary, *The Vratyas in Ancient India*, (Varanasi, India : Chowkhamba Sanskrit Office, 1964). It is interesting to note that the Hindu ceremony used today to admit non-Aryan groups of individuals into the Hindu community continues to be known as *vratyasoma.*

25. H. G. Rawlinson, *India : A Short Cultural History* (New York : D. Appleton-Century, 1938), p. 176.

26. See, for example, Professor M. N. Srinivas' study, *Religion and Society Among the Coorgs of South India* (Oxford : Clarendon Press, 1952). For a discussion of this work, also see Milton Singer, "The Social Organization of Indian Civilization," *Diogenes*, Vol. 45 (Spring 1945), pp. 84-112, and particularly, pp. 99ff.

27. See supra, Chapter IX.

28. G. Coedes, *The Making of South East Asia*, trans. H. M. Wright, (Berkeley : University of California Press, 1966), p. 55.

CHAPTER XI

CULTURE AND POLITICAL-MILITARY BEHAVIOR

THE SOCIAL SCIENTIST AND THE IDEA OF CULTURE

SOME BRANCHES of social science, notably anthropology and sociology, have made us aware that despite geographical proximity the domestic behavior of one European country oftentimes differs in major respects from that of another country. In seeking an explanation for such distinctions, anthropologists and sociologists for years have hypothesized that one society's cultural standards —its integrated collection of traits and values that are shared by the members—go a long way towards providing us with an interpretation for distinctive patterns of behavior. Many of these theories have helped us to understand why some European states and their people conduct themselves so differently from other European societies. We have accepted, for example, Weber's thesis that European countries in which Protestant ideals and ethics flourished ultimately favored the capitalistic system. Here individual frugality was encouraged, which in turn resulted in accumulated wealth for investment purposes. These individual practices, reflecting the culture of the specific area, are in marked contrast to other countries in which the teachings of Calvin did not take hold. The latter group resorted to alternate economic systems for the production of goods and services.

Cultural analysis is not limited to economic matters. Few people today challenge scholars who argue that European states which developed the most dynamic scientific community and produced the leading scientific experiments of the times were societies in which the ideas and writings of Coparnicius, Kepler, Galileo and their successors neither were censored nor banished. Other near-by countries, on the other hand, denegrated the intellectual efforts of such men and categorically refused to consider any work seeking to explain the nature of the physical world not based on divinity and mysticism. In these states, science and technology was slowed, its productivity less impressive, and, not the least important, the so-called scientific method did not enter the mainstream of societal values.

Anthropologists and sociologists, of course, have not confined themselves to the European scene. Many have specialized in the life-styles of non-Western societies, particularly primitive communities of Africa, Asia, and the Pacific Islands. Their findings have taught us much about behavorial differences relating to the family structure, social groupings, sex, as well as faith and superstition, creative forms of expression, and the ways natural resources can be exploited for the common good.

The point being stressed is that for many years some branches of social science have applied cultural analysis in an imaginative and productive fashion to further our understanding of societal traits and differences.

Until fairly recent times, however, political scientists ignored the concept of culture as a means of better appreciating differences in political-military behavior. "For a discipline that rejoices in imparting ideas," Professor Lucian Pye notes, "political science was strangely slow to incorporate the concept of culture."[1] In the late 1940s when a select group of imaginative political scientists did begin to examine cultural variations as a means of advancing and enriching political analysis, they first sought to introduce a human and biographical-psychological dimension (Lasswell, Leites) and later moved on to study the process of political socialization (Almond, Verba, et al.). The core problems these men examined dealt with the internal dynamics of a particular state and its people, that is, the basic processes of national political life as opposed to its external relations or its military conduct.

The present study has concentrated on these two areas, namely culture and foreign relations along with culture and military behavior. It has attempted to determine whether the cultural standards of a society provide a plausible, functional explanation for its political-military behavior in the international arena. Specifically, I have sought to determine whether the dominant traits and values that prevailed in the Hindu community of India prior to the mid-sixteenth century A.D. were causal determinants of the concepts that governed their behavior abroad and limited their abilities in fighting their enemies.

CONCLUSIONS

The case material presented here discloses that pre-sixteenth century Hindus, governmental leaders as well as the people in general, reached policy decisions about foreign affairs and military strategy according to cultural values and time-honored traditions that were then paramount in this society. They rejected public policies which would have led to the growth of naval-maritime power although their land faced two of the leading waterways of the pre-modern world. Their willingness to engage in internecine warfare had few, if any, rivals but their military leaders never developed a strategy that offered India security nor were they able to train Hindu men to be as skillful and able soldiers as those invading from abroad. Dozens of Hindu armies, in seriatim, suffered huuiliation and dishonor yet Hindu kings abjured efforts to combine their military forces and confront a common enemy with the combined power of an all-Hindu alliance. Finally, Hindus achieved what today remains a most impressive accomplishment : without resorting to force or other harsh techniques Hindu émigrés established themselves throughout Southeast Asia, thousands of miles from India, and implanted Hindu cultural standards permanently there. In short, the pre-modern Hindu record of managing their political-military affairs offers us, as students of inter-state relations, a case history of a important society that conducted its foreign relations and military affairs as no other polity in similar circumstances has done. How did these patterns arise and persist over nearly three millenia ?

The key to understanding the pre-modern Hindu performance is Hinduism : the distinctive religious, social, economic, legal and artistic expressions of these people which, when combined, personifies early Hindu culture. Provided with an explanation rooted in Hindu cultural standards, their political-military behavior becomes less quizotic and fatuous than otherwise. Given this key, the student of international affairs can begin to appreciate these public policies as expressions of an immeasureably complex system of ordering Hindu society and one in which the spiritual release of its adherents held a priority unknown in the West.

CULTURAL ANALYSIS AND CONTEMPORARY INTERNATIONAL RELATIONS SCHOLARSHIP

Many political scientists who today are concerned with third world countries and their political-military behavior have, tended to concentrate their research on domestic issues and internal problems, such as modernization, integration, industrialization, and governmental institutions and processes. As a group, comparative politics specialists seem to minimize the uniqueness of pre-colonial cultural patterns in the area of political-military affairs and, more often than not, tacitly assume the newly independent states of Asia and Africa reach policy decisions and manage their affairs as if these earlier policy preferences are no longer of significance. It is, therefore, legitimate to ask whether greater sensitivity to indigenous cultural standards would be a worthwhile effort among scholars concerned with today's non-Western world. Would such an approach produce new insights and greater understanding of established facts ?

The answer appears to be yes. There are indications that international relations scholars and governmental officials need to become much more knowledgeable about the cultural ideas of the third world. The argument has been expressed often but deserves repetition : We of the Western political science community must break the bonds of our ethnocentricity in order to expand our capacity for research, teaching, and service in the international field.

If the conclusions of this study apply to international relations today, we political scientists should not assume that Asians and Africans have discarded completely their traditional style of conduct in those areas despite their adoption of the Western nation state system and its leading features. Since many pre-colonial cultural standards remain a dynamic force among third world countries and, equally as important, since culture is a causal determinant of societal behavior, it is not correct to conclude that their earlier ways of dealing with the world beyond their borders and conducting military operations are dead. The typical Political Man of the third world has learned how to conduct public policy along Western nation state lines, but he is no exact replica of his European-American counterpart. Deep within his comciousness, he carries his society's pre-colonial cultural standards, and these may re-surface and influence contemporary political-military affairs when least expected.

REFERENCE

1. Lucian Pye, "Culture and Political Science : Problems in the Evaluation of the Concept of Political Culture," *The Idea of Culture in the Social Sciences,* ed. Louis Schneider and Charles Bonjean (Cambridge : Cambridge University Press, 1973), p. 65.

INDEX